THE STORY OF
BRITAIN

With special thanks to Martha Dillon for the maps

First published 2010 by Walker Books Ltd
87 Vauxhall Walk, London SE11 5HJ

2 4 6 8 10 9 7 5 3 1

This book has been typeset in Clarendon and Golden Cockerel

Printed in China

British Library Cataloguing in Publication Data:
a catalogue record for this book is available
from the British Library

ISBN 978-1-4063-1192-1

www.walker.co.uk

THE STORY OF
BRITAIN

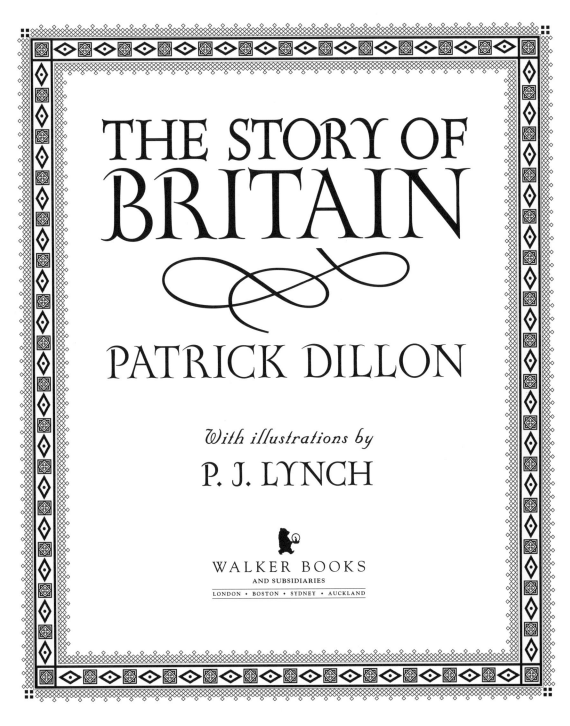

PATRICK DILLON

With illustrations by

P. J. LYNCH

WALKER BOOKS
AND SUBSIDIARIES
LONDON · BOSTON · SYDNEY · AUCKLAND

CONTENTS

INTRODUCTION 9

TIMELINE 18

THE MIDDLE AGES

❖ ❖ ❖

THE NORMAN CONQUEST 23

DOMESDAY BOOK 27

THE WHITE SHIP 29

MATILDA 31

ENGLAND'S NEIGHBOURS....... 33

THE KING AND THE
    ARCHBISHOP 36

RICHARD THE LIONHEART AND
    THE CRUSADES 40

JOHN LACKLAND AND
    ROBIN HOOD 42

MAGNA CARTA 44

SIMON DE MONTFORT AND
    PARLIAMENT 46

WOOL 48

EDWARD LONGSHANKS......... 50

THE EXPULSION OF THE JEWS.. 52

BRAVEHEART 54

ROBERT BRUCE, KING OF
    SCOTLAND 56

EDWARD II AND PIERS
    GAVESTON 59

ISABELLA AND MORTIMER...... 60

THE HUNDRED YEARS WAR 62

THE BLACK PRINCE 64

THE BLACK DEATH............ 66

THE PEASANTS' REVOLT 68

THE CANTERBURY TALES....... 71

OWAIN GLYN DWR'S
    REBELLION 72

AGINCOURT 74

THE WARS OF THE ROSES...... 75

THE PRINCES IN THE TOWER... 77

RICHARD'S DOWNFALL......... 79

THE END OF THE MIDDLE
    AGES 80

TIMELINE.................... 83

THE TUDORS

❖ ❖ ❖

HENRY VII.................... 89

JAMES IV OF SCOTLAND........ 91

YOUNG HENRY VIII............ 93

CARDINAL WOLSEY............. 95

THE REFORMATION 97

THE KING'S GREAT MATTER 99

THE DISSOLUTION OF THE
MONASTERIES 101

HENRY'S WIVES 103

THE STRIPPING OF THE
ALTARS 106

THE NINE DAYS QUEEN 108

BLOODY MARY................. 110

QUEEN ELIZABETH........... 112

MARY, QUEEN OF SCOTS....... 114

THE SPANISH ARMADA....... 119

WAR IN IRELAND 122

ELIZABETH'S EXPLORERS ...124

MERCHANTS 126

"ALL THE WORLD'S A
STAGE" 128

TIMELINE.................... 130

THE STUARTS

❖ ❖ ❖

BRITAIN UNITED 135

THE GUNPOWDER PLOT 137

THE MAYFLOWER 139

THE TROUBLES OF KING
CHARLES I................. 140

THE FIRST CIVIL WAR 143

THE SECOND CIVIL WAR 146

THE KING'S DEATH........... 148

BRITAIN WITHOUT A KING 149

LORD PROTECTOR.............. 151

THE YEAR OF CHAOS.......... 153

THE RESTORATION 154

SCIENTISTS 156

PLAGUE...................... 159

THE GREAT FIRE.............. 161

THE DUTCH WARS............. 163

THE EXCLUSION CRISIS........ 164

HUGUENOTS 166

THE GLORIOUS REVOLUTION... 167

TOLERATION 172

TIMELINE.................... 173

THE GEORGIANS

❖ ❖ ❖

SLAVERY..................... 179

THE UNION OF ENGLAND AND
SCOTLAND 183

MARLBOROUGH'S WAR........ 186

A KING FROM GERMANY 187

THE SOUTH SEA BUBBLE....... 188

ARISTOCRATS................. 191

STAND AND DELIVER!........ 192

BONNIE PRINCE CHARLIE..... 194

RULE BRITANNIA!............ 197

INDIA 199

CAPTAIN COOK................ 201

THE AMERICAN REVOLUTION..203

THE SCOTTISH
    ENLIGHTENMENT...........205

THE MADNESS OF GEORGE III..207

THE FRENCH REVOLUTION.....209

THE IRISH REBELLION........211

NAPOLEON BONAPARTE 213

NAPOLEON'S MISTAKE.........216

THE BATTLE OF WATERLOO ...218

THE END OF THE SLAVE
    TRADE....................221

THE ROMANTICS..............223

TIMELINE....................224

THE VICTORIANS

❖ ❖ ❖

BEING BRITISH 229

THE PETERLOO MASSACRE 230

DANIEL O'CONNELL...........233

THE GREAT REFORM ACT 235

THE INDUSTRIAL
    REVOLUTION................237

RAILWAYS 239

LIFE IN THE FACTORIES 241

UNIONS.......................243

BETTER LIVES................244

THE GREAT EXHIBITION 246

THE CHARGE OF THE LIGHT
    BRIGADE...................248

FLORENCE NIGHTINGALE AND
    MARY SEACOLE..............250

THE INDIAN MUTINY..........252

QUEEN EMPRESS 255

THE IRISH FAMINE...........259

HOME RULE FOR IRELAND....261

CHARTISTS AND COMMUNISTS .263

"CHANGE IS INEVITABLE" 265

SUFFRAGETTES...............267

THE EDWARDIANS 269

TIMELINE....................272

THE TWENTIETH CENTURY

❖ ❖ ❖

GERMANY......................277

THE GREAT WAR...............279

LIFE IN THE TRENCHES.......281

THE END OF THE WAR.........285

MIDDLE AGES

1066   1100   1200   1300   1400   1500

THE JAZZ AGE...................287
WAR IN IRELAND 290
THE RUSSIAN REVOLUTION 292
THE GENERAL STRIKE........294
THE GREAT DEPRESSION.......296
THE NAZIS.....................298
HITLER AND GERMANY 300
THE SECOND WORLD WAR
    BEGINS.....................303
DUNKIRK.....................304
THE BATTLE OF BRITAIN 305
THE BLITZ....................308
LIFE IN THE WAR 310
THE ALLIES 311
WAR ALL OVER THE WORLD...313
THE HOLOCAUST...............314
THE WAR IN THE WEST.......315
D-DAY........................316
THE NUCLEAR BOMB 319
THE WELFARE STATE.........321
THE END OF THE EMPIRE......323
THE COLD WAR...............326
THE SIXTIES..................329
BRITAIN IN TROUBLE 331
IMMIGRATION 333
A NEW START.................335
WHAT NEXT? 337

TIMELINE.....................340

INDEX 342

KINGS AND QUEENS IN BRITAIN
    AND IRELAND SINCE 1066....348

MAPS

❖ ❖ ❖

THE NORMAN INVASION 24
THE ARMADA 118
THE CIVIL WAR BATTLES......145
SLAVERY.....................181
THE BRITISH EMPIRE IN 1900..256
THE GREAT WAR 280
THE D-DAY LANDINGS.........317

TUDORS   STUARTS   GEORGIANS   VICTORIANS   20TH CENTURY

1600   1700   1800   1900   2000

INTRODUCTION

LONG ago, as the ice melted and continents shifted, two islands appeared on the edge of the Atlantic Ocean. Beyond the Atlantic to the west lay America, although the ocean was so wide that no one on the islands knew it was there. To the north were icy seas full of fish; to the east was the North Sea, a place of storms and sandbanks; and to the south, beyond the narrow sea we call the Channel, lay the great continent of Europe.

For thousands of years the people of the islands lived quietly, fishing, hunting and farming. We don't know much about them, because they couldn't write, but we do know they built the great stone circle we call Stonehenge, and became expert at metalwork, making gold brooches and silver daggers. Sometimes a ship appeared from the south to buy their brooches and daggers. The sailors told them of countries far larger than theirs, of cities far grander, of palaces made of stone. They told them of kings who conquered neighbouring kingdoms to build empires.

"We'll never see anything like that here," the people of the islands said. "We live on the edge of the world."

Years passed. Gradually one of the southern nations conquered all of the countries around it to become the biggest empire the world had yet seen. Its capital was a city in Italy called Rome. The Romans were better organized than anyone else and their soldiers, the legions, defeated every other army until they ruled the Mediterranean Sea and all of the lands on its shores: Spain and Morocco, Libya and Egypt, Palestine, Syria, Turkey and Greece, Serbia, Croatia, Italy itself, and the southern part of France. Of course, none of those countries had the same names in those days. The Romans called France Gaul.

One day, a Roman general called Julius Caesar decided to conquer the rest of Gaul. He marched his army north until he reached its northern coast and gazed out across the Channel at a distant island shrouded in mist.

"Britain," said an officer at his elbow.

Julius Caesar ordered his soldiers to build ships, and sailed across the Channel to Britain. In those days its people were divided into tribes. They often fought one another, and, being disunited, were easily beaten. The next year, Caesar led his legions to Britain again, and made the largest tribes sign treaties with him.

But he didn't stay. He went back to Rome, and the people of Britain went back to their farming. They didn't hear until much later how Julius Caesar tried to make himself ruler of the Roman Empire and was murdered, and terrible wars were fought among the Romans until his adopted son, Augustus, became emperor.

Nor did they hear what happened around the same time in Palestine, at the eastern end of the Mediterranean Sea, where, in the town of Bethlehem, a man called Jesus Christ was born. He said he was the Son of God, but the Romans put him to death. After his death, though, his followers, who were called Christians, began a new religion that would one day become the religion of most of Europe.

A few years after Christ's death, a Roman emperor called Claudius decided to conquer Britain properly. He gathered a great army with soldiers from Spain, horsemen from Holland and war elephants from Africa. The British fought bravely under their leader, Caractacus, but they had no chance against the Romans. General Aulus Plautius led his legions north until they reached a wide river, the Thames. On the far side they could see the Britons waiting, but they found a ford, marched across and defeated them. At this river crossing the Romans built a town which they called Londinium, or London.

The Roman Empire was divided into provinces, so London became the capital of the new province called Britannia. Britain was no longer a small island on the edge of the world; it was part of the Roman Empire. The Romans built law courts where arguments could be settled fairly, a market, and docks for the ships that sailed to Britain from all over the empire. The ships brought food the Britons had never tasted before, and luxuries they'd never even heard of. The Romans built roads so their legions could march from one end of the country to the other, and towns like Chelmsford, St Albans and York. People came from Spain, Italy and Gaul to live there and

built fine villas with central heating, baths and rich decorations.

The Britons had never seen such magnificence before; they had never been so well organized. But even so, many of them hated being ruled by people from another country.

"Foreigners!" spat Boudicca, queen of a tribe in Norfolk called the Iceni. Boudicca hated the Romans because they had killed her husband and raped her daughters. She started a rebellion, destroyed Colchester and burned London before the Romans could defeat her.

The people of northern Britain didn't want Roman rule either. The Romans called them Picts, because they painted their bodies with patterns and pictures. The Picts never gave in to the invaders. Once, the Roman Ninth Legion marched north to conquer them, setting off into the mountains with trumpets blaring and standards glinting. No one ever saw the Ninth Legion again. Somewhere in the northern forests it was defeated, and every man killed.

So the Roman emperor Hadrian built a wall from one side of Britain to the other to keep out the Picts. It marked the edge of Rome's power, and the boundary of the province of Britannia.

As time went by, most people in Britain grew to like what the Romans brought them. They lived peacefully under fair laws, traded with people all over the world, and grew rich. Many Britons copied the Romans' way of dressing and eating, and learned their language, Latin. After a while, the Romans took on the religion of Jesus Christ, and so did most Britons. A British-born Roman called Patrick was captured by pirates and taken to Ireland, where he taught the Irish to be Christians too.

For four hundred years Britannia lived in peace. Its roads stretched for miles; its legions defended the borders. It seemed as if the Roman Empire would last for ever. But nothing lasts for ever. Eventually the Romans started quarrelling among themselves. A Roman general in Britain declared himself emperor, and marched the British legions to Gaul, where he was killed. German tribesmen invaded the empire. Then two German tribes called the Angles and the Saxons sailed across the North Sea and attacked Britain. The Britons wrote to Rome asking for help, but the Roman emperor wrote back saying that Rome had its own problems to deal with, and from now on they would have to look after themselves.

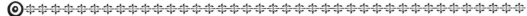

Vortigern, leader of the Britons in Kent, knew he was not strong enough to fight the Angles and Saxons. So he made a deal with two Saxon leaders, brothers called Hengist and Horsa, offering them gold if they helped fight off the other Saxons. But Hengist and Horsa cheated him. They took the gold, beat Vortigern themselves, and made Hengist king of Kent.

To start with, the Angles and Saxons had come to plunder and steal. But when they saw how rich Britannia was, they decided to stay. They brought their own language, Anglish, or English, and called the country they conquered Angleland, or England.

The Britons did their best to hold out, but had no help from Rome, for Rome itself had been burnt by invaders. It was in those years that people made up stories about a king called Arthur who fought back against the Angles and Saxons, gathering the best knights of Britain to his castle at Camelot to form them into a band called the Knights of the Round Table. But there was no real Arthur to lead the Britons, and there were no Knights of the Round Table to protect them. At last they ruled only the western parts of the island of Britain, which we now call Cornwall and Wales, while England was ruled by the Anglo-Saxons.

And so four nations took shape. Ireland was the western of the two islands at the edge of the Atlantic Ocean. It had never been invaded by the Romans. Scotland was the northern part of Britain, which the Romans also never reached (it was called Scotland after an Irish tribe, the Scots, who took part of it from the Picts). England was the part of Britain that the Anglo-Saxons conquered. And Wales was where the Britons lived on, still speaking their old language and telling their old tales.

The Anglo-Saxons divided England into seven kingdoms. Kent was the first one they conquered. Essex, Sussex and Wessex were the kingdoms of the East Saxons, South Saxons and West Saxons. East Anglia was where the East Angles lived. Mercia was the kingdom of the north-west. And Northumbria was the north-eastern kingdom that stretched as far as Hadrian's Wall. Sometimes one of the seven kings became so strong that the others agreed to obey him. Offa, king of Mercia, was the most powerful of all. He built a wall called Offa's Dyke between England and Wales, just as Hadrian had built his wall across the island to mark the boundary with the Picts.

During those years, the rest of the world seemed very distant to the people of Britain and Ireland. They hardly remembered the Romans, and almost forgot there had once been a province called Britannia. People in the north stared at the ruined wall that stretched from hilltop to hilltop, and thought it must have been built by giants. Weeds pushed through the Roman roads and choked the gates of the Roman forts. Dogs lived in the Roman law courts, whose roofs fell in and walls disappeared under mounds of ivy. The Anglo-Saxons never went to such places, which they thought were full of ghosts. They couldn't imagine building law courts. Their own towns were little more than villages, while their villas were rough halls where warriors feasted, sang and told stories of battle.

The Anglo-Saxons worshipped their own gods, but Christianity survived in those parts of the islands the invaders didn't conquer. In Ireland monks still copied out the Bible and decorated its pages with drawings of saints and dragons, while Irish pilgrims voyaged to the Faroe Islands and Iceland – perhaps even to America. And Christianity still existed in Rome, where its leader, the pope, lived. A pope called Gregory sent a missionary called Augustine to England to convert the Anglo-Saxons. Augustine landed in Kent and built a church at Canterbury (which is why the archbishop of Canterbury is still the head of the English Church). First he converted the king of Kent, and then all the other kings, until the whole of England was Christian.

Being part of the Christian Church connected Britain and Ireland to the rest of Europe again. The Anglo-Saxons started to build churches. At Jarrow and Monkwearmouth, on the Tyne, they built two great monasteries where monks could read books and study. One of the monks, Bede, decided to write the history of everything that had happened in England since the Romans left, three hundred years before. He told of the wars between Saxons and Britons, and the battles between the Anglo-Saxon kings. But now, he wrote thankfully, everyone was at peace. Britain was quiet again and the years of trouble were over.

Unfortunately for the people of Britain and Ireland, their new-found peace didn't last long.

One day, some children on the beach saw a ship approaching. Its prow was carved like a dragon's head, and its sides were hung with shields.

Forty oars lifted in unison as they drove it towards the shore. As soon as it touched land, forty men jumped into the breakers, waving swords and clubs, and ran towards the nearest village to steal, burn and kill.

The people of Britain and Ireland called the raiders Vikings. They sailed across the North Sea from Norway and Denmark, but no one could tell when they would arrive or where they would attack next. When their longships appeared on the horizon, villagers tried to hide, for Vikings killed all the men they found, and took the women away. They burned Bede's monasteries of Monkwearmouth and Jarrow. They sailed around the north of Britain, attacked Ireland, then went down the coast of Wales, plundering and destroying.

Like the Angles and Saxons before them, though, the Vikings soon noticed how rich Britain was, and decided to stay. They made their capital at York and, one by one, defeated the Anglo-Saxon kingdoms until only Wessex was left.

The king of Wessex was called Alfred. To start with, the Danes (the Vikings who settled in England) beat his army as they beat everyone else. Alfred was forced to retreat until he reached the island of Athelney, in the Somerset fens. By then he hardly had any soldiers left, and no palace to live in, so he knocked on the door of a farmhouse and asked for shelter. One day – so people said afterwards – the farmer's wife left him to watch her cakes baking while she went to market. Alfred sat down to think how he could beat the Danes and was concentrating so hard he forgot about the cakes. He didn't notice them burning until the farmer's wife ran in shouting what a fool he was. Only then did he see how low he had sunk. The farmer's wife hadn't even realized he was a king.

But Alfred did come up with a plan. The Danes raided villages, so he made people live in fortified towns called *burhs*, or boroughs. The Danes came by sea, so he built a navy of his own to protect the island against them. In that way he defeated the Danes and became the first king of all the free English. The Danes still ruled the north and east of England, which was known as the Danelaw, but thanks to Alfred – who became known as Alfred the Great – they advanced no further.

At this time, the other kingdoms of Britain and Ireland took shape as well. Kenneth Mac Alpin, the king of the Scots, defeated the Picts and

made Scotland into one kingdom. The Scots were a nation of two parts. The south, where many Saxons had settled, was gentle farmland, while the mountains of the north belonged to fierce clans who spoke the Gaelic language they had brought with them from Ireland. Mac Alpin was a brave king, strong enough to keep the Vikings at bay.

The Welsh were united by Rhodri Mawr (Rhodri the Great), king of Gwynedd, who defeated the other Welsh kings and beat an army of Vikings that attacked from the sea. Unfortunately Rhodri's kingdom didn't last. The Vikings came back and killed him, and Wales broke up into smaller kingdoms again. But Rhodri's grandson, Hywel Dda, ruled much of Wales, and gave the Welsh laws that lasted for many centuries.

The Irish suffered from the Vikings even more than the other nations. Viking kings took over the east of Ireland and founded a great city they called Dublin.

The four nations of Britain and Ireland don't all have the same history. If this book could be longer, it would tell the stories of them all – of the Irish heroes, the Welsh kings, and the chieftains of the Scottish clans. Britain's story was written by all the people of the two islands, and only makes sense if you understand that Britain has never been a simple place, but a family of four different nations.

But in that family England was always the biggest, strongest and richest kingdom; and in time, England would come to dominate the others. So to understand how Britain came together, England's story is the thread we have to follow most closely, always remembering that it is only one of the threads that make up the story of Britain.

After Alfred died, English kings kept fighting the Danes, and almost drove them out of England. Unfortunately they weren't all as wise as Alfred. King Ethelred was known as "the Unready", because he did nothing to prepare ships or fortify boroughs. Instead of standing up to the Danes, he paid them to go away. But the Danes took his money and attacked anyway. First the Danish king, Svein Forkbeard, beat him, then Forkbeard's son Cnut drove Ethelred out of Wessex and made himself king of England.

By now, more than a thousand years had passed since Julius Caesar first set eyes on Britain, and one thousand and sixteen years had passed since Jesus Christ was born. That is the year we measure dates from, so the date was 1016 CE – Common Era (you also see it written AD or Anno Domini). From 1016 there were about another thousand years to go until today.

Cnut's son Harthacnut had no children, and after he died an Anglo-Saxon became king of England again. His name was Edward. He was Ethelred's son and had grown up in France, at the court of the duke of Normandy. King Edward founded a great abbey at Westminster and was so devout a Christian that people called him Edward the Confessor.

He kept England at peace, but had no sons. "Who should rule England when I die?" he wondered.

Many kings wanted to rule England, which was a rich country, with forests full of game and seas full of fish. The king of Norway, Harald Hardrada, said Harthacnut had promised him the throne, and he should have been king instead of Edward. William, duke of Normandy, said Edward had promised *him* England when he died, because Edward had been brought up at the Norman court. And the most powerful family in England, the Godwins of Wessex, wanted to be kings as well. The Godwins were so rich they already behaved like kings. Harold Godwinson had led an army into Wales, and beaten the Welsh in the king of England's name.

If I announce that any of them will be king, Edward thought to himself, the others will complain and attack England. And I am too old to fight them.

So he said nothing at all.

At last Edward the Confessor realized he was about to die. He lay in bed with priests kneeling by the door muttering prayers. Harold Godwinson, earl of Wessex, sat by his bedside day and night. He never left the dying king until Edward beckoned him closer and whispered something in his ear. Only then did Harold rise and go out.

"King Edward has made his decision," he announced. "I will be the new king of England."

The English cheered at the thought of having an Englishman as king, rather than a Frenchman or Viking. But the other candidates were furious. In Norway Harald Hardrada ordered a hundred longships to be built to carry his army to England. And in France Duke William of Normandy called his brother Odo and his advisers to a council of war.

"Many years ago," he told them in a voice thick with rage, "Harold

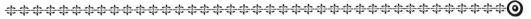

Godwinson came to Normandy and promised he would help me become king after Edward died. He has broken his word, and he will be punished."

The forests of Normandy echoed to the sound of axes chopping down trees, of shipwrights sawing wood to build ships and armourers sharpening swords. Carts rolled in from the countryside bringing barrels of food and wine for the soldiers. And Duke William stared out across the Channel towards England.

William was a giant of a man, head and shoulders taller than any other knight. Others trembled when they heard his name, for the duke of Normandy had never been defeated.

The year was 1066, and that is where our story begins.

TIMELINE

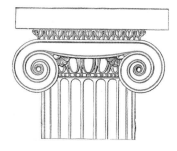

55–54 BCE ❖ Julius Caesar raids Britain.

43 CE ❖ The Romans invade Britain and make it the province of Britannia.

122 ❖ The Romans start Hadrian's Wall to defend the northern border of Britannia.

410 ❖ The Roman legions leave.

432 ❖ St Patrick goes to Ireland to convert the Irish to Christianity.

457 ❖ Hengist defeats the Britons. The Angles and Saxons are here to stay.

about 490 ❖ The Battle of Mount Badon. The Britons fight back.

500s ❖ The Scots move from Ireland to the land of the Picts, which we now call Scotland.

597 ❖ Sent by the pope, Augustine arrives in Britain

to convert the Anglo-Saxons to Christianity.

664 ❖ The Synod of Whitby. All the Christians in Britain agree to obey the pope.

731 ❖ Bede writes his history of the Anglo-Saxons.

757–96 ❖ Offa, king of Mercia, builds Offa's Dyke on the border between England and Wales.

789 ❖ The Vikings arrive. They make their first raids on Britain and Ireland.

840–58 ❖ Kenneth Mac Alpin unites the Picts and Scots and becomes the first king of Scotland.

?–878 ❖ Rhodri Mawr, king of Gwynedd, unites Wales, but is killed by the Vikings and his kingdom breaks up again.

871–99 ❖ Alfred the Great, king of Wessex, fights back against the Danes and becomes the first king of England.

?–950 ❖ Hywel Dda, Rhodri Mawr's grandson, gives the Welsh laws.

1014 ❖ The Danish king, Svein Forkbeard, attacks Ethelred the Unready, who flees to Normandy.

1016 ❖ Cnut, Svein Forkbeard's son, becomes king of England.

1042 ❖ Cnut's son has no children, so Edward the Confessor, Ethelred's son, becomes king of England.

1066 ❖ Edward dies. Harold Godwinson, earl of Wessex, becomes king and defeats Harald Hardrada, but is beaten by William the Conqueror, duke of Normandy. The Normans take over England.

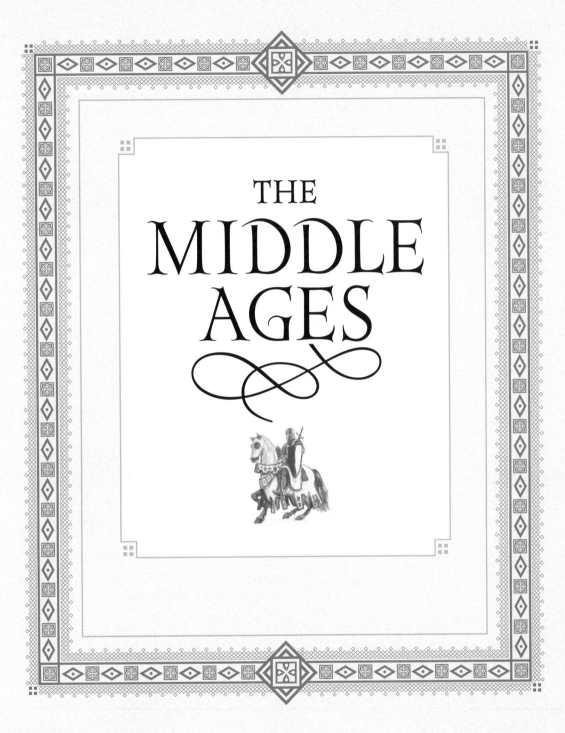

THE
MIDDLE
AGES

William I

CONQUERED
ENGLAND

Henry II

ATTACKED
THE CHURCH

Robert Bruce

SAVED
THE SCOTS

Richard
the Lionheart

INVADED
THE HOLY LAND

Black Prince

THE GREATEST
KNIGHT

Geoffrey Chaucer

TOLD STORIES
FOR EVERYONE

Owain Glyn Dwr

FOUGHT FOR
FREEDOM

Prince Edward &
Prince Richard

MURDERED IN
THE TOWER

THE MURDER OF THOMAS BECKET

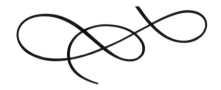

❖ The Norman Conquest ❖

HARALD Hardrada was the first to invade. He landed in Yorkshire with a great army of Vikings. With him was Harold Godwinson's brother Tostig, who had quarrelled with Harold the year before and wanted to get his own back.

Harold Godwinson gathered his army and marched north as fast as he could. "We must beat the invaders one at a time," he told his advisers. "First we will defeat Hardrada, then march back south to face the Normans."

His speed took the invaders by surprise. Hardrada and Tostig were holding a feast to celebrate their landing when the Anglo-Saxons arrived; their men didn't even have their armour with them. The Norwegians fell back to a place called Stamford Bridge but the Anglo-Saxons' best soldiers, the "Housecarls", made a wall of shields that no one could break through. Both Hardrada and Tostig were killed and hundreds of Norwegians slaughtered.

Panting, still smeared with blood from the battle, Harold addressed his soldiers. "No time to rest!" he shouted. "The Normans will soon attack England as well. We must march south tonight."

The English Channel is so narrow that on a clear day the white cliffs of Dover can be seen from France. But its storms can quickly overwhelm sailing ships, and several times Duke William had to delay his invasion while he waited for better weather. At last his chance came and the Normans set off across the Channel by night.

The Normans spoke French, but they were descended from Vikings – Northmen, or Normans – who had landed on the coast of France and made their home there. They had defeated many enemies before, but the invasion of England was the greatest challenge they had ever faced. As the soldiers stared ahead into the darkness, only William and his brother Odo seemed unafraid.

When the ships touched land it was William himself who jumped onto

THE NORMAN INVASION

stamford Bridge

River Humber

NORWAY

N

ENGLAND

London

Hastings

Pevensey

Calais

River Somme

FRANCE

- - - HAROLD HARDRADA
- · - HAROLD GODWINSON
○○○○ WILLIAM OF NORMANDY

the beach first. Men scrambled down the ships' sides. Soldiers stood up to their waists in water, making human chains to pass ashore barrels of arrows and racks of swords. Then the Norman army was ready to fight.

Meanwhile, Harold marched south.

When they first set off, the excitement of beating Hardrada had cheered up the housecarls and they sang songs as they marched. But as the miles stretched out, they grew tired. Their shields and swords seemed to grow heavier, and each hill was greeted with a groan. By the time they reached the agreed gathering place near Hastings on the Sussex coast they were exhausted. Knowing the Normans were near by, some began grimly sharpening their swords, but others were too tired even to do that, and fell asleep with their packs still slung across their backs.

Next morning, Harold drew up his housecarls along a ridge. Normans filled the valley below. He could see Duke William, the tallest of them, ordering the horsemen into line, for the Normans fought on horseback as well as on foot.

Then the ground began to shake as the Normans charged.

When their cavalry reached the Anglo-Saxon line, the shock seemed to make the earth itself quiver. For a moment, there was a terrible confusion of whinnying horses and screaming men as the Anglo-Saxons staggered back. Then the housecarls recovered, and before they knew it, the Normans were retreating back down the hill.

That wasn't the last charge, though. Again and again the Normans thundered towards the line of shields on the hill. Waiting in the rear, the women who followed the Anglo-Saxon army knew nothing of what was happening in the battle. Sometimes they heard cheers from the front, and sometimes groans. The fighters who came to refresh themselves with gulps of water were smeared with grime, and their swords red with blood. They had no time even to exchange a word before snatching up their shields to run back to the battle. As the day wore on, the women noticed more and more of them were wounded. But it wasn't so much the terrible wounds that troubled them as the empty look in the fighters' eyes.

"How is the battle going?" they asked. "Have we won yet?"

Earlier in the day the men might have shouted, "Soon!" Now they merely shook their heads before returning to the fray.

But towards the end of the afternoon, Harold's men saw a change.

"The Normans are retreating!" someone yelled.

With a shout of relief the housecarls broke their line. King Harold yelled at them not to move, but the soldiers streamed downhill to pursue their enemy.

That was when Duke William gave the signal to turn round.

Running away had only been a trick to break the Anglo-Saxon line. Now the Normans turned and fell upon their pursuers. Only a small remnant of the Anglo-Saxon army made it back to the top of the hill. Locking arms, they tried to form a shield wall, but there were many gaps in it. They barely had time to regroup before the Normans charged again.

"Arrows!" someone cried. Arrows dropped from the sky like hornets. And the next moment a murmur ran along the line.

"The king ... the king has been hit... Harold Godwinson is dead..."

Afterwards some said that an arrow had hit Harold Godwinson in the eye; others thought he had been struck down by a Norman knight. Whatever happened, the shock was enough to make hope desert the Anglo-Saxons. They lowered their shields; first one man dropped his weapon, and then another. Screams went up from the women in the rear as they saw Normans appearing out of the evening gloom. And among them, head and shoulders above any other man, was Duke William of Normandy.

The Anglo-Saxons had ruled England for five hundred years, ever since conquering it after the Romans left. At the Battle of Hastings, on 14 October 1066, their rule came to an end. England had new masters, French masters. And it had a new king – William the Conqueror.

❖ Domesday Book ❖

WILLIAM the Conqueror hoped that defeating Harold would make the Anglo-Saxon leaders, who were called earls, accept him as king. But he was in for a disappointment. Survivors of the battle gathered together in forests and marshes and attacked the Normans wherever they could. An Anglo-Saxon leader called Hereward the Wake hid in the Cambridgeshire fens, raiding Peterborough and other towns. Whenever Normans came to fight him, he and his followers retreated into the marshes, using hidden causeways his enemies didn't know about.

So William took land away from the Anglo-Saxon lords. After all, he had plenty of French followers who wanted their reward for fighting at Hastings. Normans became earls; Norman knights took over Anglo-Saxon villages and built manor houses where the servants had to listen to the strange sound of French being spoken. William built a castle by the river Thames to make sure that London obeyed him. He called it the Tower of London.

Meanwhile, his brother Odo ordered a great tapestry to be made, telling the story of the Norman Conquest of England. It showed the Normans preparing their ships and armour, and the moment when Harold was killed. The tapestry can still be seen in Bayeux, in Normandy.

But despite all William had done, another rebellion began in the north of England. This time William was furious. He led an army to the north to punish the rebels and destroy their land.

"They will never raise their swords against me again," he said.

His soldiers rode from village to village, tearing down barns, slaughtering cattle and destroying crops. Palls of smoke drifted across the moors. In the towns through which William passed, women crouched in the streets, weeping next to the bodies of their husbands.

But frightening people is not the same as governing them. William decided that if he was to rule England successfully, he had to know more about the country he had conquered. So one year, just after Christmas, he ordered his officials to make a list of everything in England and write it down in a book.

"Everything?" the officials asked.

William nodded. "Everything."

So every town and every village was listed in William's book; every field and pasture was measured. The book listed how many cattle there were in each herd and how many sheep in each flock. When it was finished, people called it Domesday Book, because it was like the list that would be made at the Day of Judgement – Doomsday – when Christians believed the world would come to an end.

After that, the Anglo-Saxons realized there was nothing in England their new king didn't know about. *"Not one ox,"* they muttered sorrowfully to each other. *"Not one cow. Not one pig!"* *

And at last they understood that they hadn't just been beaten in a battle. The Normans were here to stay.

* Quotations in italics are from historical sources.

❖ The White Ship ❖

IN those days kings ruled everything. They commanded the nobles (the earls and the lesser lords, who were called barons); the nobles commanded the knights; the knights commanded the ordinary people. In that way, the poorest child in England did what the king wanted. But what happened when a king died? Quite often everyone started quarrelling about who should be king next.

William the Conqueror had three sons. He left Normandy to the eldest, Robert; and England to the second, who was called William Rufus because of his red face. William Rufus was a strong leader and a brave fighter. He soon quarrelled with Robert and took Normandy for himself. But one day, while he was hunting in the New Forest, he was accidentally killed by an arrow.

Accidentally? Some people whispered that the youngest of William the Conqueror's sons, Henry, had murdered William Rufus because *he* wanted to be king. That was the trouble with giving so much power to kings. People would do almost anything to become king themselves.

Henry I was a thoughtful leader. He ended the bitterness between Normans and Anglo-Saxons by marrying an Anglo-Saxon princess. He improved the way the country was run by keeping proper accounts of all the money he gathered in tax and spent on the government. The clerks who added up his money used a chequered tablecloth to do their sums on, and that gave the accounts office the name it still has today: the Exchequer. Fortunately Henry had a son, so everyone hoped that when he died there would be no argument about who should be king next.

Henry was duke of Normandy as well as king of England, so he and his son, William, often had to cross the Channel between Normandy and England. One day, Henry gave Prince William a new ship. It was fast and beautiful. Because of its white sails and white hull, people called it the *White Ship*, and William couldn't wait to sail in it. He arranged to meet his new ship at Barfleur in Normandy, but when he arrived he was told he would have to wait for the tide. While he waited, William feasted and drank with his friends, and they invited the sailors to join them. No one noticed that the wind was getting stronger and the waves were rising –

they were all too drunk. When it was time to leave, the harbour master tried to stop them, because it was too dangerous.

"Nonsense!" shouted Prince William.

The sailors were so drunk they could hardly hoist the sails, and the harbour master watched in terror as the *White Ship* headed out to the sea. A moment later, a squall whistled out of the darkness, and the ship was picked up like a toy boat on a pond and hurled towards the rocks. For a second, it soared above the waves like a gull; then it was gone and all the harbour master could see was twisted rope and men struggling amid the wreckage. Prince William's body was washed up on the beach the next day.

King Henry grieved for the son he had lost. But he also saw trouble ahead, for his only other child was a daughter, Matilda. And England had never had a queen before.

❖ Matilda ❖

IN those days women and men weren't seen as equal. Most people thought women were there to have babies. Poor women cooked and cleaned; rich women played music and sewed. The idea that a woman might run a kingdom seemed mad.

Matilda didn't agree. She was used to getting her own way. Matilda was hardly a little girl, after all. At the time of the *White Ship* disaster she was already grown up and married to the Holy Roman emperor, who ruled most of central Europe. Why shouldn't she become queen of England after her father?

To avoid arguments Henry made all the earls and barons promise to obey Matilda after he died. But in private they all shook their heads. And after Henry's death, Matilda's cousin Stephen gathered them together.

"None of us want a woman as ruler," he said. "Make me king instead."

Stephen was popular and a good fighter, so they agreed. They didn't think Matilda would make a fuss. After all, she was only a woman! But they soon discovered how much they had underestimated her. First she gathered an army and conquered Normandy. Then she invaded England, just like her grandfather William the Conqueror. Matilda's husband, the emperor, had died by then, and when she married again, she had chosen the richest nobleman in France, Geoffrey Plantagenet. That meant she didn't have to worry about money, and could concentrate on beating Stephen.

Stephen could have won the war by capturing Matilda as soon as she landed, but despite his brave appearance he turned out to be weak and indecisive. He said it wouldn't be right to take a woman prisoner. When his army was beaten in battle, though, Matilda didn't worry about capturing Stephen. She threw him in jail and rode to London to be crowned "Lady of the English".

It seemed as if her dream had come true at last. But Matilda soon threw away her advantage, for she was proud and had a terrible temper. She screamed at earls and treated barons like servants until the English started muttering that they would rather have Stephen back; so when he escaped from jail, the war began again.

This time Matilda called on her son Henry to help. Henry, who was as

brave and strong-willed as his mother, arrived from Normandy with a new army. Despite his assistance, the war went badly for Matilda, but it was then, when her fortunes were at their lowest, that she showed just how brave a woman leader could be.

That winter, her army was trapped inside Oxford. It was freezing cold, the fields were covered in snow, and Stephen's soldiers surrounded the town. Matilda ordered her followers to lower her down the walls in a basket so she could escape.

"You'll be seen against the snow!" they protested.

So Matilda put on a white cloak as camouflage. She climbed into her basket, escaped through the snowdrifts and went on fighting.

The war continued to go badly, though, and at last Matilda realized she would never defeat Stephen and become queen of England. But she was determined her son Henry would be king. So in return for ending the war, she made a deal with Stephen. And when Stephen died, Matilda's son, Henry Plantagenet, was crowned king of England – just as his mother had wanted.

❖ England's Neighbours ❖

WHEN William the Conqueror and the Normans invaded, they only planned to take over England, but it wasn't long before they started looking greedily at the countries that lay beyond – at Scotland, Wales and Ireland.

William the Conqueror invaded the Scottish Lowlands and forced King Malcolm III to accept him as overlord. After Malcolm's death, the Scots quarrelled about who should be king next.

"We'll have no more Englishmen," cried Malcolm's brother, Donald Ban, "and no more Normans!" And he drove away Malcolm's son Duncan and became king himself.

Duncan escaped to England, travelled to London and asked the English king, William Rufus, to help him win his kingdom back. The war that followed between Duncan and Donald Ban was as bitter as the war between Stephen and Matilda. When Duncan was killed, his younger brother Edgar took over. Edgar captured Donald Ban, blinded him, and became king of Scotland himself. After Edgar's death a third brother, Alexander, became king, and then a fourth, called David. But most of them needed English help to keep their thrones. From now on there were always Normans at the Scottish court, and the kings of England were always looking for opportunities to extend their power. Malcolm IV, who followed David, was too weak to resist. When Henry II, Matilda's son, demanded that Cumbria and Northumbria should become part of England, the Scots told Malcolm he ought to fight back. He just sighed and shook his head.

"What can I do?" he said. *The king of England always has the better of it, by reason of his much greater power."*

The Welsh were next to find out how hard it was being England's neighbour.

Wales wasn't a single kingdom. Gwynedd, Powys, Morgannwg and Dyfed each had their own king, and that made it much harder for the Welsh to stand up to invaders. Not long before the Normans arrived, Gruffudd ap Llywelyn, king of Gwynedd, overcame all the others to make himself king of Wales. But when Harold Godwinson brought an army to beat him, Gruffudd's rivals turned against him, and he was killed.

The Normans invaded Wales as well, but the Welsh fought back, retreating into the mountains when the Normans sent soldiers, and winning their country back when the Normans were occupied with troubles of their own. During the civil war between Stephen and Matilda, Owain, King of Gwynedd, called all the Welsh leaders together and united Wales, making himself king.

So Henry II set out to humble the Welsh just as he had humbled the Scots. First he commanded Owain to accept him as overlord. Then, when Owain refused his orders, he invaded Wales, and the Welsh had to retreat back to their mountains. They stayed free, but it was clear they would never live peacefully next to a country as powerful as England.

Finally, having dealt with Scotland and Wales, Henry turned his attention to Ireland.

Ireland had never been conquered by the Romans or Anglo-Saxons. The Vikings had settled there, but the country was still divided between different kings. Dermot Mac Murrough, king of Leinster, wanted to make himself king of Ireland, but when his ally, Muirchertach o Mac Lochlainn, was killed, Dermot had to flee across the Irish Sea to Britain. There he made friends with a Norman, Richard de Clare, earl of Pembroke, a powerful fighter everyone called Strongbow.

"If you help me win Ireland," Dermot told Strongbow, "you can marry my daughter Aoife, and I will reward you with rich lands."

Strongbow agreed. He gathered soldiers and knights, told them of the wealth they would find in Ireland, and led them across the sea. One by one he defeated all of Dermot Mac Murrough's enemies. But then, finding a country of green fields and rich valleys, Strongbow and his men decided to stay. And when Henry II heard of Ireland's wealth, he was furious that Strongbow hadn't asked him to help, so he too led an army to Ireland. English soldiers marched across the countryside, burning and looting; English lords claimed valleys for themselves; English knights seized castles and divided up the fields.

"It was easy to ask the English in," the Irish whispered to each other. "But how will we ever make them leave?"

Indeed, it would be almost a thousand years before Ireland was free again. In those years, many English armies would pass through Ireland,

and many Englishmen would seize Irish land and make their fortunes. And many hard centuries would pass before the people of Britain and Ireland learned to live together in peace and dignity.

By conquering Ireland, Henry II became the most powerful ruler the islands had known since the Romans. His empire stretched far beyond Britain and Ireland. Thanks to Matilda, he was duke of Normandy; from his father, Geoffrey Plantagenet, he inherited much of western France; and when he married the richest heiress in France, Eleanor of Aquitaine, he took over all of south-west France as well. You could walk from Newcastle to Spain without leaving Henry's lands.

But even an empire wasn't enough for Henry II. Henry was as fiery and proud as his mother, the sort of person who wants everyone to do as he says. So when he realized there was something in his empire he couldn't control – the Christian Church – he began to brood. And he decided not to rest until the Church obeyed him as well.

❖ The King and the Archbishop ❖

APART from a small number of Jews, everyone in Britain and Ireland was Christian, and the most important building in every village was the church. The Anglo-Saxons had built some churches of stone, but they were nothing compared with the churches constructed after the Normans arrived. Every village soon had a fine stone church, while in the most important towns the Normans built huge cathedrals whose walls rose high above the rooftops.

Cathedrals took years to finish, and hundreds of men to build them. Masons laboured in the stoneyards, some squaring blocks while others worked the stones which would be fitted to water spouts or pinnacles, carving them into flowers, animals or monsters. Cathedral architects were always trying to come up with new ideas, many of which they copied from France. At Durham Cathedral the central aisle grew so tall that the masons felt dizzy as they looked down at the pavement below. Instead of covering the roof in wood, the architect ordered them to build a vault of stone, so that people entering the cathedral felt as if they were walking into a great stone forest. In Henry II's time, architects learned how to build pointed arches instead of round ones. The new style was called Gothic. Then they worked out how to stretch windows upwards until walls seemed to have more glass in them than stone. In the setting sun, the stonework glowed like gold, and light glinted off the glass.

Cathedrals were the greatest and most beautiful buildings in the whole of England, but they didn't belong to the king – they belonged to the Church. And the people who prayed in them every Sunday were not doing the king's bidding, but that of their priests and bishops.

And that made Henry II furious.

"You may be king of England," bishops said to him, "but our master is the king of heaven."

"You may tell your earls what to do," said the archbishop of Canterbury, "but my orders come from God himself."

At last Henry came up with a plan.

It is lonely being a king, and Henry, with his raging temper, only had one friend. His name was Thomas Becket. He was not much older than

Henry and, like him, loved hunting, feasting and fine food. He was the only person able to stand up to Henry, for he was just as stubborn as the king himself. Henry decided to make his friend archbishop of Canterbury.

"If I make you its leader," he told Thomas, "the Church will do as I say!"

People who knew Becket laughed at the thought of him as an archbishop. He wasn't even a priest! Becket himself wasn't sure about the idea. But when the old archbishop of Canterbury died, Henry made his friend archbishop in his place.

Eagerly the king looked forward to his first meeting with Archbishop Thomas. They would enjoy a fine feast together, he decided, and work out how to deal with the Church once and for all. But when Becket arrived, the king could hardly believe his eyes. His friend had turned into a proper churchman. He wore a rough brown cloak and his feet were bare. He refused to touch any of the rich food the king's cooks had prepared.

When Henry told Becket to control his priests, Becket said his master was the king of heaven. When Henry shouted that he expected the bishops to obey him, Becket replied that his orders came from God himself. The two men, who had once been such close friends, became deadly enemies. At last, in a towering rage, Henry banished Becket from the kingdom.

When he was gone, though, Henry regretted what he had done. His rages never lasted for long, and Becket had once been his closest friend. So envoys were sent to tell Becket he could return.

But it wasn't long before the archbishop and the king were arguing as much as ever. The king demanded to be obeyed; the archbishop said he would obey only God. One night at dinner, after hearing of Becket's latest refusal to follow his orders, the king rose from the table in a furious rage.

"Will no one rid me of this turbulent priest?" he shouted.

Henry was not the only one who found Thomas Becket irritating. Plenty of knights at court were jealous of him, and longed for revenge. Four of them, sitting at the back of the room, nodded at each other, then slipped out so quietly that the king didn't even see them go. They saddled their horses and took the road to Canterbury.

Thomas Becket was praying with his monks when the knights broke into the monastery. The monks pulled him into the cathedral for safety, but he wouldn't let them bolt the door.

"It is not right to turn the house of prayer into a fortress," he said.

Evening service had started in the cathedral, but everyone stopped singing when the four knights strode in, brandishing swords. Becket stood by an altar to pray, with his monks around him. One of the knights furiously struck at his head, almost cutting off a monk's arm. After two more blows Becket slumped to the ground, and a third blow cut his head open. Then, grinding their heels in the blood on the cathedral floor, the knights strode out into the darkness.

By this time Henry had quite forgotten his rage. When the knights came in and told him what they had done, he shouted for them to be seized as murderers.

Their leader didn't even flinch. "But it was you who told us to do it," he said. "Have you forgotten your own words? *'Will no one rid me of this turbulent priest?'"*

Stunned, the king stole away to his bedroom, where he lay all night wide awake. How could he sleep? He had ordered his own friend's death.

In the days that followed he had to endure the shocked looks of his courtiers, and angry messages from kings abroad. Pilgrims flocked to Canterbury to pray at the tomb of Thomas Becket, and the pope declared him a saint.

And so Henry never did become master of the Church. Instead he had to endure his own guilt until he too took the road to Canterbury. There, the most powerful man in Europe was whipped publicly by the monks of Canterbury, and forced to pray for forgiveness at his friend's tomb.

Not everything Henry II did was bad. He improved the way laws worked by setting up proper courts and sending judges all over the country to settle arguments. However, his temper never got any better, and he never found a friend to replace Thomas Becket. He quarrelled with his wife, Eleanor of Aquitaine; he quarrelled with his five sons. Although he had been such a powerful king, Henry died knowing that not even his own family loved him.

After his death his eldest son, Richard, became king. Richard was a famous fighter, and as he marched through London to be crowned, the crowd cheered and called him Richard the Lionheart. Everyone looked forward to his reign. But Richard passed hardly any of his time in England. Instead he spent it fighting far away, sometimes in France or Germany, but most of all in the Holy Land of Palestine, on crusade.

❖ Richard the Lionheart and the Crusades ❖

HUNDREDS of years before, not long after the fall of Rome, the prophet Muhammed began a new religion in the countries to the east of the Mediterranean Sea. He called it Islam. After Muhammed's death his followers, called Muslims, spread Islam among the Arabs. Inspired by their new faith, the Arabs expanded their empire until it reached the eastern shore of the Mediterranean. Muslims conquered Egypt and northern Africa. They even crossed the Mediterranean, invaded Spain and marched north as far as France. In the countries they conquered, Muslims maintained the civilized way of life of the Roman Empire. They built great cities and beautiful mosques. However, most people in Europe hated and feared them because they were not Christian.

Along the way, the Muslims conquered Palestine, the country on the eastern shore of the Mediterranean where Jesus Christ had lived. They took over Bethlehem, where Christ was born; and Jerusalem, where he died. Christians hated Muslims owning these holy places, so the pope, head of the Christian Church, declared a holy war against Muslims. He ordered all Christian kings and knights to go to the Holy Land and win it back.

The knights wore the Christian symbol, the cross, on their armour, so they were called crusaders. They marched to the Holy Land, defeated the Arabs and founded a Christian kingdom in Jerusalem. But the Arabs fought back. They didn't see why Christians from Europe should govern part of their lands. Besides, Jerusalem was just as holy to Muslims as it was to Christians and Jews. So they attacked the kingdom of Jerusalem, and knights from France, Germany, England and Spain set off on crusades to defend it.

The crusaders had a shock when they arrived in the east. They had been brought up to think Muslims were barbarians; instead they found most Arabs were more civilized than they were. Muslim scholars studied mathematics and astronomy; their architects designed gardens filled with the sound of fountains and the scent of orange trees, and rooms decorated with beautiful tiles and carpets. The Christian knights, with their shaggy beards and rusty armour, seemed as savage to them as the Viking raiders once seemed to the English.

But the Muslims were great fighters as well. And just before Richard the Lionheart became king of England, they recaptured Jerusalem from the Christians. Their leader was Saladin, sultan of Egypt.

As soon as he became king, Richard the Lionheart swore he would win Jerusalem back. So he gathered his knights and set off for the Holy Land on crusade. Richard conquered Cyprus, captured the town of Acre, and even beat the mighty Saladin in battle. He became famous for his courage and daring. He could not capture the city of Jerusalem, however, so at last he made a truce with Saladin and turned for home.

Unfortunately Richard had quarrelled with some of the other crusaders, who were jealous of him, and on his way home one of them captured him and locked him up in a castle. In England everyone waited for news of the king. But years passed and Richard the Lionheart did not return.

In the meantime England was governed by Richard's younger brother, Prince John.

❖ John Lackland and Robin Hood ❖

MOST of our story so far has been about kings, earls and knights. But most people weren't kings or knights; they were just ordinary men, women and children. And in the Middle Ages most of them were very poor.

Life then was much harder than it is now. There were no proper doctors or hospitals, so people who fell sick often died. There were no cars or trains, so the only way to get about was by horse or on foot. There was no electricity, which meant no fridges, so food went bad quickly, and no light, so people rose at dawn and went to bed at sunset, to make the most of the sun's brightness. They worked in the fields, ploughing and harvesting by hand because they had no machines. Their backs grew crooked and their shoulders bent, until young farmers looked like old men of eighty.

Most people weren't free. They had to work for the knight who ran their village. The knight had to obey the local lord (a baron or an earl), and the lord obeyed the king. The king was at the top of everything. It wasn't so bad if the king was wise, generous and honest. Unfortunately John, who governed England while Richard was away, was not wise, generous or honest. People called him John Lackland because he had no land or money of his own. And as soon as he took charge of England he set about making himself rich.

"Put up the taxes!" he roared at his chancellor.

The people had already been taxed to pay for Richard the Lionheart's crusade. They had hardly anything left, but John taxed them anyway. After that, the poor had nothing left to eat, so they sat around their fires and told stories instead. The stories they loved best were about a bandit called Robin Hood, who refused to pay John's taxes and lived in Sherwood Forest as an outlaw. He robbed rich people on their way through the forest and gave their money to the poor. As time went by, other bandits came to join him in the forest. Robin's friends – Much the Miller's Son and Alan-a-Dale, Friar Tuck and Little John – became almost as famous as Robin Hood himself. The villains in the Robin Hood stories were Prince John's sheriff at Nottingham, and the baron Guy of Gisbourne.

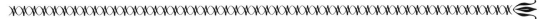

Unfortunately there was no real Robin Hood to feed the poor. When the stories ended, children's stomachs were still empty, and the fire was still cold.

"Never mind," they said. "Richard the Lionheart will soon come back to look after us."

Then came news from France that made every poor man and woman in England tremble. Richard the Lionheart had been released from prison, but killed soon afterwards fighting in France. John Lackland was the new king of England.

❖ Magna Carta ❖

JOHN was even worse as king than he had been as governor. He became more crafty, and more untrustworthy. Some people believed he murdered his own nephew, because he was jealous of him. When the king of France seized his lands in Normandy, John didn't even fight back, as Richard the Lionheart would have done, but let Normandy go. After that he was known as John Softsword.

While a good king might run things well, a bad king is worse than useless. John taxed people and wasted the money. He threw his enemies in jail for no reason. He changed laws without asking anyone's opinion. At last even his barons had had enough.

"Why should we give up our wealth to a king who wastes it?" they asked. "Why should we obey John Softsword when even the poor people hate him?"

And so the barons drew up a great charter. They wrote down everything that was wrong with John's rule, and described how England ought to be governed instead.

It was the first time people had really thought about what made government fair, and what made it unfair. The barons decided kings couldn't do just as they pleased. They had to obey rules, like everybody else. They couldn't seize someone else's property, or lock people up just because they didn't like them. In fact, they decided proper law courts were the most important things of all, because everyone had a right to a fair trial.

"To no one will we sell, to no one will we deny or delay right of justice," they wrote. That meant that no one should bribe judges, that everyone had a right to a fair trial, and that they couldn't be kept in jail for years waiting for it.

The barons wrote down their rules, sixty-three of them, and signed their names at the bottom. They called their document Magna Carta, the Great Charter.

"Traitors!" squealed John when he heard about it.

He summoned an army, but no one obeyed him any more. Then the barons seized London, and John realized he had to do as they asked. He

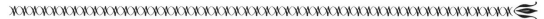

met them at a field called Runnymede next to the Thames.

"Give us your word you will obey the Great Charter!" they ordered.

"Traitors," John hissed between his teeth. But he set his seal to it anyway.

Some of Magna Carta is still law today. And still, eight hundred years later, everyone in Britain expects justice in the courts, and wants the government to be fair to everybody. That is the basis of everything that happens in this country.

Of course, John tried to go back on his word soon afterwards; the barons had been right not to trust him. He didn't get far, though, for John Lackland died the next year, unloved and unmourned.

❖ Simon de Montfort and Parliament ❖

ONCE people had started thinking about how the country should be run, it was hard for them to stop. Who should make laws? Everyone had to live by them, so why shouldn't everyone have a say in making them? Should kings ask advice, or make decisions by themselves? Should barons have a say in what happened, or did they have to do as they were told? Of course, kings hated the idea of being given rules. Henry III, John's son, kept trying to wriggle out of Magna Carta. And that meant he too began arguing with the barons.

Henry III was not as grasping or cowardly as his father, but he was just as foolish. For example, he decided he wanted to own Sicily, a rich island in the Mediterranean where crusaders often stopped on their way to the Holy Land, so he offered to buy it from the pope. The pope was surprised, as Sicily didn't belong to him, but he took Henry's money anyway. Only then did Henry realize what a stupid mistake he had made.

"You might as well try and buy the moon," growled his brother, Richard.

Richard would have made a much better king than Henry, but he was only a younger brother. As time went by, and Henry came up with one pointless scheme after another, the barons became more and more annoyed. Eventually they called a great meeting at Oxford. The country shouldn't be governed only by the king, they declared, but by a great council. They called their proposals the Provisions of Oxford.

Some of the barons wanted to go even further, and change the way everything in England was run. That was too much for others, so they began to quarrel. Seeing his enemies argue among themselves, Henry summoned an army and declared war on all of them.

That was a mistake. At a great battle at Lewes, in Sussex, the king was beaten and taken prisoner along with his son, Prince Edward. Simon de Montfort, the barons' leader, became the most powerful man in England.

De Montfort was among the barons who felt Magna Carta hadn't gone far enough. It was all very well to say the king had to govern by certain laws, he thought, but shouldn't everyone have a chance to agree to the laws before they were passed? So he summoned all the lords (the earls and barons) to London. He couldn't summon all the ordinary people (the commons), so he called representatives instead. Two knights from every county and two citizens from every town in England set off for London. The House of Lords and House of Commons met as a parliament for the first time in 1265, and agreed that no law could be passed unless they approved it.

Unfortunately not all the barons liked what Simon de Montfort had done. They weren't sure about ordinary knights and townspeople helping to decide laws, and a lot of them were jealous of him.

"He wants to be king!" they whispered.

So when King Henry's son, Prince Edward, escaped from jail, many of them joined him. They fought a battle at Evesham in Worcestershire, killed Simon de Montfort, and put Henry back on the throne.

All the same, the idea of parliaments didn't go away. For Prince Edward could see that parliaments might help kings as much as everyone else. If Parliament agreed to the laws the king wanted, then people wouldn't be able to complain about them. If Parliament agreed to taxes, people would have to pay them.

And Edward decided that when he became king, he would summon Parliament himself.

❖ Wool ❖

TAXES mattered more than ever before, because England was getting richer. Cathedrals and churches were being built everywhere, and architects had come up with a new style of building. Instead of using plain stone, they ordered stonemasons to decorate every surface with carvings of flowers, leaves and animals, and twist the stone around the windows into elaborate patterns. Today we call it the Decorated Style. Meanwhile the towns were becoming more crowded. In those days Britain had fewer people than it has today; but even so, villages were growing, and on almost every hilltop a windmill spun its sails, grinding up the corn to make flour for bread.

England was getting richer because of wool.

Wool was almost the only cloth people had in the Middle Ages. All clothes, all sheets, all blankets were made of wool. And the best wool in Europe came from England. If you stood on a hillside in the Cotswolds you could see sheep grazing the fields in every direction. In Norfolk and Suffolk huge flocks surrounded every village. Warehouses in seaports were piled high with bales of wool, and their owners, the wool merchants, became rich. They used their money to build palaces, and competed to see who could construct the most lavish churches.

Knights and lords hated that. "Some of those merchants are richer than we are," they muttered.

In London, they peered through the windows of counting houses and saw rows of men bent over account books. Fighting still mattered more than anything else, and for that you still needed knights. But money was starting to matter too. Hundreds of years before, the Romans had shown how people could get rich by trading instead of fighting. It had almost been forgotten in the centuries after the end of Rome, but during the Middle Ages merchants started to amass wealth again. Their ships sailed to France, to Italy and Spain, carrying wool and bringing back spices and wine.

In those days, long sea voyages were dangerous. But at around this time a new invention, the compass, made them much safer. It came from the east, and passed quickly from merchant to merchant until it reached England.

"It's just a wooden box," said sea captains, who gathered in harbours to talk about it.

But inside the box was a tiny metal needle, and whichever way they turned it, the needle kept pointing in the same direction.

"North," said the captains.

A captain with a compass always knew which way north was, so he could find his way home – even if he sailed as far as China. Sea voyages were still dangerous. Ships were small, with only sails or oars to drive them, and out on the empty sea it was easy to get lost. That was why nobody in Europe ever ventured far from the shore. They'd never heard of America or Australia, and sailing to Africa would have been like going to the moon. But from now on, people could sail further round the world than ever before, carrying wool, and bringing back goods from far away.

❖ Edward Longshanks ❖

WHEN Henry III died, his son, Prince Edward, became king. Edward I was a soldier, grim-faced, unsmiling, and so tall he was known as Longshanks. When he was young he went on crusade and made a name for himself as a fighter. None of the barons dared quarrel with him. The only soft thing in Edward was his love for his queen, Eleanor. She was a Spanish princess, whose title was Infanta of Castile. When she arrived in London, Londoners tied their tongues in knots trying to say it right.

"The Fantastic Cattle."

"The Elephant and Castle."

There is still a place in London called Elephant and Castle where they put up a sign to greet her.

Edward adored his queen. When she died, much later, he ordered stone-masons to carve crosses to his *chère reine* or "dear queen" wherever her funeral procession stopped. Many people think that Charing Cross, in London, is named after a Chère Reine Cross.

However Edward planned to spend most of his reign leading his army. He knew whom to fight: the Welsh and the Scots – for he had decided to make the whole island of Britain obey England.

Because wars are expensive, Edward knew he would need a lot of money, and that was when he remembered the idea of calling Parliament. If Parliament agreed to the taxes he asked for, then no one could complain about paying them. So he summoned Parliament to London to discuss his laws and vote for his taxes. Then, when Edward had enough money, he was ready to start fighting.

He began by attacking Wales.

The English had never managed to conquer the Welsh. Harold Godwinson defeated them, but they didn't become Saxon. The Normans conquered them, but Owain of Gwynedd drove the Normans out. Henry II subdued them, but not for long. King John tried to overcome them, but while he was quarrelling with his barons over Magna Carta, Llywelyn ap Iorwerth won back what John had taken. His grandson, Llywelyn ap Gruffudd, did the same while Henry III was quarrelling with Simon de

Montfort. For hundreds of years, then, the Welsh stayed free – until King Edward came.

Edward built castles all round Wales – at Harlech, Caernarvon and Conwy – to keep the Welsh under control. They were enormous, with towering battlements and walls several metres thick. The Welsh had never even heard of castles like that.

"How could anyone attack such a thing?" they gasped as they peered up at the battlements.

Nor had the Welsh seen an army like Edward's. His columns of soldiers seemed to march by for ever. And even in stories they had never heard of a fleet as powerful as the one that sailed up the coast of Wales, landing wherever its captains pleased.

"This time the English are coming to stay," said Llywelyn ap Gruffudd's brother Dafydd gloomily.

"Nonsense!" shouted Llywelyn. "We'll fight them, and when they've gone, we'll win back what we've lost!"

But in his heart of hearts even Llywelyn knew this time was different. He was still fighting bravely when the English killed him in battle.

"From now on," Edward announced, "Wales will be part of my kingdom."

He passed a law, the Statute of Rhuddlan, to say so, and made his eldest son prince of Wales. Since then, the eldest son of the king or queen of England has always been called prince of Wales, and Wales has always been ruled as one country with England.

Edward wanted to do the same to Scotland. But first he turned his attention to another people, a race inside England itself. He made his decision just after Queen Eleanor died, when everyone said he was becoming harsher than ever.

Edward decided to drive out the English Jews.

❖ The Expulsion of the Jews ❖

JEWS had lived in England for centuries. There weren't many of them, and they mostly lived in a few towns so as to be near each other. Usually they were forced to live in special parts of towns, called ghettos. One of the most important was the ghetto in York.

Jews weren't allowed to own land; most were poor tailors and craftsmen. A few grew rich, though, by lending money to Christians and charging them interest. Christians weren't allowed to do this, because the Bible said it was wrong. The Christians didn't *have* to borrow money, of course, but it didn't stop them hating the Jews they paid interest to.

Today we hardly see the difference between British Jews and British Christians, but in those days Jews stood out because of their different language and dress.

"They can't be trusted," English Christians said. "They're not like *us*."

"They care more about their religion than this country."

People often fear anyone who isn't like them, and fear often turns into hatred. On the Sabbath, Jews went to their synagogues to follow the rituals they had practised for thousands of years, but Christians started a rumour that their Sabbath ritual was to steal Christian babies and drink their blood.

The Jews in York knew that people outside the ghetto hated them. Often, when they went into town, people spat at them or trod on their cloaks. Jewish children were told terrible stories about what had happened in the past.

"When Richard the Lionheart was crowned, two Jews went to London to give him presents from the Jews of York. But people turned on them in the street, and when news got back to York, the Christians attacked Jews here as well. They drove them into the castle and burned it down. Every Jew in York was killed."

Now Jews were attacked again. First King Edward made them wear yellow badges on their clothes; then he decided to get rid of them altogether. He had orders pinned up in every marketplace saying that Jews had to leave England immediately, and if they stayed they would be put to death.

Jews gathered anxiously in their homes in the ghetto.

"The king can't throw us out! We're English! We've been here for centuries."

But their leaders only shook their heads. "He can do what he likes," they growled. "He's the king."

The Jews weren't even allowed to take all their possessions with them – Edward kept any money that was owed to them. They sold what they could, but their Christian neighbours laughed and paid almost nothing for linen, tables and chairs. From every ghetto, columns of Jews set out, with children perched on the tops of wagons, chair legs poking out from under blankets, and chickens squawking as they tried to balance on chests of clothes. Behind them soldiers scoured the empty ghettos to make sure every Jew was gone. The candles went out in the synagogues, and boys broke in and played on the platforms where prayers had once been said. It would be hundreds of years before Jewish prayers were heard in England again.

There are many different faiths in the world. Today we know that the only way to live in peace is to respect those who think differently. The suffering of the Jews showed how cruel people can be when they use religion as an excuse to persecute others.

Meanwhile, Edward turned to his next enemy: the Scots.

❖ Braveheart ❖

FROM Edward's point of view, it was lucky that just then the Scots had troubles of their own and were in no state to fight back. Scotland's king had died without a son, and the next ruler was a little girl called the Maid of Norway. When she died as well, aged only seven, thirteen different people claimed the throne, and everyone in Scotland began arguing about who had the best right to be king. To avoid a civil war, the thirteen claimants agreed that Edward should choose between them, for by now it was quite usual for Scottish kings to recognize the king of England as their overlord.

Edward chose a nobleman called John Balliol, but, after choosing him, behaved as if he had become master of Scotland himself. Every week he sent orders from London, until John Balliol felt more like a servant than a king. Eventually he declared he wouldn't obey Edward any more, so Edward invaded Scotland, beat John Balliol in a battle at Dunbar, and locked him in the Tower of London.

"He planned it all along," growled William Wallace, a Scottish lord. "He wants Scotland for himself, just as he conquered Wales."

Edward's army was the most powerful in Scotland. Scottish lords had no choice but to bow down and promise to obey him. Only William Wallace refused. Wallace was a stubborn man, and a brave one. He didn't want an English king. He knew his men were proud, and would fight alongside him.

He gathered a little army of Scottish fighters from the hills who knew how to hide in the heather, march along glens, and set traps at river crossings. Wallace's army ambushed the English while they were crossing Stirling Bridge. When half of the English were across the river, they heard shouts and looked up to see figures in plaid hurtling down the hillside like demons. Before they could form themselves into line, the Scots were upon them and the English were beaten. William Wallace became the hero of Scotland.

But maybe that victory went to Wallace's head. He started to think he could beat any army the English sent.

"English knights are riding north," his advisers warned him. "They have archers as well, hundreds of them."

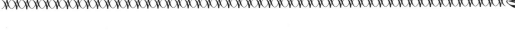

"We're Scots!" Wallace shouted. "We'll beat them just as we did at Stirling Bridge!"

Even Wallace hesitated, however, when he saw the size of the English army drawn up against him at Falkirk. Banners waved above massed lines of horsemen, while to either side, troops of archers grimly prepared their bows. Someone shouted an order and the sky turned dark with arrows, which fell as thickly as a storm of rain. The Scottish spearmen could only cower under them as the English knights began their charge.

This time, the English army was too much for the Scots. They were defeated and Wallace taken prisoner. Edward had him carried to London, tortured and put to death.

But William Wallace never gave in, and never accepted Edward as king. Although the Scots had lost their leader, they would always remember his courage and defiance.

❖ Robert Bruce, King of Scotland ❖

ONCE William Wallace was dead, it seemed as if Scotland was bound to become part of England. The new Scottish king, Robert Bruce, tried fighting Edward, but was defeated and became an outlaw. English soldiers searched castles and farms while the king of Scotland lurked in the hills in disguise.

Many of the Scots said there was no point fighting any longer. Every time they fought the English they were beaten. The English king would simply take over the country, they said, as he had taken over Wales. Maybe he would call his eldest daughter princess of Scotland.

Meanwhile, Robert Bruce hid in a cave. People brought him news of his supporters being arrested and his family sent to jail. Robert Bruce stared out of his cave and wondered whether it was worth fighting on. Then something caught his eye. A spider was weaving its web in a corner. Back and forth it went, unfurling its silken thread behind it. Just one vein of thread crossed the cave to start with, but the spider wove patiently until it had made a perfect web. Then it settled down to wait for flies to fall into the trap.

I must be as patient as that spider, Robert Bruce thought. If I take on the English in a pitched battle, they will always win. I must be more patient.

So he collected a small force of men, and captured the smallest English castle he could find.

"Tear it down," Bruce ordered.

His soldiers looked startled. "But we've only just captured it!"

"And the English will capture it back. Tear it down and they will have nowhere to defend."

One by one Robert Bruce's little army attacked castles and destroyed them. They swooped on isolated detachments of English soldiers. They seized carts taking supplies to garrisons, so that soon the English began to grow hungry. And whenever they found themselves facing a larger English army, they disappeared back into the hills.

I must be like the spider, Robert Bruce thought.

Hearing of his success, Scottish lords started to join him. He attacked larger castles and destroyed them as well. People began to whisper that Scotland could survive.

Then the Scots had a stroke of luck. Edward, the soldier king of England, died. He was buried in Westminster Abbey and on his tomb were carved the words *Scottorum Malleus*, Hammer of the Scots. Edward's son, Edward II, gathered an army and marched north to carry on beating the Scots like his father.

"We should fight!" some of Robert Bruce's advisers urged him. "We're strong enough now, and Edward II is nothing like as good a soldier as his father!"

"And lose everything we've won?" said others. "The English always win battles. We're better off waiting till they've gone."

All of them fell silent when Robert Bruce stood up. He thought of the spider waiting in its web, waiting – and then striking.

"We will fight," he said.

Some Scots wished he had decided not to when they saw the English army drawn up opposite them at a place called Bannockburn. They couldn't even count the knights – there were too many of them. Troop after troop of archers marched out to take up positions on the flanks. The king's banner flew above a tent in the centre.

If Robert Bruce was afraid he didn't show it. Nor did the Scottish spearmen who waited grimly in the heather. They spoke to one another in the Gaelic of the Highland people, wishing each other luck. Then a trumpet blared somewhere across the valley and the English line rolled forward.

"Wait," ordered Robert Bruce. He knew he could only win by being patient. And he knew the Scots would fight to the death.

On their side, the English weren't expecting much of a battle. The Scottish infantry would wave their swords fiercely enough, but melt away into the heather when the knights charged. They would ride down the Scottish spearmen. The English always won battles.

But this time it didn't work. However often they charged, the Scots didn't give way.

"What shall we do, sire?" a knight asked the new king.

Edward I might have thought up some clever strategy; his son just gave the order to charge again. The English charged until they were exhausted, but still the Scots stood firm. And when Robert Bruce's men attacked in their turn, the English broke, knights turning headlong,

archers dropping their bows and fleeing for their lives. The king himself only just managed to escape on a fast horse.

Bannockburn was a great victory for the Scots. The next year Robert Bruce invaded England, and eventually the English recognized him as king of Scotland.

The Scots knew England would always be larger and more powerful than Scotland. But they had not given in to English force – and they never would. A few years later, the Scottish barons wrote a letter to the pope. It is known as the Declaration of Arbroath, and is one of the proudest statements ever made by people of these islands:

> *For as long as a hundred men remain alive we will never in any way be bowed beneath the yoke of English domination; for it is not for glory, riches or honours that we fight, but for freedom alone, that which no man of worth yields up, save with his life.*

❖ Edward II and Piers Gaveston ❖

EDWARD II went back to England in disgrace. As he entered his palace, the barons muttered behind his back.

"His *father* would never have been beaten," they whispered.

Weak kings are worse than no kings, and Edward II turned out to be England's weakest king. He was no good at fighting. When his chancellor of the Exchequer started talking about money, he got muddled. When advisers told him what to do, he got angry. To make matters worse, he fell in love with a young man called Piers Gaveston.

"Isn't Piers good-looking!" he exclaimed to his courtiers. "Aren't his jokes funny? Doesn't he sing well?"

In those days people didn't think much of men who fell in love with other men. And they didn't think much of Edward. Edward gave Piers Gaveston presents; he threw parties for him; he made him earl of Cornwall. At last the barons ran out of patience.

"Remember Magna Carta?" they said. "Kings can't just do what they like."

So a group of them got together in a society called the Ordainers. They drew up a set of rules for the king to follow, and forced him to get rid of Piers Gaveston. The king did send his favourite away for a time, but he found he couldn't live without him, so Piers Gaveston came back. Then the Ordainers captured Piers Gaveston and put him to death.

Edward just fell in love with someone else.

His new favourite's name was Hugh Despenser. Hugh and his father were the greediest men in England, and they decided to use the king's love for Hugh to make themselves rich and powerful. When people complained, Edward just laughed. The Ordainers rebelled, but their army was beaten.

Then Edward showed he was not only foolish but cruel as well, by putting many of his enemies to death. Everyone complained, but Edward didn't care. He was king of England and would do what he liked – kill his enemies, reward his friends, spend all day with Hugh Despenser if he wanted to! There was no one left to stop him.

Unfortunately Edward had forgotten about one person – his wife.

❖ Isabella and Mortimer ❖

PEOPLE called Edward's wife, Isabella, the French She-Wolf. She was very beautiful, but behind her lovely face Isabella was as fierce and cruel as a wolf. She hated being married to Edward. She was the most beautiful woman in Europe, but every day she had to watch him laughing and joking with Piers Gaveston or Hugh Despenser. After a few years, Isabella returned to France and announced that she wasn't coming back.

Then she met Roger Mortimer. Mortimer was charming and clever, and Isabella fell in love with him.

"Why do you put up with Edward?" Mortimer whispered to her as they lay in bed together. "You would be much better at running England than he is."

"But I am a woman," Isabella objected.

Roger Mortimer smiled. "Then we could run it together!" he said.

So Isabella and Mortimer invaded England. Isabella took her eldest son, Edward, prince of Wales, with her. By now, everyone in England hated Edward II and his favourites, so no one defended him. Edward was captured and forced to give up the throne. Isabella and Mortimer threw him into prison and made Isabella's son Edward III.

"We'll rule England in his name," Mortimer said.

But Isabella and Mortimer proved to be just as greedy as the Despensers. Mortimer made himself earl of March; Isabella spent a fortune on fine clothes. They killed their enemies and gave presents to their friends.

As he grew up, Edward III became more and more ashamed of his mother. One day he burst into the bedroom where she and Roger Mortimer were lying together.

"Arrest them," he ordered the soldiers he had brought with him.

"Edward!" his mother cried.

"I'm seventeen years old," Edward said coldly. "It's time I ruled as king."

Mortimer was put to death. Isabella was allowed to go on living – she was the king's mother, after all – but the French She-Wolf never had any power again.

And what happened to Edward II? Isabella and Mortimer had ordered him to be killed in secret. Edward, who had once been king, came to an end so nasty I won't even tell you about it. It happened at Berkeley Castle, where fortunately the walls were so thick that no one outside could hear his screams.

❖ The Hundred Years War ❖

EDWARD III couldn't have been more different from his father. He was a fighter. He had read stories about his grandfather Edward I, and longed to be like him. He visited his grandfather's tomb and read the inscription that called him Hammer of the Scots. He hoped that when he died, people would talk of him as a strong king who beat his enemies. But whom should he fight? Wales was conquered and Scotland had shown itself too strong to defeat. Whom else could he attack?

That was when Edward thought of France.

In the old days the English kings had owned a lot of France. William the Conqueror had been duke of Normandy; Henry II's father had owned Anjou; and Henry had won even more of France by marrying Eleanor of Aquitaine. Since then, King John had lost Normandy, and the other English lands had grown smaller.

But I could become king of France, Edward thought. I could take back everything we have lost – and the rest of France as well!

And so the war began. Edward declared himself king of France, gathered an army, and sailed across the Channel. Neither he nor his army knew that the war would still be going on when they died. It would still be going on when their children and grandchildren died. Today we call it the Hundred Years War.

For England to attack France was like a small dog attacking a bull. France was the richest kingdom in Europe. It had more people than England, more knights, more castles. And to start with the war went badly for England. It cost a fortune – as wars always do – and Edward didn't win anything. People started to mutter that it was all a waste of time.

But the English had a secret weapon – the longbow.

French archers used crossbows. They were very accurate, but took a long time to load. English and Welsh archers used longbows instead. With a longbow, a skilled archer could shoot so fast that his next arrow was in the air even before the first landed. Archers practised for hour after hour on village greens, where barrels were set up as targets. Edward wanted every man in England and Wales to be a trained archer, so he banned them from playing all other sports – even football.

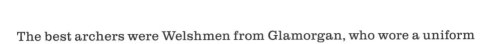

The best archers were Welshmen from Glamorgan, who wore a uniform of green and white. Edward took thousands of them with him when he went to France in 1346. But the French paid no attention. They thought beating the English and Welsh was going to be easy.

"We are the best knights in the world," they boasted. "One charge from us and Edward's soldiers will soon run away!"

They didn't even bother to make a plan before the battle. They were too busy arguing about who would capture the most English knights. Next morning they lined up near a village called Crécy, where the English and Welsh were waiting. Their armour glittered in the sunlight; their horses tossed their manes. No one even gave the French the order to charge. They just galloped forward, each one trying to get in front. The line became a terrible mess as they cursed and swore at each other.

And then arrows started to fall.

King Edward had put his archers on high ground at the side of the battlefield. Grimly they strung their bows, and stuck arrows into the grass in front of them so they could snatch them up more quickly. They didn't fire until the order was given. But when it came, their arrows turned the sky black.

The French knights didn't understand what was happening. Jostling against each other, turning this way and that in their confusion, they felt searing pain as the arrows stung them. Knights fell from their chargers, who kicked out and whinnied, mad with terror. The knights in front tried to retreat; those at the back pushed forward. And through it all, the torrent of arrows kept raining down as archers took aim and fired.

In the end, one charge by English knights was all it took to sweep the French from the field. The Battle of Crécy was a great victory. The French knights – supposed to be the best in the world – had been defeated.

Perhaps, after all, Edward III had a chance against mighty France.

❖ The Black Prince ❖

EDWARD went back to England and celebrated his victory with a tournament. Brightly coloured tents sprang up on the fields around his castle at Windsor. The air filled with the noise of blacksmiths shoeing horses and sharpening swords, the whinnying of horses, and the bustle of squires hurrying to and fro with their knights' armour.

Edward loved tournaments, which were the best test of a knight's fighting skills. Knights spent all their lives learning how to fight, first as squires to other knights; then, when they had proved their own courage, being knighted themselves. Once they were knighted, they could wear their family's coat of arms on their shields and tunics – a falcon's head, perhaps, or a fist in chain mail. The best knights had armour so skilfully made that when they wore it, they became like steel men. It was expensive to be a knight, because fine horses and armour were not for the poor, but knights were admired by everybody. They were supposed to be not only brave but chivalrous, which meant never breaking your word, never running away, and always behaving graciously – particularly to ladies.

After the victory at Crécy, Edward wanted to prove that English knights were the best in the world. He wanted people to think of them like King Arthur's Knights of the Round Table, so he founded his own version of the Round Table. It was called the Order of the Garter, and his twenty-six bravest knights were chosen to join it. The bravest knight of all was his own son, the prince of Wales.

The prince of Wales was named Edward, like his father and grandfather, but everyone called him the Black Prince because of his black armour. No one ever defeated him in a tournament. At the Battle of Crécy he led the final charge. People said the Black Prince was the greatest knight in the Christian world – *the greatest knight in Christendom*.

And it was the Black Prince who won England's next victory. He took an army to France and led it through the countryside, capturing castles and burning towns. At Poitiers he fought a battle against the French king, John II, beat him, captured him, and brought him back to London as a prisoner. That was a victory even greater than Crécy. Without a king, people said, the French were bound to give up.

But sometimes, after a string of triumphs, everything suddenly goes wrong. And that was what happened to England. After two great victories, it entered a century of trouble, the worst it had known since the Norman invasion.

❖ The Black Death ❖

THE first disaster struck even before the Battle of Poitiers. A plague came from the east, devastated Europe, and finally reached Britain. Merchants heard the first reports of sickness from their sea captains. Returning from voyages, they brought stories of a new disease that killed everyone who caught it. The merchants wrote to their trading partners in the east for more details, but got no reply.

Then news came of a Spanish seaport where a ship from the east landed, and everyone in the town fell sick. Like a shadow stalking ever closer to Britain and Ireland, new rumours of the sickness kept arriving, first from Italy, then from France. Doctors were powerless against the new disease, people said. Anyone who caught it found terrible swellings under their arms, vomited and soon died.

Most people refused to believe the rumours. Everything was going so well! Britain was richer and more populous than ever before. Villages were bigger, and the bawl of new babies seemed to come from every window. The countryside, which had once seemed empty, was almost overcrowded. You couldn't take a step without coming across a farmer chopping wood or cutting hay, and the thump and creak of watermills echoed along valleys.

And then a ship arrived in Dorset.

It came from France, and no one paid much attention to it at first. The captain said one of his men was sick, but it was nothing serious. However, the next day the man was dead, and when the harbour master came to visit, he saw that the captain looked terrified.

The harbour master went home. He ate with his family and played with his little daughter. Just before going to bed he said he had a sore throat. His wife was woken by the sound of someone being sick. She lit a candle. Her husband's face was so distorted that she hardly recognized him. Sweat started from his forehead, and he gasped for air. When she pulled off his nightshirt to cool him, she saw hideous black swellings under his armpits.

The news spread quickly. People gathered in marketplaces to hear the latest: the plague was all over Dorset; it had reached Bristol. They shared ghastly descriptions of the victims' suffering. But what could anyone do?

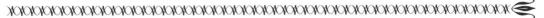

Doctors couldn't think of a cure. No one in those days knew anything about how diseases worked, or how they were passed from one person to another. They hardly knew anything about science.

"It's a punishment from God," priests said. "And we must pray for God to save us."

So churches were packed with offerings and candles, and people stayed on their knees all night, begging God to deliver them from the plague.

It made no difference. The plague reached London, and in street after street, people could be seen staggering out of doorways, clutching their throats and vomiting. Doctors hurried from house to house to help, but they caught the plague and died as well. There was no time even to bury bodies; they were flung into great pits outside towns, with hardly a prayer to remember them. Ordinary life came to a halt. No one harvested the wheat; no one milked the cows. Markets were deserted and shops empty. Abandoned dogs roamed the streets.

"Our Father in heaven," people prayed, "please take pity on us!"

When winter came everyone hoped the plague would end, but people kept dying. The ground was too hard to dig, so bodies were buried under mounds of straw. Not until next spring did the plague finally relax its grip.

Then the survivors looked around them. They saw abandoned farms, houses boarded up, and alleyways inhabited only by cats. They saw empty streets and deserted villages. To this day no one knows exactly how many died in the plague we call the Black Death – perhaps one in every three. Before it, about six million people lived in England, Wales and Scotland. It would be centuries before that many lived in Britain again.

❖ The Peasants' Revolt ❖

UNFORTUNATELY the Black Death was only the beginning of England's troubles.

Edward III grew old and his wife died. He took a mistress called Alice Perrers, but everyone hated her. They said she twisted the old king round her little finger. The war with France started up again, and like his grandfather, Edward I, King Edward summoned Parliament to grant the taxes he needed to pay for it. But one year, Parliament refused. No one likes paying tax, so everyone called it the Good Parliament and cheered the lords and MPs when they passed them in the streets.

Then the Black Prince fell ill. His arms and legs swelled, and he became so weak he could no longer walk. One day, there was a riot in London and the Black Prince was carried into the street to calm the crowd. When people saw *"the greatest knight in Christendom"* turned into a poor invalid who couldn't walk, they all went home in silence.

The Black Prince died. Then old King Edward died; and the Black Prince's son, Richard, became king. But Richard was just ten years old. And he had only been on the throne a few years, when the poor people of England rose up in rebellion.

The lives of peasants – the men and women who worked in the fields – were harder than ever. They laboured until their backs were bent, and never had enough food to eat or firewood to keep them warm. Poor families suffered more than anyone else in the Black Death. When it was over they hoped things might get easier.

"Now there are less of us to do the work," they said, "each of us should get paid more!"

But the king passed a law to say that the poor should be paid the same as before. Then, to raise money for his war, he demanded a poll tax of twelve pence that everyone in the country had to pay, no matter how poor. In those day twelve pence was a lot of money.

A man called Wat Tyler was at home in Essex when he heard about the poll tax. He quickly put on his coat and went out. Villagers were already gathering around the tavern to complain.

"Twelve pence!" they shouted. "Where will we get twelve pence?"

"Let the people who own land pay tax – not us!"

Wat Tyler pushed his way to the front. "It's wrong," he said quietly. "And we won't pay."

Everyone looked worried at that. "Shh," someone whispered. "They'll send soldiers!"

"Let them," Wat Tyler replied. "Knights may have armour and horses, but there are more of us. It's time those kings and lords listened to what we say!"

News of Wat Tyler's speech soon spread to the surrounding villages. Poor people became more and more angry as they thought how unfair their lives were. They didn't have a say in Parliament – the House of Commons was for knights and rich townsmen, not peasants. Why should they spend their lives being told what to do by knights and lords?

"We'll go to London," Wat Tyler said, "and force the king to listen to us!"

So he and his supporters set out from Kent and Essex, tramping along the muddy road to London with sticks, hoes and pitchforks as their weapons. Soldiers came to meet them, but turned back when they saw the great crowd. It was just as Wat Tyler said – if the peasants got together, the lords would have to give in.

They reached London and gazed in awe at the lords' palaces, thinking of their own homes, where a whole family lived in a single room. When townsmen pointed out the houses of the most unpopular ministers, they broke in and burned them, tearing down tapestries and smashing furniture. Eventually they reached Smithfield, the great field just outside the city wall where farmers brought animals to market. There the peasants halted. In front of them stood a group of soldiers headed by the lord mayor of London. Next to the mayor was the slight figure of a boy – the king, Richard II.

The king had never looked at a peasant before. He had seen them out of the window of his carriage, of course. And he knew that *somebody* had to plough the fields. But he had never really looked at one. He saw men with backs bent by work and faces burnt brown by the sun. He saw hands twisted from holding tools, and bodies scarred by disease and injury.

How angry they look, he thought.

Wat Tyler had never seen a king. He had heard stories about kings; he had prayed for the king in church – but he had never seen one.

He's only a boy, he thought.

And, on the day he had been waiting for ever since the revolt began, Wat Tyler suddenly felt uncertain. He knew that many of the peasants had already gone home, worried about what they were doing, and he wondered how his revolution would end. They were only peasants. They couldn't run the country – they didn't know how.

But at least, he thought, we've made them listen!

The lord mayor of London drew his sword and struck Wat Tyler a dreadful blow across the neck. Soldiers ran forward to attack, and the other leaders of the revolt, Jack Straw and John Ball, were quickly arrested. By the end of the day, the Peasants' Revolt was over.

However, no one would ever forget Wat Tyler. Lords and knights had all the power, but ordinary people outnumbered them by far. And one day the country would belong to them!

❖ The Canterbury Tales ❖

THE Peasants' Revolt reminded people that not everyone was a knight or a fine lady. The country was full of ordinary people: millers and merchants, carpenters and farmers, lawyers, sailors and cooks. And just after the Peasants' Revolt a writer called Geoffrey Chaucer decided to write some stories about them.

He set his stories among a group of pilgrims who were going to Canterbury Cathedral to see Thomas Becket's tomb. They met at a pub in London and agreed that each of them would tell a story to pass the time on the journey.

In those days most books were written in Latin or French, but Geoffrey Chaucer wrote in English so everyone could understand. Most stories were about knights and ladies, but Chaucer told stories of all different kinds. In his book a nun told a story about a miracle, a knight told a story about fighting, and a miller told a rude story. He described all his characters at the beginning:

> The Miller was a strong fellow, be it known,
> Hardy, big of brawn and big of bone;
> He was stoutly built, broad and heavy;
> His beard, as any sow or fox, was red,
> And broad it was, as if it were a spade.
> Upon his nose, right on the top, he had
> A wart, and thereon stood a tuft of hairs,
> Red as the bristles in an old sow's ears...

Chaucer called his book *The Canterbury Tales*. Lots of people couldn't read in those days, so they had it read aloud to them. Some of the stories were funny, some were magical, and some were sad. And people loved it from the first, because here, at last, was a book that told stories for everybody.

❖ Owain Glyn Dwr's Rebellion ❖

BUT stories didn't solve England's troubles. Everyone in the country still felt restless. In fact, everyone in the world seemed restless. French peasants started a rebellion. In Rome the pope quarrelled with the French king, who ordered a new pope to be elected. *His* pope moved from Rome to France, and then a third pope was elected – so there were three at once, and no one knew which to obey. Meanwhile in England there was trouble with the king.

English kings seemed to alternate between strong and weak. Edward I had defeated the Welsh and Scots, but his son Edward II was weak. Edward III fought the Hundred Years War, but Richard II grew up weak and became more and more unpopular. Eventually his cousin Henry Bolingbroke led a rebellion against him and made himself King Henry IV. However, because of the way Henry stole the throne, people often complained about him and the two kings who followed him, his son Henry V and grandson Henry VI. Were the Henrys proper kings? Or cheats?

When Henry IV became king, two rebellions started against him. The first was led by Henry Percy, earl of Northumberland, and his son, a famous knight whom everyone called Hotspur. Henry IV did manage to beat Hotspur, but a second rebellion began in Wales, where Owain Glyn Dwr was determined to rescue his country from English rule.

When news arrived that the English were fighting among themselves, Owain called the Welsh leaders together.

"While the English are quarrelling," he said, "we can free Wales, drive out their soldiers and tear down their castles!"

Soldiers joined Owain from all over Wales, proclaimed him prince of Wales, and followed him to the great English stronghold of Harlech.

When they saw the Welsh coming, the English soldiers just laughed. "Why should we worry about some Welsh farmers?" they jeered. "The walls of this castle are a hundred feet thick!"

Yet the Welsh were so determined that even the walls of Harlech Castle couldn't keep them out. Owain led the final charge, and tore down the English king's banner. He captured Aberystwyth Castle as well. It seemed as if Wales really might become free.

But then Henry IV, who had just beaten Hotspur, arrived in Wales with his army.

"We'll fight them!" Owain promised his followers. "And one thing I swear: they'll never catch me alive!"

But Owain didn't know about Henry's new weapon – gunpowder.

The English laid siege to the Welsh in Harlech Castle. From the battlements the Welsh watched their enemies huddle over something on the hillside.

"It looks like a new kind of battering ram," one of them said.

Suddenly the English ran back; there was a roar of flame, a crack like thunder, and a moment later something crashed into the wall beneath them with a force that made the whole castle shake.

"What was that?" gasped one of the Welsh soldiers, who had been sent sprawling by the blast. "Was it a dragon? It breathed fire!"

"No," whispered their sergeant, whose face had turned chalk white. "I have heard of this before. That thing is a *gun*. It can hurl rocks so hard they will knock down the walls of any castle ever built!"

With guns to help them, the English soon won back their castles, captured Welsh strongholds, and defeated Welsh armies. But they couldn't capture Owain Glyn Dwr.

"Have you found him yet?" King Henry asked his officers after each battle. His officers just shook their heads.

The Welsh remembered what Owain Glyn Dwr had told them: "They'll never catch me alive!"

"Where is he?" English knights shouted at them. "Where is Owain Glyn Dwr?"

But the Welsh never betrayed their leader. Even when the last army had been beaten and the last castle surrendered, Owain Glyn Dwr was never caught. Indeed, to this day no one knows what happened to him, and some say Owain Glyn Dwr is still living in the mountains, waiting to lead his people again.

❖ Agincourt ❖

ALTHOUGH Henry IV beat both the rebellions against him, he still felt guilty for stealing the throne, and people still muttered that he wasn't a proper king. When he died, his son Henry V decided the only way to stop them was to go to war and win a great victory. So he led his army across the Channel to France and the Hundred Years War began again.

To start with, nothing went well for Henry. His scouts reported that the French army was the biggest ever assembled, with so many knights that their banners filled whole valleys. Then it began to rain and Henry's soldiers fell sick. They tried to get back to their ships, but the French closed in on them, and eventually the English could go no further. At the village of Agincourt Henry ordered his men to prepare for battle.

That night there was much feasting in the French camp. Lords boasted about tournaments they had won in the past. Knights prepared their armour and sent squires to sharpen their swords. No one gave the English a chance.

In the morning the French knights drew up for their charge. They watched the English through the eye slits of their helmets. There were so few of them on the hillside above that they hardly looked like an army at all.

But what followed was just like the Battle of Crécy, years before. The French started to charge without any order. One knight followed another, each shouting his battle cry, and when the English archers began to fire, the proud French knights became a rabble of screaming, quarrelling men. It seemed to them as if the sky was full of vicious birds. Horses reared; knights fell – and when they did, they found it impossible to get up again in their heavy armour. Before the French knew it, English soldiers were among them, hacking at the fallen and stripping armour from the dead.

Agincourt was the greatest English victory of the war. Hundreds of French knights were killed or captured. Henry reconquered Normandy and married the French king's daughter. For a time it looked as if the Hundred Years War was over.

The victory didn't last, though. Henry V grew sick and died, and his son, Henry VI, was a weakling who couldn't rule or fight. So England's troubles began again.

❖ The Wars of the Roses ❖

HENRY VI was only a baby when his father died, but courtiers soon noticed there was something wrong with him. He couldn't learn his sums; he didn't seem able to concentrate. A rumour went round that the king was weak in the head.

"We always said the Henrys weren't proper kings," people muttered.

The French quickly won back what they had lost in the war. A farm girl called Joan of Arc dressed as a knight and led their army. The English were driven out of France (though they kept the town of Calais) and the Hundred Years War finally came to an end.

The English were furious about losing the war. In Kent a man called Jack Cade started a rebellion. Even though Jack Cade was killed and the rebellion ended, it didn't stop people complaining. Meanwhile Henry VI lost his mind completely. It was as if England didn't have a king at all.

At last, seeing how feeble Henry was, his cousin Richard of York decided to take over. He declared he had a better claim to be king than Henry, and gathered an army. Richard's family were dukes of York, and the emblem of York was a white rose, while Henry's family were dukes of Lancaster, with a red rose as their emblem, so the struggle between them became known as the Wars of the Roses.

The Yorkists and Lancastrians fought a battle at St Albans, and another at Blore Heath, near Wales. Richard of York was killed, but his son Edward kept fighting. At Towton, in Yorkshire, the two sides fought a battle so bloody that, by the day's end, the rivers ran red and soldiers stood dazed on the field, too exhausted even to raise their swords. At the end of the battle Henry fled and Edward, who was just eighteen years old, was crowned King Edward IV.

Everybody liked Edward. He was good company, and loved feasting and parties. But the new king had a secret. He had fallen in love with a widow called Elizabeth Woodville, and married her without telling anyone. When the secret came out, everyone was shocked. Kings were supposed to marry princesses! England had never had an *ordinary* woman as queen! Edward began to argue with his most powerful supporter, the earl of Warwick, who had helped him become king. Eventually Warwick swapped sides, Edward

fled to France, and Henry VI became king for the second time. Warwick became known as "the Kingmaker", because whoever he supported became king.

But Edward was determined to return. He may have loved good company and feasting, but he was also a skilful soldier. He gathered a new army, defeated Warwick the Kingmaker, then captured Henry and beat the Lancastrian army at the Battle of Tewkesbury. Henry's son was killed in the battle, and to make sure the Wars of the Roses didn't go on, Edward put Henry to death as well. There was no one left to challenge him.

"Congratulations!" said Edward's younger brother Richard, a thin, secretive man who always seemed to be smiling to himself.

It looked as if the Wars of the Roses really were over. What Edward didn't realize was that his younger brother had a secret ambition of his own. He too wanted to be king.

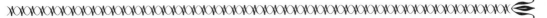

❖ The Princes in the Tower ❖

EDWARD didn't survive long. His life of feasting and drinking took its toll on him. He died, and his son, Edward, who was just twelve years old, set off for London to be crowned, with his younger brother, Richard, accompanying him. But at the gates of the city they were stopped by their uncle Richard.

"I'm worried there may be a riot," he said. "I'm going to send you somewhere you will be safe."

"Where?" asked Edward, trying to sound as much like a king as possible.

His uncle smiled. "To the Tower," he said.

Ever since William the Conqueror built it, the Tower of London had stood guard over the river Thames. No windows relieved its walls. Soldiers stood on every tower. But the castle no longer kept out the king's enemies, it had become a prison.

The boys arrived by boat in the dead of night. Someone helped them up the steps and they followed a soldier with a flaming torch along stone corridors that dripped with moisture. They were too scared to speak. Edward kept his arm round his brother's shoulder. The soldier led them to an office where the keeper of the Tower was waiting next to a huge man in a leather jerkin, the chief jailer.

Edward tried to make his voice sound commanding. "I am king of England," he said. "I demand that you send for my uncle at once."

"Maybe tomorrow," said the keeper of the Tower, and added as an afterthought, "Your Majesty."

The jailer laughed. Beside him, Edward heard his brother give a sob.

They were taken to a room without a window, and the jailer locked the door behind them. Edward hammered on the door with his fists but nobody answered the twelve-year-old king of England.

Days passed. Edward tried to keep his brother's spirits up.

"Uncle has put us here for our own safety," he said. "Perhaps the Lancastrians have started the war again. He will send for us soon."

But their uncle didn't send for them. In fact, he was busy spreading a rumour that Edward IV hadn't really married Elizabeth Woodville, so his

sons were illegitimate and Edward couldn't be king. Richard had begun to call himself lord protector.

One night, the boys weren't brought any food. Edward yelled through the keyhole, but nobody came. The torch went out, leaving them in darkness. Edward couldn't believe it. He was king of England and he was sitting in a cell in darkness! As the night drew on, it grew colder. The boys hugged each other to stay warm, but cold seemed to seep up from the floor and drip from the vaulted ceiling until they were both shivering.

Then they heard the sound of footsteps coming down the stairs. Iron boots scraped on stone. A key grated in the lock. When the door was kicked open, the glow of torches seemed blinding after the pitch darkness of the cell. Edward had to shield his eyes with one hand.

"Uncle?" he said.

But it wasn't his uncle Richard. A group of soldiers stood in the doorway, holding drawn swords.

Outside the Tower, a boatman was rowing his boat towards London Bridge that night. The massive shape of the Tower loomed out of the darkness on his right-hand side. Suddenly he heard a scream. It was so faint that it might have been one of the river birds, but something about it made him stop rowing. A moment later, there was a second scream. The boatman stood up, staring wildly into the darkness, but he heard no other noise.

And no one else in London heard a thing.

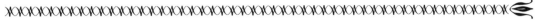

❖ Richard's Downfall ❖

SOON after that, the princes' uncle Richard declared himself King Richard III. But most people spat on the ground when they heard his name.

"Murderer!" they hissed. "What happened to the princes in the Tower?"

Meanwhile, the last of the Lancastrians gathered to fight back. Their leader was a Welshman called Henry Tudor. He was descended from Edward III through his mother, but on his father's side he came from Owain ap Maredudd ap Tudor and the old kings of Wales. Henry gathered his army in France, then landed in Wales, at Milford Haven. Welsh soldiers and English lords hurried to join him. Henry marched east into England, and the Wars of the Roses began again.

Henry's army met Richard's at Bosworth Field in Leicestershire. Richard's army was smaller than usual, because not even the Yorkists wanted to help a man who had killed his own nephews. Before the battle began, he was told even more of his soldiers were deserting. But at least Richard was no coward. He gathered his last supporters, charged Henry Tudor's army, and was killed in the thick of the fighting.

Henry Tudor marched on to London, where he was crowned King Henry VII. To finish the Wars of the Roses once and for all, he married Edward IV's daughter, Elizabeth of York. So the families of York and Lancaster were united, and Henry VII took as his emblem a rose coloured both red and white.

At last England and Wales were at peace, under a family of Welsh kings – the Tudors.

❖ The End of the Middle Ages ❖

ENGLAND had been ruined by the Wars of the Roses, so Henry VII's first task was to make the country rich again. Fortunately there was still plenty of wool to sell. All over the Cotswolds and East Anglia, sheep dotted the fields. And, just as before, the money that wool merchants made was spent on fantastic new manor houses and churches. Indeed, the churches of Henry VII's reign were the most magnificent yet, with windows so big that their insides were bathed in light, stone vaults so delicate that they looked like trees arching overhead, and soaring towers that could be seen for miles across the fields.

But the buildings of Henry's reign were the last to be built in the Gothic style. For while he was king, great changes took place in the world. The time we call the Middle Ages finally came to an end.

Sailors in Cornwall and Ireland used to stare westwards towards the Atlantic Ocean, sure that the ocean went on for ever and Ireland was the edge of the world. But not long after Henry VII became king of England, a rumour went round that there was another country beyond the ocean, one no one had heard of before.

It was found by an Italian sea captain called Christopher Columbus. In 1492 the king of Spain paid Columbus to take three ships and sail west as far as he could. A year later he returned to say he had discovered a new land. He called it America.

Columbus wasn't expecting to find America. When he set off, he thought he was going to arrive in India. Most people understood that the earth was round, like a very large ball. That meant that if you went west you'd end up in the east, Columbus said. He hadn't realized that before you got to India, you reached America first. The world was much bigger than anyone thought.

People shook their heads when they heard about America. What else could they discover that no one knew about? More new lands? More ways around the world?

All through the Middle Ages, people believed that nothing ever changed.

"Peasants obey knights," said knights as they sat in their manor houses. "Knights obey lords. Lords obey kings."

"The world is God's," said monks, rising for their morning prayers. "God made it. God decides what happens in it."

"Nothing changes," said scholars surrounded by their dusty books. "Things have always been the same."

That wasn't true, of course. Once, things had been very different. There had been a province called Britannia, and a great city called Rome, with an empire that covered half of Europe. In Northumbria people could still see the wall the Romans had left behind. In Italy ruins of Roman villas and temples were scattered across the landscape.

People started wondering what life had been like for the Romans. They began reading books the Romans had left behind. And they discovered that things hadn't always been the way they were in the Middle Ages. People hadn't always lived in castles. They hadn't always worn armour and fought. They hadn't always gone to church.

In that case, people thought, why couldn't they change things now?

So the rich started to build villas instead of castles. Sculptors copied Roman sculpture. Philosophers read books in Latin and Greek. Scholars called this shift the rebirth of ancient learning. In French the word for rebirth is *renaissance*, and that is what we still call the change that took place at the end of the Middle Ages. King Henry's eldest son, Arthur, learned Latin and Greek so that he could read ancient books. Desiderius Erasmus, the most famous thinker of the age, came to England to spread new ideas.

Those new ideas would not have spread very fast, however, if it wasn't for a new invention that was made not long before America was discovered. It was even more important than the compass or the gun. Some think it the most important machine ever invented – the printing press.

The first printer in Britain was called William Caxton. He had learned his skill in Europe, and his shop was in an alley near Westminster Abbey. When Caxton's neighbours heard strange noises coming from the shop, they asked what he did there. Caxton told them he made books. The neighbours had never heard of books being made in a shop. Books were made by monks or scribes, who copied them out word by word, taking

months to finish each volume. Caxton told them he had just made two hundred copies of Geoffrey Chaucer's *The Canterbury Tales* in a week. They didn't believe him, so he showed them one of the copies. The pages weren't covered with handwriting, like in an old-style book. Instead words were stamped crisply on the page, so clear that anyone could read them.

Caxton invited them into his shop to see how he did it. Hunched over a table, he took up little pieces of metal with tweezers, one by one, and dropped them into a wooden frame. When the frame was full, he stepped back so they could see.

One of the neighbours, who knew how to read, pushed forward to look at the frame. "It's backwards!" he declared.

Caxton just smiled. He dipped a roller in sticky ink and rolled it over the frame. Then he laid a sheet of paper on the frame and pressed down hard. When he peeled it off and held it up to them, it was covered in words – the right way round.

As they watched, he laid another sheet of paper on the frame, then another. In half an hour he made ten perfect copies of the same page – a job that would have taken a scribe all day. Looking around Caxton's shop, the neighbours saw stacks of frames, piles of paper and cases of half-bound books. When they bent to look at the titles, they saw that Caxton was making books of all kinds – prayer books, law books, storybooks, books of poetry. Books, they suddenly realized, no longer needed to be rare and secret – and nor did the ideas they contained. If books could be printed quickly, the words in them could be copied again and again, shared, passed from hand to hand and passed on again until everyone had read them.

And when that happened, the world really would begin to change...

TIMELINE

1069 ❖ The harrying of the north – William the Conqueror puts down Saxon rebellions in the north of England.

1085 ❖ William orders a book listing all the land and property in England – Domesday Book.

1087 ❖ After William dies, his son William Rufus becomes king of England.

1093–97 ❖ Donald Ban seizes the Scottish throne. Civil war in Scotland. His nephews Duncan, Edgar, Alexander and David throw him out with Norman help.

1099 ❖ Crusaders capture Jerusalem from the Muslims.

1100 ❖ William Rufus is killed in a hunting accident, and Henry I becomes king.

1120 ❖ Henry's son drowns in the disaster of the *White Ship*. Now his daughter, Matilda, will be queen of England.

1135–54 ❖ Civil wars in England between Matilda and her cousin Stephen, who seizes the throne. In the end they agree that when Stephen dies, Matilda's son will be King Henry II.

1157 ❖ Owain of Gwynedd and Malcolm IV of Scotland accept Henry as overlord.

1168 ❖ Strongbow's soldiers invade Ireland, invited by Dermot Mac Murrough, king of Leinster.

1170 ❖ Henry's knights murder Thomas Becket, archbishop of Canterbury.

1171 ❖ Henry II conquers Ireland.

1180s ❖ A new kind of architecture with pointed arches arrives in Britain. – Gothic.

1187 ❖ Saladin, sultan of Egypt, captures Jerusalem from the Christians.

1189–99 ❖ Richard the Lionheart becomes king and sets off on crusade to win Jerusalem back. While he is away, his brother Prince John governs England. The people start to tell stories of Robin Hood. When Richard is killed, John becomes king.

1215 ❖ John's barons force him to agree to Magna Carta. When he dies, next year, his son becomes Henry III.

1258 ❖ The barons agree the Provisions of Oxford, saying Henry should rule according to Magna Carta.

1258–67 ❖ While Henry and his barons are quarrelling, Llywelyn ap Gruffudd frees Wales.

1264 ❖ Simon de Montfort defeats Henry.

1265 ❖ Simon de Montfort calls Parliament after beating Henry at the Battle of Lewes. But Henry's son, Edward, defeats and kills him.

1272 ❖ Edward I becomes king of England.

1276–84 ❖ Edward conquers Wales. He passes the Statute of Rhuddlan to make Wales part of England.

1290 ❖ All Jews are expelled from England.

1292 ❖ The Scots ask Edward to settle the Great Cause – who should be king of Scotland. He chooses John Balliol; but when Balliol stops obeying him, he takes over most of Scotland.

1297 ✧ William Wallace fights back and beats the English at Stirling Bridge.

1305 ✧ William Wallace is defeated and killed.

1306 ✧ Robert Bruce, the new king of Scotland, is defeated and goes into hiding.

1307 ✧ Edward dies and his son becomes Edward II. The next year he marries Isabella, the She-Wolf of France.

1312 ✧ The Ordainers, barons opposed to Edward, kill his favourite, Piers Gaveston.

1314 ✧ Robert Bruce defeats the English at the battle of Bannockburn.

1320 ✧ Scottish barons write the Declaration of Arbroath, proclaiming Scottish freedom.

1327 ✧ Isabella and her lover, Roger Mortimer, murder Edward and rule England in the name of Isabella's son, Edward III.

1330 ✧ Edward III takes power himself, and kills Mortimer.

1337 ✧ Edward III attacks France, starting the Hundred Years War.

1346 ✧ The English and Welsh beat the French at the Battle of Crécy.

1348 ✧ The Black Death kills millions of people all over Europe.

1356 ✧ The Black Prince captures the king of France at the Battle of Poitiers.

1376 ✧ The Good Parliament stops the king taxing people too much. Death of the Black Prince. The next year, Edward III dies and Richard II becomes king at the age of ten.

1381 ✧ Wat Tyler leads the Peasants' Revolt.

1380s ✧ Chaucer writes *The Canterbury Tales*.

1380s ✧ John Wyclif and the Lollards challenge the pope.

1399 ✧ Henry Bolingbroke kills Richard and becomes Henry IV.

1403–08 ✧ The rebellion of the Percys, earls of Northumberland. Henry Percy – Hotspur – is killed in 1403.

1404 ✧ Owain Glyn Dwr captures Harlech Castle. The English don't win it back for five years.

1413 ✧ Henry dies, and his son becomes Henry V. Two years later he attacks France and starts the Hundred Years War again.

1415 ✧ The English win the Battle of Agincourt, their greatest victory of the war.

1422 ✧ Henry V dies and his son becomes Henry VI.

1453 ✧ The English lose everything in France except Calais. The Hundred Years War is over.

1455 ✧ The start of the Wars of the Roses, between Henry of Lancaster (Henry VI) and Richard of York.

1461 ✧ Richard of York's son defeats the Lancastrians and becomes Edward IV.

1470 ✧ Warwick the Kingmaker, who has changed sides, beats Edward, and Henry VI becomes king again.

1471 ✧ Edward returns, beats Warwick and kills Henry VI.

1476 ✧ William Caxton sets up the first printing press in Britain.

1483 ✧ Edward dies. His sons are sent to the Tower of London by their uncle Richard, who becomes Richard III.

1485 ✧ Henry Tudor, last of the Lancastrians, invades England and kills Richard at the Battle of Bosworth Field.

1492 ✧ Christopher Columbus discovers America.

THE
TUDORS

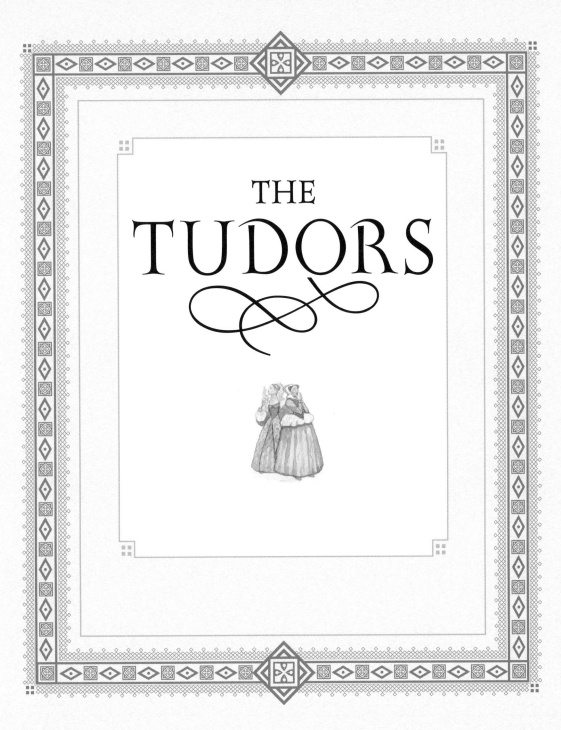

Henry VIII
❖❖❖❖❖❖❖

SEIZED THE
CHURCH

Lady Jane Grey
❖❖❖❖❖❖❖

RULED FOR NINE
DAYS

Elizabeth I
❖❖❖❖❖❖❖

LED ENGLAND
TO VICTORY

Thomas More
❖❖❖❖❖❖❖

DEFIED THE
KING

Mary Queen
of Scots
❖❖❖❖❖❖❖

LOVER AND QUEEN

John Knox
PREACHED A NEW FAITH

Francis Drake
SAILED ROUND THE WORLD

William Shakespeare
WROTE PLAYS FOR EVERYONE

ELIZABETH I AT TILBURY

❖ Henry VII ❖

ALTHOUGH Henry Tudor brought peace to England and Wales, some people hated the idea that a mere Welsh lord should be king of England, so they kept searching for claimants who had a better right to the throne than Henry. Once, a priest called Richard Symonds announced that he had found Edward IV's nephew. He took him to Ireland, proclaimed him King Edward VI, then invaded Lancashire with a small army. As it happened, Edward IV's real nephew was in London, so Henry could prove it was a trick. The impostor was actually a boy called Lambert Simnel, and after defeating the rebels Henry had him brought to his palace and put to work in the royal kitchens.

Next, a rumour arrived from Burgundy, in France, that one of the princes in the Tower had actually escaped and was still alive. He arrived in Ireland calling himself King Richard IV, then landed in Cornwall and gathered an army. But he ran away when the king's army approached, and was revealed as another impostor, whose real name was Perkin Warbeck. Henry had him taken to the Tower and executed.

Other claimants followed. Henry dealt with each one as best he could and tried to concentrate on his main task – to make England rich again.

For the other kings in Europe were getting much richer. Spain was becoming the most powerful nation in the world. A Spanish princess married the son of the emperor who ruled Austria, Belgium and Holland, so their son, the emperor Charles V, governed half of Europe. Then the Spanish conquered America, ending the ancient empires of the Incas and Aztecs, and seized its gold and silver mines. After that, galleons laden with treasure sailed across the ocean to make the king of Spain even richer.

France was wealthy too. Its glamorous young king, Francis I, loved Renaissance ideas, and persuaded Leonardo da Vinci, the most famous artist in the world, to work in France. Instead of old-fashioned castles he built Renaissance palaces decorated with paintings and sculptures.

The world was changing and Europe's kings were becoming more powerful. Barons no longer dared challenge them, because kings had cannon that could batter down the walls of their castles. Ordinary lords couldn't afford guns, but kings collected as many as they could, and their armies became stronger and stronger. Compared with Spain and France, it looked as if the kingdoms of England and Scotland might get left behind. That was why Henry Tudor worked so hard at his accounts and spent so long in meetings with his bankers. He was determined to save all he could and make England rich again.

But the kings of Scotland were more interested in spending money than saving it. And their ambition eventually drove their kingdom to disaster.

❖ James IV of Scotland ❖

THE kings of Scotland came from a family called Stewart, who had taken over when Robert Bruce's son died without any children. The Stewarts were determined to make Scotland as famous as any country in Europe.

King James II made Scotland powerful by collecting guns, buying hundreds of them. He died when a gun blew up as he practised firing it. His grandson James IV was even more ambitious. He wanted to be admired as much as Henry VIII, the handsome young king of England who was crowned after Henry VII died.

First James hired architects and sculptors to make Stirling Castle as magnificent as the Renaissance palaces Francis I was building in France.

"Scotland won't be left behind!" he told his courtiers proudly.

Then he built Scotland a navy. He ordered two huge new ships, the *Margaret* and the *Great Michael*. Most ships in those days were quite small, but the *Margaret* and *Great Michael* were like floating castles, with towering masts and sides bristling with guns. They were far bigger than any of the king of England's ships. James IV had the first proper navy in Britain.

All this time, Scotland and England went on quarrelling as much as ever, even though James married Henry VII's daughter Margaret. When Henry VIII and Francis I began to argue, the French easily persuaded James to declare war on England. After all, the Auld Alliance between Scotland and France had bound the two nations together for centuries.

James forgot that, from the French point of view, the Auld Alliance was just a useful way to get England attacked from behind. He forgot that Scotland was a small country, and a poor one, and thought only of the power and glory he could win by beating the English. Proudly he led his army, with its great collection of guns, into Northumberland.

But then it began to rain. The roads became muddy, and the guns were too heavy to drag through the mud, so the Scots had to leave most of them behind. James took up a position at a hill called Flodden, but the English marched round to attack him from the side, and when the battle began, it was the English cannon that roared the loudest. James ordered the Scots to charge again and again, but the English guns kept firing until the whole battlefield was covered with smoke.

If James had been a wise general he would have given the order to retreat; instead, he thought only of glory.

"A king never retreats!" he shouted, then gave a great war cry and led his army back into battle.

The fighting soon came to an end. And when the smoke cleared from the battlefield, it revealed a terrible sight. The Scottish army was destroyed. Five thousand Scots lay dead on the field of Flodden. And among them, still clutching his sword, lay King James IV.

❖ Young Henry VIII ❖

HENRY VII had two sons, Arthur and Henry. Arthur was the elder, and was expected to inherit his father's throne. But he fell ill and died, so Henry became king instead.

Henry looked and behaved exactly as a king should. He was tall and handsome, wrote poetry and music, and was a fearless fighter and a fine sportsman. He seemed to have enough energy for ten men. He could spend hours hunting with his friends, and in tournaments rode faster and charged harder than anyone else. At the end of the day, when other fighters slumped to the grass exhausted, Henry roared for more opponents. When the tournament was over, his courtiers begged for rest, but Henry never allowed them to stop.

"Music!" he bellowed.

And his musicians stayed up late into the night, playing song after song while the king and his friends feasted, danced and drank.

Thanks to his father, Henry VIII didn't have to worry about money and could live as grandly as any king in Europe. He hated the Scots having a better navy than his, so he ordered two great ships of his own, the *Mary Rose*, and the *Henry Grace à Dieu*, which everyone called the *Great Harry*, after their king. He hated Francis I having all the best artists, so he persuaded the painter Hans Holbein to come and work in London. Holbein painted a portrait of Henry standing proudly in his royal clothes with his chest puffed out and one hand on his dagger.

Francis and Henry, the finest young kings in Europe, were always competing. They led their kingdoms to war against each other, and it was during a sea battle against the French that the *Mary Rose* capsized and sank, drowning every sailor. They didn't stop competing, even when they made peace and agreed to meet at a field near Calais, where each side would put up tents.

"My tents must be the most magnificent!" Henry shouted.

So his designers planned tents of gold cloth with silver poles. But of course Francis wanted *his* tents to be the most splendid as well. When the day of the meeting arrived, the field was so covered with gorgeous tents, banners and flags that it became known as the Field of the Cloth of Gold.

Back in England, Henry planned a great palace that he called Nonsuch, because he wanted there to be none such palace in the whole world. And he threw himself into extravagant pleasure, gathering a group of favourites called "the minions" who hunted and feasted with him. He wrote more songs, one of which, "Greensleeves", is still famous today. In fact, with all his hunting, feasting and music, Henry hardly had any time left to run his kingdom, so he had to find someone else to run it for him. Fortunately he chose a brilliant politician who was only too pleased to make the decisions Henry couldn't be bothered with.

But Henry's minister wasn't a great lord. The second most powerful man in England and Wales was a butcher's son from Ipswich. His name was Thomas Wolsey.

❖ Cardinal Wolsey ❖

IN those days, if you didn't come from a great family, the only way to become rich and powerful was to join the Church, so Thomas Wolsey became a priest. Because he was clever and ambitious, people soon noticed him and asked him to help with their affairs. He managed things so well that they gave him more and more important jobs, and eventually one of them introduced him to the king.

Wolsey was brilliant at flattering the boastful young king.

"No one is better at tournaments than Your Majesty," he told him. "No one writes better music than Your Majesty. Anything is possible for Your Majesty."

Gradually Henry left more and more of his business to Wolsey. It was Wolsey who read the king's accounts and answered the king's letters. It was Wolsey who decided who got which job in the government.

In return, Henry made Wolsey archbishop of York, the second most important bishop in England, and then allowed him to become a cardinal, the highest rank in the Church under the pope. Lords and earls who had once sneered at the butcher's boy bowed when he passed in his carriage. And as he grew more powerful, Wolsey became rich. His cardinal's robes were made of red silk, and the rings on his fingers were studded with rubies. He built a palace at Hampton Court that was grand enough to make even the king jealous.

But then, at the height of Wolsey's power, everything went wrong.

All over Europe cardinals like Thomas Wolsey lived in palaces and dressed in fine clothes. In Rome the pope behaved like an emperor, dining off golden dishes. But some people started to mutter that it was wrong for men of the Church to enjoy such power and wealth. Shouldn't holy men be humble?

"Jesus Christ was poor," they muttered. "Jesus didn't eat off golden dishes."

People had complained about the Church in the past. Long before, an Englishman called John Wyclif had started a campaign to make the Church more humble. He told Christians not to listen to everything the pope said, but to read the Bible instead. But he and his followers, the Lollards, were silenced.

This time, though, the complaints grew louder and louder, until they turned into the greatest argument Europe had ever known - an argument that split the Church, caused wars for the next two hundred years, and still leaves the continent divided today. It became known as "the Reformation".

❖ The Reformation ❖

THE Reformation began in Germany. One day, a priest called Martin Luther marched up to the church at Wittenberg, took out a piece of paper and nailed it to the church door. The piece of paper listed everything Luther thought wrong about the Church. He hated its love of finery. He hated its dishonesty and greed. Christians believed that if they did something wrong, they would be sent to hell when they died. So the Church sold them pardons, telling them they could do what they liked and still go to heaven.

"Only God can pardon people!" Luther said.

The Church told everyone to do as the pope commanded.

"The pope is a man, just like any other," Luther said. "If you want to know what God wants, read the Bible!"

Most people couldn't read the Bible, because it was written in Latin and the pope wouldn't let anyone translate it. Many years before, John Wyclif and the Lollards had wanted to translate the Bible into English, but the pope had stopped them.

Luther thought that was wrong.

"The Bible is God's word," he said. "Everyone should be able to read it in their own language." And he translated the Bible into German so it could be used in churches all over Germany.

The pope was furious with Martin Luther, and so were many Christians. The Church ought to be rich and glorious, they said – it was God's kingdom on earth. They loved the Latin Bible and the sound of Latin prayers. They loved the idea that all over Europe, from Madrid to Glasgow, worshippers believed the same things and prayed in the same words. Kingdoms were divided, but everyone in Europe belonged to the Church – French and Italian, Portuguese and Irish, German and Swede. And the pope, their leader, was God's representative on earth. Disobeying him was like disobeying God himself!

Because of Luther's protest, he and his followers became known as Protestants. The argument between Protestants and Catholics became more and more bitter until towns were divided and families split apart.

The pope called a council, or *diet*, at the town of Worms, in Germany.

He wanted Luther to admit he had been wrong, but Luther refused. *"I do not trust either in the pope or in councils,"* he told the Diet, *"I am bound by the Scriptures. I cannot and will not retract anything. Here I stand. I can do no other."*

Nothing is more bad-tempered than an argument about religion, because what people believe matters more to them than anything. It matters so much that they will fight, kill or die for their faith – as people still do today.

The Protestants became more extreme. They declared that everyone was the same in God's eyes, from the humblest beggar to the pope himself. A French Protestant called John Calvin went even further.

"Why not do without the pope altogether?" he demanded. "And get rid of bishops and priests as well!"

"And if we're all equal," some Protestants muttered, "why not get rid of kings too?"

At last the Church split in two. Luther declared he wouldn't obey the pope any more, and began his own Protestant Church which most people in Germany and Scandinavia joined. Calvin went to Geneva, in Switzerland, and started a Church of his own. Meanwhile, in countries where Protestants and Catholics lived alongside one another, like France, arguing turned into fighting.

For a long time, though, people in Britain and Ireland didn't seem interested in the Reformation. An Englishman called William Tyndale translated the Bible into English, but that got him into trouble and he ran away to Germany. King Henry VIII wrote an article in favour of the pope, and was given the title Fidei Defensor – "Defender of the Faith". FID DEF or FD, is still printed on British coins today. All over England and Wales, Scotland and Ireland, people went on praying in Latin and obeying the pope. In fact, the Reformation might never have reached Britain at all, if King Henry hadn't begun it himself.

It wasn't because he agreed with Martin Luther. He quarrelled with the pope because his marriage ran into trouble. And to Henry that meant only one thing: he had to get rid of the pope.

❖ The King's Great Matter ❖

WHEN Henry's elder brother, Arthur, died, Henry married his widow, a Spanish princess called Catherine of Aragon. Spain was the most powerful country in the world then – a bit like America today – and it seemed a good idea for the king of England to keep in with Spain. Henry and Catherine were married for many years, and had a daughter called Mary. But as time went by, Henry started to complain.

"She's ugly," he grumbled. "She's boring. She spends all her time in church."

Like most Spaniards, Catherine was a devout Catholic and hated Protestants.

Thomas Wolsey noticed the king eyeing the pretty young women at court. One of them in particular caught his fancy. Her name was Anne Boleyn, and she had just come back from France, where she had picked up all the latest French fashions. She was clever, she was funny, and she had beautiful auburn hair.

By this time, twenty years after becoming king, Henry was no longer young or handsome. He had grown fat from years of feasting. Each spring he had to buy a new suit of armour because he could no longer squeeze into the old one. His temper had got worse, and he glanced suspiciously about the court as if he no longer trusted anybody.

Wolsey knew why Henry was so angry with the queen. She hadn't given him a son to rule after him when he died. Henry wanted the Tudors to rule for generations, like the Plantagenets.

"If I divorced Catherine," he muttered, "I could marry someone else and have a son." And he licked his lips and glanced at pretty Anne Boleyn.

But in those days divorce was hardly ever allowed.

"Quite impossible, Your Majesty," Wolsey said. "The pope would never permit it."

Henry swung his bristling red beard towards Wolsey and his piggy little eyes flashed nastily. "You once told me anything was possible," he hissed. "See to it!"

Wolsey did his best. He wrote to the pope, pointing out that men weren't usually allowed to marry their brothers' widows, so maybe Henry's marriage to Catherine didn't count and he was free to marry again. But the pope refused to listen and Henry was stuck with Catherine.

Then Henry's friends – who were jealous of Wolsey – whispered that Wolsey had let the king down, and Henry grew angry.

"Get out of my sight!" he roared at Wolsey one day.

In a panic Wolsey did everything he could to get back in the king's favour. He even gave Henry his great palace at Hampton Court. But it was no good. Cardinal Wolsey, who had once been the second most powerful man in England, was arrested for high treason. On his way back to London to stand trial, he fell ill.

"If I had served God as diligently as I have served the king," he muttered sadly, *"he would not have given me over in my grey hairs."*

But at least he died before Henry could execute him.

"Someone must think of a way I can divorce," said the king.

Then a young man called Thomas Cromwell stepped forward. Thomas Cromwell had been a servant of Wolsey's. He was very quiet, with cold black eyes, and most people were afraid of him.

"The pope won't let you divorce Catherine," he murmured to Henry, "but why must you obey the pope?"

"You sound like a Protestant!" roared Henry, thrusting out his beard.

Cromwell just smiled coldly. "If the pope is no longer head of the Church," he said, "you can be head of the Church yourself. You can divorce Catherine and marry Anne Boleyn. If you become head of the Church, you can do anything you like!"

❖ The Dissolution of the Monasteries ❖

KINGS had always been jealous of the Church. Hundreds of years before, Henry II had wanted to run it, which was why he argued with Thomas Becket. Now, thanks to the Reformation, Henry VIII had a chance to take it over completely. England became Protestant not because ordinary people wanted it, but to give the king more power.

Henry appointed Thomas Cromwell his new minister, and got Parliament to pass an Act of Supremacy that made him head of the Church in England and Wales. He divorced Queen Catherine and married Anne Boleyn. He chose a Protestant called Thomas Cranmer as archbishop of Canterbury, and ordered the Bible to be translated into English.

As head of the Church, he also took over the Church's property. And that gave Henry and Thomas Cromwell an idea. They couldn't sell cathedrals or seize village churches. But monasteries were a different matter.

Before the Reformation, England was full of monasteries, and everyone was used to the sight of monks with their robes and shaven heads. Monks were supposed to live simply, like Jesus Christ, but in fact, monasteries were rich. They owned huge estates, and when people died they left them money so the monks would pray for them – and that way monasteries grew even richer.

"If you shut them down," Cromwell whispered to Henry, "you can take their lands and sell them. All their wealth will be yours!"

Henry had used up all his father's money by now, so he jumped at the chance to become rich again. Cromwell passed an Act to close the monasteries and take their land, and royal officers went from one to another, driving out monks and locking doors. They counted up the wealth of each monastery, its income, gold and silver. Ancient halls, where monks had lived for centuries, were stripped of their valuables and fell silent.

The monasteries weren't particularly popular, but that didn't mean people wanted to shut them down. They were used to the sight of monks visiting town or working in the fields. For centuries they had been woken by the sound of bells ringing and the chanting of monks at morning prayers.

"The monks used to pray for us!" they said.

Some people in the north started a rebellion. All their lives they had

honoured monks as holy men; now they were told they were frauds. All their lives they had obeyed the pope; now they were told he was a villain. Surely something was wrong! They didn't want to be Protestant. They wanted the king to put things back the way they had been before. Calling themselves pilgrims – people who were making a journey in God's service – they began a rebellion that became known as the Pilgrimage of Grace.

Then Henry showed how cruel he had become. He pretended to come to an agreement with the rebels, then arrested and killed them. And he went on closing monasteries until none were left.

Hardly anyone was brave enough to challenge the king after that. Only one man dared stick up for the old Church and the old Catholic ways – Henry's chancellor, Thomas More. More was famous all over Europe for his wisdom and learning, and he didn't think it right for Henry to take over the Church. He knew the king might kill him if he complained, but decided to stand up for his principles. So he resigned as lord chancellor and refused to work for Henry any more. Henry arrested More and sentenced him to death.

The night before he was killed, More wrote a letter to his daughter Margaret. *"Farewell, my dear child, and pray for me,"* he wrote, *"and I shall for you and all your friends, that we may merrily meet in heaven."*

The next morning, he was taken to a platform outside the Tower of London. He saw the executioner waiting on the platform, holding the axe, but stayed calm.

"See me safe up," he joked to the soldier who helped him climb the ladder to the platform. *"As for coming down, I can shift for myself!"*

Henry didn't even feel guilty about killing Thomas More. He ruled both kingdom and Church, both what people did and what they thought. What Cromwell said had come true: he could do anything he liked!

❖ Henry's Wives ❖

QUEEN Anne Boleyn became pregnant. At the time for her to give birth, people gathered in the corridors of the palace, hoping Henry would get the son he wanted. But when a child's cry was heard, a rumour quickly spread along the corridors and around the streets of London.

"A girl! The queen's given birth to a girl!"

The child had auburn hair, like her mother. They called her Elizabeth, but Henry would hardly even look at her. He didn't want a girl; he wanted a son to follow him as king! When Anne Boleyn returned to court, Henry complained that her looks had faded, and snapped at her when she spoke.

"Get rid of her," he hissed to Thomas Cromwell.

So Cromwell made up a story that the queen had betrayed Henry by taking a lover, and Anne Boleyn was arrested and executed.

Then Henry spotted a pretty courtier called Jane Seymour. Jane was sweet-faced and stupid. Henry married her, and the next year she gave birth, and this time the baby was a boy. They named him Edward, and let off fireworks to celebrate the birth of a prince. But the queen grew sick. Giving birth was dangerous in the days before proper doctors and medicine, and Queen Jane died, so Henry was alone again.

By now he had grown so fat he could hardly walk. He sat slumped in his throne, breathing noisily through his mouth. His face looked like a slab of raw beef, and his mean little eyes darted suspiciously around the court. Were people laughing at him? Were they plotting against him? Many people think it would be wonderful to have absolute power. In fact, hardly anyone enjoys it. Just as misers always want more gold, rulers never have enough power to satisfy them.

Cromwell persuaded the king to marry again. He suggested the daughter of the duke of Cleves, an important town in Flanders, and sent Hans Holbein to paint Anne of Cleves's portrait. Holbein's picture showed a delicate young woman with fine features, and the king was delighted. Unfortunately Holbein had made Anne look a lot prettier than she really was. When she arrived in England, Henry took one look at her and stormed out of the room.

"She looks like a horse!" he screamed at Cromwell. "*A Flanders mare! Get rid of her!*"

Cromwell arranged yet another divorce, but the king never trusted him after that. Soon Cromwell was arrested, and the minister who had killed so many others was executed himself.

So the king had had four wives in seven years: Catherine of Aragon: divorced; Anne Boleyn: beheaded; Jane Seymour: died; Anne of Cleves: divorced. Everyone wondered what would happen next.

Catherine Howard was beautiful, young and empty-headed. Her relatives made sure she caught the king's eye, and Henry soon fell in love with her and they married. He didn't notice how his courtiers sniggered when they saw them together, for Henry was old and fat, while Catherine, who was just nineteen, was the prettiest girl at court. Unfortunately she could only think of the fine clothes and jewels she would have as queen, and was too stupid to realize that she ought to stop seeing her old lovers. When someone told the king Catherine was cheating on him, he was furious. After just two years as queen, she too was taken to the Tower and executed.

"Divorced, beheaded, died," chanted children in the London streets. "Divorced, beheaded..."

Henry married once more before he died. Katherine Parr was a sensible lady of the court; there was no danger of her taking a lover. She did her best to make Henry happy, but he was old by now, and while on the outside he grew more bloated, on the inside he was eaten up by suspicion. He didn't trust his advisers. He refused to do any work. He lay in bed, too fat to walk, feared by everybody, and so eaten up by his own power that he could enjoy nothing.

Meanwhile, great changes were taking place in the rest of Europe. More people became Protestants, and bitter wars broke out between Protestants and Catholics. More and more people in England and Wales became Protestant too. They wanted the Church of England to turn into a proper Protestant Church, like the ones Martin Luther and John Calvin had started.

"The Church of England is neither one thing nor the other," they complained.

But Henry wouldn't let them change it. He had got rid of the pope, but didn't want a proper Reformation.

Katherine Parr was a Protestant, though. So were Thomas Cranmer, the archbishop of Canterbury; and the lords who brought up Prince Edward, the king's son. So when King Henry VIII died, the Reformation arrived. England and Wales would never be the same again.

❖ The Stripping of the Altars ❖

ONE day, not long after Edward VI became king, a horseman rode into the little village of Morebath, on Exmoor. A man in black robes dismounted and entered the house of the vicar, Christopher Trychay.

The villagers gathered in the street outside. It wasn't often that people in Morebath had visitors. They waited several hours before the man in black came out and rode away. Then Christopher Trychay appeared, looking as if he had aged ten years in a single afternoon.

"We have orders from the king," he told the villagers sadly. "We must change our church."

The villagers were proud of their church. They had all paid to make it as grand as possible, with a stained glass window, a statue of Christ's mother, Mary, before which they always kept a candle burning, fine robes for the vicar and a screen shining with gold. Now Christopher Trychay told them they had to sell the robes, dismantle the screen and blow out the candle.

"We'll soon get used to it," he said sadly.

The villagers spent Saturday taking down the screen and removing the statue. By Sunday morning their church was as bare as a barn. They hardly recognized it as the place they loved.

Edward VI and his advisers sent commissioners all over the country to make England Protestant. Everything Catholic had to go: candles, incense, statues and screens, Latin Bibles and jewelled robes. If a church had stained glass windows, Protestants threw stones at them and broke them. If its entrance was decorated with statues of saints, they hacked off the saints' faces, and if its wall had a painting of the Day of Judgement, when the dead would rise from their graves, they made the villagers paint over it with whitewash. Protestants wanted churches as simple as possible.

The archbishop of Canterbury, Thomas Cranmer, announced that church services would no longer be held in Latin but in English, and wrote an English Book of Common Prayer to replace the old Catholic service. The first day it was used, everyone stared at one another in astonishment. Some were delighted. They had never before understood what they were praying for, and it was right, they said, that ordinary people should understand what was said in church – hadn't Christ's own disciples been ordinary working men? But others said it was wrong to get rid of things people had believed in for so long.

It was they who rebelled against the king, first in Cornwall, then Norfolk. Robert Kett led an army from Norwich towards London. But, just as in King Henry's time, the king's soldiers defeated the rebels and hanged their leaders. Edward VI and his advisers were determined to change what the English believed, so they sent out more Protestant commissioners who smashed more stained glass windows and tore down more statues.

When the commissioners were gone, the families of Morebath and other villages found themselves kneeling in bare white churches and muttering awkward prayers in English. And they felt as if their whole world had come to an end.

❖ The Nine Days Queen ❖

BUT if Protestants thought they had driven Catholics out of England and Wales for ever, they were wrong. Edward had always been sickly, and as he grew up he became thinner and paler. He began to cough. Eventually his doctors called in Edward's advisers and gave them terrible news – the young king was dying.

Protestants faced disaster. For Henry VIII had written in his will that if Edward died without any children, the throne of England should pass to his eldest daughter, Mary. And Mary was a Catholic.

"Mary must not become queen!" the advisers whispered.

So they agreed a plan with Edward. To keep out Mary, he left the throne to his cousin, a girl called Jane Grey. Jane Grey was plain and quiet, and never expected to become queen. She was horrified when her father called her into his study to tell her what had been decided.

"I don't want to be queen!" she exclaimed. "What about Princess Mary?"

"Never mind Princess Mary!" her father ordered. "Do as you are told!"

But as Jane Grey rode through London to be proclaimed as queen, she couldn't help noticing how people stared at her. She knew they were thinking the same as she had: What about Princess Mary?

People had always felt sorry for Mary, because Henry VIII had divorced her mother, Catherine of Aragon, and treated her badly. When Mary, who was in Suffolk, announced she was going to go to London to make herself queen, huge crowds came to cheer her on her way. By the time she reached it, nine days later, hardly anyone supported poor Jane Grey.

"Where is the girl who dares call herself queen?" Mary asked as she rode triumphantly into London.

Soldiers arrested Jane Grey and her father and took them to the Tower of London. First they executed her father, then told Jane that she too had to die.

"But I never wanted to be queen!" Jane sobbed.

She had only ever wanted to be plain Jane Grey; instead she had been caught up in arguments about power and religion that she never really understood. But it made no difference. The next morning, Jane was led to Tower Hill, blindfolded and forced to kneel down with her head on a block of wood. Then the executioner raised his axe and brought it down on the neck of the Nine Days Queen.

So Mary became queen. And the first thing she did was declare England Catholic again.

❖ Bloody Mary ❖

A lot of people were pleased to go back to the old ways. The villagers of Morebath put their statue back up, and the smell of incense filled their church once more. But Protestants were horrified. And everyone became worried when Mary announced she wanted to marry Philip II, who ruled England's worst enemy, Spain.

Spain was the richest and most powerful country in Europe – and the most Catholic. The king of Spain had sworn to stamp out Protestants in his empire, and Mary set out to do the same in England. She sent Protestant vicars to the Tower and declared the archbishop of Canterbury, Thomas Cranmer, a "heretic" – an enemy of the Church. The punishment for heresy was to be tied to a stake and burnt alive.

Cranmer had written the first prayer book in English. In the last few years many had grown to love it because the prayers were as beautiful as poetry, and they found it easy to remember them. Even most Catholics thought it wrong to burn the archbishop of Canterbury, but Cranmer was arrested and locked in a prison cell.

He lay awake at night imagining what it would be like to be burnt alive. He imagined he could already smell smoke and hear the crackle of flames. Sometimes, in the days that followed, he wondered if Mary was just trying to frighten him, but every week he heard news of Protestants being arrested and burnt alive. Some screamed as the fires were lit, he was told, while others, the brave ones, just closed their eyes and prayed to God. Cranmer didn't think he had the courage to do that, so at last he wrote the queen an apology for his English prayer book, and for what the Protestants had done. He felt guilty afterwards, but at least he was alive.

But Mary didn't let him go. She had decided to kill him anyway. When Cranmer realized this, he was so angry he forgot his fear. He didn't scream when the soldiers tied him to the stake, but made a speech saying how much he regretted the cowardice that caused him to write his "apology". And as the flames rose, he thrust his right hand into them. *"This was the hand that wrote it,"* he cried, *"therefore it shall suffer first punishment!"*

Mary was queen for five years, and killed hundreds of Protestants.

Soon people began to fear her instead of respecting her. And they started to give her a new nickname: Bloody Mary.

❖ Queen Elizabeth ❖

ALTHOUGH Catholics were pleased at the triumph of their faith, they were worried about the future. Mary had no children, so England's next ruler would be Henry VIII's youngest daughter, Elizabeth, who was Protestant. Mary hated Elizabeth. She arrested her, sent her to the Tower, and visited her cell to scream abuse at her.

"You are plotting against me, sister!" she shouted. "Plotting to bring back the Protestants!"

Fortunately Elizabeth was just as clever as her mother, Anne Boleyn, and just as proud and determined as her father, Henry VIII. She was too intelligent to be caught out by Mary's questions, but answered her quietly, giving Mary no excuse to accuse her of treason.

Then Elizabeth was told she wouldn't be queen after all, for Mary had announced she was pregnant. But the months passed, no baby appeared, and Mary's doctors looked more and more worried. At last they realized the truth. The queen wasn't pregnant, but ill with a terrible disease of the stomach. Not long afterwards, Bloody Mary died, and Elizabeth became queen in her place.

As queen, Elizabeth needed all her intelligence, because England and Wales were now divided between Protestants and Catholics who hated one another. In France the two sects had begun fighting, and she didn't want that to happen in her country. So she tried to find a compromise.

She made herself head of the Church of England instead of the pope, just as her father had done. She brought back Thomas Cranmer's English prayer book. But she didn't get rid of bishops, as many Protestants wanted, and she wasn't as stern as King Edward about destroying statues and candles.

Unfortunately compromises sometimes leave everyone unhappy. The most fiery Protestants, who were called Puritans, said God had made everyone equal, so they hated bishops and wanted churches to be as plain as possible. Meanwhile, Catholics kept trying to bring back the old religion, holding services in secret and hiding priests in "priests' holes" in their houses. Captured priests were tried and executed until Catholics claimed Elizabeth persecuted them as much as Mary had persecuted Protestants.

Apart from keeping the peace between people of different beliefs, Elizabeth had a second problem to deal with. She had to put up with rumours about whom she would choose to marry. Until Mary, England had never had a queen, and people couldn't get used to the idea of being ruled by a woman.

"When's she going to fall in love?" courtiers whispered.

In fact, Elizabeth already was in love. As a girl she had fallen for a handsome young earl called Robert Dudley. She longed to marry him, but knew that if she did, Dudley would order her around, and all the other lords would be jealous.

I'm the queen, she told herself. No one will tell *me* what to do! So she forced herself to stop thinking about Robert Dudley.

Her advisers suggested she marry the king of France's son.

Then the French will want to run England, Elizabeth thought, and the Spanish will attack us. So she refused to marry him, either.

Instead she devoted herself to the task of being queen. She travelled from town to town and spent hours in meetings with her advisers. Gradually her looks faded. Her face grew wrinkled, so she covered it in white make-up; her hair turned grey, so she put on a red wig. People started to call her the Virgin Queen.

"I'm married to my country," Elizabeth said.

And however sad or lonely she felt, she never regretted her decision. For her cousin Mary, Queen of Scots, got married three times, and Mary's husbands brought her – and Scotland – nothing but trouble.

❖ Mary, Queen of Scots ❖

AFTER King James IV of Scotland died at the Battle of Flodden, his son James V became king and married a French lady called Mary of Guise. James was desperate for a son, because having only daughters would end his royal line, just as it had ended Robert Bruce's. Mary of Guise became pregnant, but soon afterwards James fell ill, and was close to death when the bad news arrived. His wife had given birth to a girl.

"It cam' wi' a lass and it will gang wi' a lass," James muttered sadly, then turned his face to the wall and died.

He didn't know that his baby daughter would become one of the most famous of all monarchs: Mary, Queen of Scots.

Mary of Guise ruled Scotland while her daughter grew up. It was even harder to rule than England. Its barons were more quarrelsome, its arguments about religion even more bitter. Mary of Guise was a Catholic, but some Scots were determined to make Scotland Protestant. They attacked Catholic leaders, and Mary of Guise had to send for French soldiers to help her.

One of the Protestants, John Knox, was captured and sent to be a slave in the French navy. After he was released – hating Catholics even more – he went to Geneva, whose leader, John Calvin, had thrown out bishops and made the whole town Protestant. John Knox dreamed of making Scotland the same, and wrote a book attacking both Mary of Guise and Bloody Mary, who was queen of England at the time. He called it *The First Blast of the Trumpet against the Monstrous Regiment of Women*!

By then Mary of Guise had sent her daughter to France to protect her from the English. When she was only a child, Henry VIII had decided to make her marry his son, Prince Edward. Most princes sent their lovers jewels, but Henry sent an army to force the Scots to agree. Scots called his attack the *"rough wooing"*.

In France she was safe, and Mary spent her whole childhood there. She grew up to be very beautiful, married the French king's son, Francis, and became queen of France. Unfortunately Francis, who had always been sickly, fell ill and died, and when her mother died soon afterwards, Mary decided to return home as queen of Scotland.

By then Mary could hardly remember what Scotland was like. She behaved and dressed like a Frenchwoman, and spoke French better than English. As her ship sailed north, she and her ladies-in-waiting shivered on the deck, watching the sea turn grey and the sky cloud over. When Scotland's bare mountains came in sight, she thought she had never seen so wild and frightening a place in her life.

Even more frightening, though, was John Knox, who was waiting for her in Edinburgh. Knox hated the idea of a Catholic queen, and hated Mary's extravagant habits.

"Look at her rich dresses!" he screeched. "Look at all her jewels! A true Christian should care about her soul, not her wardrobe!"

In the end Mary decided the only way to fight back was to meet him, so she invited Knox to her palace of Holyroodhouse to argue about religion with her. Not surprisingly they disagreed about everything. Mary thought it was right for a queen to wear rich clothes, while Knox wanted everyone to live harsh, simple lives with no luxury. Mary liked the way the Catholic Church was organized, with the pope at the top, then his cardinals and bishops, then the priests. But Knox thought everyone ought to be equal. There should be no bishops, he shouted, just ordinary people.

As he spoke, he grew more and more angry, his eyes burning and his beard shaking. Mary tried not to let anyone see how frightened she was, and whether they liked her or not, everyone agreed she was brave to argue with John Knox. In fact, she might have become popular in Scotland, if she hadn't spoiled everything by falling in love.

She fell in love with her cousin, a handsome Scottish nobleman called Lord Darnley. She looked after him when he was sick, married him, and they had a baby son together. Unfortunately, although Darnley was good-looking, he turned out to be stupid, vain and bad-tempered, and poor Mary was miserable.

"I hate Scotland," she whispered, "and I hate Darnley."

To comfort herself, she spent evenings with her secretary, an Italian called David Rizzio. Rizzio reminded her of the happy days in France by singing songs and playing the guitar. But Darnley soon grew jealous.

"I'm sure she's having an affair with that greasy foreigner!" he shouted.

One day, while Mary was having supper with Rizzio, Darnley and his friends burst into the room brandishing pistols and knives. Rizzio screamed, begged for mercy, and tried to cling to Mary's skirt, but Darnley's friends dragged him from the room and stabbed him to death.

Darnley tried to take over the government, so Mary had to turn to someone else for help. She chose a rough, fearless soldier called the earl of Bothwell, who decided to make the queen fall in love with him and marry her himself.

One winter night, while the city of Edinburgh slept, some men in black cloaks slipped through the alleyways as silently as they could, heading towards Kirk o' Field, where Darnley was staying. Edinburgh was quiet at night. The only sounds were the footsteps of nightwatchmen, and the creak of frost on the church roofs. But suddenly an enormous explosion tore through the darkness from the direction of Kirk o' Field. When rescuers hurried to the scene, they found the building blown to rubble by gunpowder, and Darnley's body lying in the garden.

Everyone knew Bothwell had arranged it, but by now Mary had fallen in love with him. When Bothwell was arrested for murder, she let him off, then announced she was going to marry him.

"I told you she was evil!" screamed John Knox in triumph. "She's had her husband killed, and married the murderer!"

The Scots rebelled against Mary, her army was defeated, and she escaped to England to beg her cousin Queen Elizabeth for help. Elizabeth couldn't decide what to do. If she protected Mary, people would accuse her of helping a murderess. If she punished her, they would blame her for harming her cousin. To make matters worse, English Catholics began plotting to make Mary queen of England.

When Mary was tried and found guilty, Elizabeth had to decide whether to execute her or not. For eighteen years she dithered. It didn't help that she had always been jealous of Mary, who was younger and prettier than her, and who knew what it was like to love and get married. When Elizabeth gazed in the mirror, she saw an old lady plastered in make-up who looked more like a statue than a living person.

One day, Elizabeth's spies told her of a new plot to kill her and make Mary queen. Afterwards most people thought the spies had made the plot up, but Elizabeth decided Mary should be executed.

Dressed in black, Mary looked as beautiful as ever when her jailer at Fotheringhay Castle led her to the platform where she was to be beheaded. As Mary kneeled, one thought comforted her. Her little son, James, had been made king of Scotland, and since Elizabeth had no children, he would one day inherit the throne of England too.

Mary, Queen of Scots, faced death, but her son would unite England and Scotland at last.

❖ The Spanish Armada ❖

ELIZABETH always felt guilty about executing Mary, Queen of Scots. She worried about not marrying or having children, and about whether people really respected her. But she finally had her chance to show how good a queen she was when the king of Spain attacked England.

Spain was the most powerful country in the world. Gold and silver from South America filled the king's treasury, and Spanish soldiers seemed unbeatable. King Philip, who had once been married to Elizabeth's sister, Mary, decided to attack Elizabeth, conquer England and make it Catholic again.

Most people didn't give England a chance against mighty Spain, but English sailors, who were famous for their skill and bravery, attacked Spanish ships and ports, and even sailed across the Atlantic Ocean to raid Caribbean islands like Jamaica that belonged to Spain. The most famous English captain of all, Sir Francis Drake, actually sailed into the Spanish harbour of Cadiz and sank Philip's fleet.

"I've singed the king of Spain's beard," he boasted, and everyone laughed.

So Philip ordered his admirals to prepare a great fleet – called an *armada* in Spanish – to invade England. It was the biggest fleet the world had ever seen. Its galleons bristled with guns, and at each end they had fortified towers that looked like miniature castles. Every ship was crammed with armour, horses and ammunition.

But the English fleet was almost as large, and its sailors were more skilful. They were used to the dangerous waters of the English Channel, where storms and tides pushed unwary ships onto the rocks. Francis Drake, one of the commanders, was at Plymouth when news came that the Armada was approaching. There is a story that he was playing bowls on Plymouth Hoe when the messenger arrived, out of breath, with his eyes starting out of his head in terror.

"The Spanish are in sight!" he shouted. "The sea is covered with their sails!"

Drake saw some of the captains glance nervously at one another. He knew the most important thing was not to let them panic. So he calmly picked up his bowling ball.

"There is plenty of time to win this game, and to thrash the Spaniards too," he remarked, and played the game to the end before leading the captains down to the port.

Out at sea, the Armada was a frightening sight. Its ships spread out in a huge crescent, and to start with the English couldn't get close enough to fight. The Spanish plan was to sail up the Channel and pick up soldiers who were waiting for them in Belgium. But when the Spanish anchored off the town of Gravelines, Drake saw that the wind was blowing straight into the bay, and ordered fireships – old ships packed full of wood and gunpowder – to be prepared. He gave his instructions carefully.

"Sail as close as you can before setting fire to the wood," he told the captains.

The Spanish had lookouts on their ships, but they didn't think the English would dare attack by night. Suddenly one of the lookouts saw a spark of flame in the darkness. Before he could say anything, the fire spread, shooting up the rigging until the outline of a blazing ship could be seen drifting down the bay.

"Fire!" he shrieked.

Other fireships burst into flame. Look-outs screamed warnings, bells rang, and sailors ran up on deck.

"Cut the anchor ropes!" the Spanish captains shouted. "Make sail as quickly as you can!"

All the ships escaped, but their crescent formation was broken, and when the sun came up they were scattered far and wide. Then, at last, the English ships could come among them and batter them with their cannon. All the Spanish could do was sail out into the North Sea. Their invasion plans were ruined.

The English attacked until they ran out of ammunition. Then the weather became stormy. The Spanish couldn't sail back down the Channel, so they decided to go all the way round Britain, and back past the west coast of Scotland and Ireland. It was autumn by then, and the storms grew worse. The Spanish didn't have any charts of Ireland and soon got lost. Ship after ship was wrecked. Irish villagers ran down to the shore to see mighty galleons crashing onto the rocks. Scottish fishermen rowed out to wrecked ships to pick up golden crosses and Spanish coins. The Armada was defeated and few of King Philip's ships ever reached home.

All through the crisis Queen Elizabeth led and encouraged her people bravely. At Tilbury, just outside London, she made a famous speech to the sailors who were setting off to join their ships:

I know I have the body of a weak, and feeble woman, but I have the heart and stomach of a king – and of a King of England too.

❖ War in Ireland ❖

AFTER that, Elizabeth sent soldiers abroad to fight the Spanish wherever they could. The Dutch rebelled against Spanish rule, so Elizabeth sent an army to help win their freedom. And she also sent an army to Ireland.

By now, it was four hundred years since King Henry II had conquered Ireland. But in those days, when there were no telephones and it wasn't easy to send messages, it was difficult for the kings of England to govern Ireland, so the king's authority quickly shrank to an area around Dublin called the Pale. In the rest of Ireland, Henry's Norman followers built huge estates, got used to living alongside Irish chiefs, and stopped obeying the king. During the Reformation, when England, Wales and Scotland became Protestant, the Irish stayed Catholic, and so did the old Norman families who lived among them.

Henry VIII was the first of the Tudors to try to win Ireland back. In the years that followed, Protestant settlers were sent from England and Scotland to take over Irish land, but the Irish fought them off, burned down the settlers' farmhouses and set fire to their crops. Soldiers arrived to help the settlers, until eventually Hugh O'Neill, earl of Tyrone, decided to free Ireland from English rule once and for all. He began a rebellion in the northern province of Ulster, defeated the English at the Battle of the Yellow Ford, and offered the throne of Ireland to Philip, king of Spain.

Queen Elizabeth sent Robert Devereux, earl of Essex, with a huge army to beat Tyrone and win Ireland back. Unfortunately the earl of Essex was weak, cowardly and knew little about fighting. When he got to Ireland he made a truce with Tyrone, then returned to London, leaving his army behind. Elizabeth was furious. Essex had always been a favourite of hers. He was charming and handsome, and made her laugh at his jokes, blush when he flattered her and gasp at his boastful stories. Now she realized she had been fooled. She sent him to the Tower, and when he escaped, recaptured him and put him to death.

To take Essex's place she sent a new general to Ireland, Lord Mountjoy, who defeated Tyrone. In the years that followed, Tyrone and Tyrconnel, the leaders of the rebellion, fled abroad, and the governments of England and Scotland gave Ulster to Protestant settlers. The city of Derry was given to the Corporation of London and renamed Londonderry. Protestant settlers burned Irish villages, and drove their inhabitants away as if they were wild animals, not people. They seized Irish farms and, in their place, laid out plantations where they planted their own crops and set the Irish to work.

The hurt and anger which the English and Scottish caused in Ulster endures today. Catholics and Protestants still quarrel there, even though they live in peace elsewhere. And the people of Ulster are still divided, with Protestants wanting it to be British, and Catholics, Irish.

Ireland's story shows how the world we live in now is created by what happened in the past. Wise decisions can bring lasting peace, but bad ones lead to centuries of bitterness.

❖ Elizabeth's Explorers ❖

THE defeat of the Spanish Armada showed how skilful British sailors were. After all, Britain and Ireland are islands, and have always been home to sailors. Now they had ships able to sail the deepest oceans, British sailors longed to go exploring, just as Columbus had done, and see what other lands they could find at the furthest ends of the world.

Captain Martin Frobisher thought he could reach the Pacific Ocean by going between the North Pole and the top of America. So he sailed north until ice cracked around his ship, and icicles a yard long hung from the rigging. At night the sailors could hear the hull creak as the ice gripped it, and they saw polar bears and walruses. No one from Europe had ever sailed so far north. Frobisher didn't find the North-West Passage, but he was the first European to meet the Inuit people, who lived on the ice, fishing and catching seals.

Captain John Hawkins sailed south along the coast of Africa. Europeans knew about black Africans from traders, and a few black people had even travelled to northern Europe, but no English ship had sailed that far south before. Hawkins was the first Englishman to see the heat haze hanging over the African coast. In river towns where he landed, he met African merchants, and was shown the tusk of an elephant.

Sir Walter Raleigh, one of Elizabeth's courtiers, tried to start a colony on the coast of North America. He called it Virginia, after his Virgin Queen. His colony failed so he led an expedition to South America to search for the fabled city of El Dorado. Raleigh didn't find it, but came back with breathtaking stories of the city of gold.

But the most famous of all Elizabeth's sailors was Francis Drake, who decided to sail all the way round the world.

Most people knew the world was round, like a ball. In theory that meant you ought to be able to sail right round it and arrive home in the opposite direction from which you started. But only one ship had ever done that. It belonged to a Portuguese captain called Ferdinand Magellan, and sailed round the world in three years although Magellan died on the way. In those days sailing round the world was a bit like flying to the moon. There was no one to help sailors if they got into trouble. They had no charts, and their small ships were easily sunk by ocean storms.

Despite all the danger, Drake decided to sail round the world, so he gathered six ships and looked for a crew.

"We'll be gone for years," he warned them. "We may never come back."

One after another, though, men joined the crew until at last Drake was ready to set off. First he sailed south across the Atlantic. He reached the equator, and the ships' decks cracked in the burning sun. But so many of Drake's men fell sick that he didn't have enough for all six ships. So he sank two of them and sailed on. He reached the bottom tip of South America, where the Atlantic Ocean touches the Pacific. There Drake discovered one of his ships was rotten, so he burned it and sailed on.

He reached the Pacific Ocean, but one of his ships was sunk in a storm, and another so badly damaged that it had to return to England. Then Drake had to sail on in the last ship he had left, the *Golden Hind*.

The *Golden Hind* headed up the coast of South America, where Drake captured a Spanish treasure ship full of gold. He sailed north, further than the Spanish had ever gone, and reached California, where he landed and said prayers for Queen Elizabeth. It grew cold as the *Golden Hind* sailed north, and when Drake reached Alaska he had to stop because the sea was blocked with ice.

Instead, he turned west across the Pacific, reached Indonesia and crossed the Indian Ocean. He sailed round the Cape of Good Hope, at the southern tip of Africa, and at last, after three years, the *Golden Hind* sailed back into Plymouth.

Queen Elizabeth knighted Drake on the deck of the *Golden Hind*, making him Sir Francis Drake. Everyone passed on stories of what he had seen on his voyage round the world. And for the first time, they realized how huge the world was, and how wide the oceans in which their islands lay. But they also realized that those oceans could be crossed. Their ships could go anywhere in the world.

❖ Merchants ❖

IF ships could travel the world to explore, they could travel the world to buy and sell things too. Merchants already sent ships far across the seas to sell wool. And as explorers like Francis Drake sailed further, they went further as well. They sailed to India, where they found towns that smelled of spices; and China, whose warehouses were piled high with silk, a cloth so rare in England that only the richest nobles owned it. At home people ate from rough clay plates and drank from heavy tankards, but in China merchants found cups so delicate they hardly dared touch them, porcelain so white they could almost see through it, and plates patterned with beautiful pictures. They were so much better than anything in Europe that we still call plates and cups "china".

Queen Elizabeth started an East India Company to trade with India and China. Its captains came back with stories of richly spiced food and painted palaces, and descriptions of "brown" people and "yellow" people who spoke languages no one in Europe had ever heard.

"They drink hot water flavoured with leaves!" they said when they got home. "They call it tea!"

It took months for ships to reach China. It was worth it, though, for when they got there, merchants could fill them with china and silk they could sell in London for a fortune. They brought back tea as well, and casks of precious spices. Soon nutmeg and cinnamon could be smelled in the streets of London. Meanwhile, from America they brought back new vegetables like potatoes and tomatoes, and a leaf you put in a pipe to smoke: tobacco. When Walter Raleigh's servants first saw him smoking, they poured a bucket of water over him because they thought his head was on fire.

With so many merchant ships sailing to and from London, there were fortunes to be made not only for merchants but for shipbuilders, rope-makers and sailmakers. The city grew rich, and, hearing of the wealth they could make, people flocked there from all over the country. More houses were built; the streets became more crowded. London was dirty, but it was exciting as well. People of all sorts were crammed together there: ladies carried through the streets in litters; craftsmen working by candlelight in tiny workshops; courtiers in brilliant clothes and lawyers in black coats; beggars, countrymen, thieves and peasants; foreigners bewildered by the constant din.

In London it really felt as if a new world was coming alive.

❖ "All the World's a Stage" ❖

NOWHERE in London was noisier than Southwark, on the south bank of the Thames. People went there to gamble and drink in huge taverns, and there was always something going on - a pig running loose in the streets, a thief being whipped as he was dragged behind a cart, a group of children pelting someone with mud. Most of all, the streets echoed to the noise of sawing and hammering as new buildings were put up. And one summer, a particular building site attracted crowds every day.

The new building was round, three storeys high, and had a thatched roof but no windows. Inside, galleries surrounded an empty circular courtyard into which a platform jutted out with two pillars painted to look like marble. The building was a theatre.

Everyone knew the theatre's story. The company of actors who owned it, the Chamberlain's Men, used to work on the other side of the river, but had an argument with their landlord so they had to move. Then one of them pointed out that although the landlord owned the ground, the theatre itself belonged to them. So one morning they turned up with a team of carpenters, took down the theatre and carried it away. They put it back up in Southwark and called it the Globe.

The actors often came to watch the builders at work. Some of them were stars, and people craned their heads to see them push their way through the crowd. They pointed out Richard Burbage, who always played the hero; and Will Kemp, a famous comedian. Sometimes the theatre was visited by a dark man with thinning hair, a beard and one earring. He wasn't the most famous actor, but wrote the best plays. His name was William Shakespeare.

Shakespeare wrote plays like *Romeo and Juliet* that made audiences cry, comedies like *Much Ado About Nothing* that made them roar with laughter, and histories like *Richard III* that made them hiss at the king who murdered his nephews. Just like Geoffrey Chaucer, Shakespeare was good at writing about ordinary people as well as kings and queens. And he showed how English could be used to describe anything in the world.

Londoners loved plays. On performance days, crowds gathered outside the Globe at dawn, and by the time the play began, the yard or "pit" where poor people stood was packed, and the galleries were crowded. Then, with a blast of music, the performance began, and Shakespeare's words took the audience into another world: to ancient Rome in *Julius Caesar*, Scotland in *Macbeth*, or Prospero's magical island in *The Tempest*.

By the end of Elizabeth's reign Londoners were surrounded by people and things that had come from far away. Southwark was full of foreign sailors; ships sailed up the Thames from China and Africa; warehouses were packed with Indian tea and Russian furs. A lot had changed since the end of the Middle Ages. And the people of England felt more and more proud of their island, which had fought off Spain and sent ships all over the world.

It was Shakespeare, of course, who found the best words to describe it:

> *This royal throne of kings, this sceptr'ed isle,*
> *This earth of majesty, this seat of Mars,*
> *This other Eden, demi-paradise,*
> *This fortress built by Nature for herself*
> *Against infection and the hand of war,*
> *This happy breed of men, this little world,*
> *This precious stone set in the silver sea.*

TIMELINE

❖ ❖ ❖ ❖ ❖ ❖ ❖

1487 ❖ Lambert Simnel claims to be Edward IV's nephew. Ten years later Perkin Warbeck, who claims to be one of the princes in the Tower, is caught and executed.

1509 ❖ Henry VII dies and Henry VIII becomes king of England.

1513 ❖ James IV of Scotland is killed by the English at the Battle of Flodden.

1515 ❖ Thomas Wolsey becomes chancellor of England.

1517 ❖ Martin Luther protests against the pope, and the Reformation begins.

1520 ❖ Henry VIII meets Francis I, king of France, at the Field of the Cloth of Gold.

1521 ❖ Martin Luther and the pope quarrel at the Diet of Worms.

1527 ❖ Henry declares he wants to divorce Catherine of Aragon.

1529 ❖ Thomas Wolsey is dismissed and Thomas More becomes chancellor.

1533 ❖ Henry marries Anne Boleyn, and the pope excommunicates him.

1534 ❖ Henry becomes head of the Church of England, and the next year Thomas More is executed. Thomas Cromwell is now chief minister.

1536 ❖ Henry starts to close down monasteries. People in the north of England protest against the Reformation in the Pilgrimage of Grace.

1540 ❖ Henry doesn't like his new wife, Anne of Cleves, and Thomas Cromwell is executed.

1540s ❖ John Knox begins the Reformation in Scotland.

1542 ❖ James V of Scotland dies, leaving the throne to his baby daughter, Mary, Queen of Scots.

1547 ❖ Henry VIII dies. His son becomes Edward VI and gives orders to make England Protestant. Soon

after, rebellions begin in Cornwall and Norfolk.

1553 ❖ Edward dies. Lady Jane Grey is queen for nine days before Mary arrives in London to claim the throne.

1556 ❖ Archbishop Thomas Cranmer is burnt at the stake.

1558 ❖ Mary dies and Elizabeth becomes queen.

1561 ❖ Mary, Queen of Scots, returns to Scotland. Seven years later, she flees to England.

1587 ❖ Mary, Queen of Scots, is beheaded.

1588 ❖ The Spanish Armada tries to conquer England.

1594–1603 ❖ Tyrone's rebellion. In 1599 Elizabeth sends the earl of Essex with an army to Ireland. The rebellion ends in 1603.

1599 ❖ Shakespeare and his actors build the Globe Theatre in Southwark.

1600 ❖ The East India Company is founded by merchants trading to India and China.

1603 ❖ Queen Elizabeth dies. James VI of Scotland becomes King James I of England.

THE
STUARTS

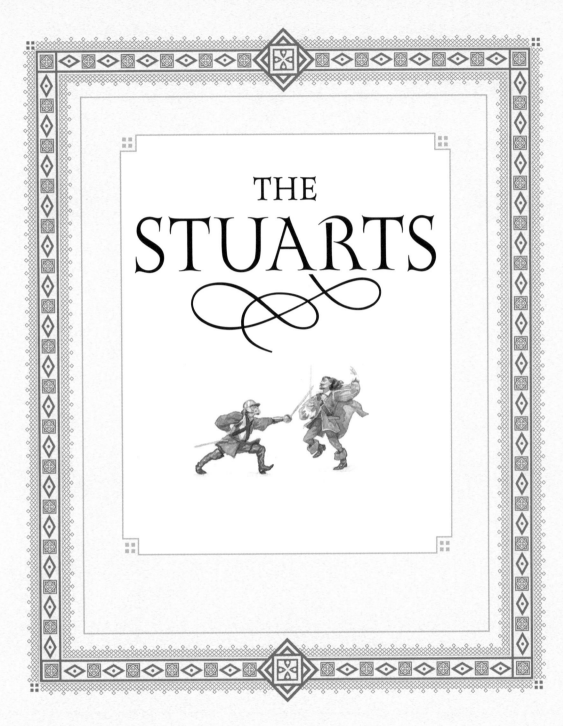

Guy Fawkes

PLOTTED TO BOMB
PARLIAMENT

Charles I

KILLED BY HIS
PEOPLE

Charles II

WON BACK THE
THRONE

Oliver Cromwell

RULED A REPUBLIC

William & Mary
THE LAST INVADERS

Isaac Newton
EXPLAINED THE HEAVENS

John Locke
PREACHED UNDERSTANDING

THE FIRE OF LONDON

❖ Britain United ❖

WHEN Queen Elizabeth died, the throne passed to her cousin King James VI of Scotland, so England, Wales, Scotland and Ireland were united for the first time under a Scottish king. Although England and Wales were one kingdom and Scotland another, people began to talk about them together as Britain.

Everyone cheered as James rode south to be crowned. At his coronation he made a famous speech: *"Hath not God made us all one island, encompassed with one sea? These two countries are now united, whereby it is now become like a little world within itself."*

Until then, the English and Scots had fought each other for centuries. Sometimes Scotland won, and sometimes England, but in fact, the two nations were never as different as they thought. Scottish kings were descended from Normans, while people in the Scottish Lowlands were much like those across the border in Cumberland or Northumberland.

James Stewart (in England he began spelling his name "Stuart") was clever, wrote books and liked discussing politics. As King James VI of Scotland he had ruled his kingdom well. Although he angered highlanders, who lived in the northern mountains, by making them give up tartan, bagpipes and speaking Gaelic, he stopped the Scottish barons fighting and kept Scotland mostly at peace. But when he became King James I of England as well, he found ruling the three kingdoms of Scotland, England (which included Wales) and Ireland much harder. All the arguments about religion that had been going on since the Reformation were getting worse, not better, and every country in Europe was descending into rebellion and warfare. The fighting across central Europe was so long and bitter it became known as the Thirty Years War, and although James's kingdoms stayed out of that conflict, they had problems enough of their own. In the next hundred years, they would face revolution and

civil war, military takeover and religious persecution. One Stuart king would be killed, and another driven from his throne, while for ten years Britain would have no king at all, but be ruled by religious fanatics and an army general. James's reign saw the beginning of those troubles. And although he was learned, James was impractical and had no common sense.

"He's the wisest fool in Christendom," joked Henry IV of France.

James wanted everyone to join either the Church of England or the Church of Scotland, and ordered a new translation of the Bible into English, the Authorized Version or King James Bible, which was used for the next three hundred years. But Puritans hated his churches. Scottish Presbyterians demanded an end to bishops, while English Puritans wanted the whole country to be run by the law of the Bible. Dressed in black, the women wearing headscarves, they even refused to go into village churches.

"Built by Catholics!" they spat.

They prayed at home, banned dancing and drinking, and if they heard someone swear in the street, shook their heads and hissed, "Sinner!" They called themselves "the Saints", for they believed God had chosen them to go to heaven, while everyone else would go to hell. To them, James's churches, with their bishops and fine robes, might as well have been Catholic.

Meanwhile, real Catholics – not that there were many left in England, Wales or Scotland – hated James as well. They had expected him to treat them less harshly than Elizabeth had done. But James did nothing to help them.

People who believe too strongly in religion can never compromise with anyone else. Certain that God is telling them what to do, they persuade themselves the most terrible things are justified. And sure enough, not long after James became king of England, a small group of Catholics turned to violence.

They decided to blow up the king and Parliament.

❖ The Gunpowder Plot ❖

ONE day, the people who lived in the courtyard next to the Houses of Parliament met a new neighbour.

"John Johnson," he said. "Pleased to meet you."

In those days Parliament wasn't closed off behind railings, and there were houses and shops right next to it. John Johnson moved into an apartment by Parliament steps, saying he was looking after it for a merchant friend of his. Every day barrels were delivered for the merchant, and Johnson rolled them down into the cellar. The neighbours were too busy to think much about him, for it was late October, the time of the yearly opening of Parliament, when lords and MPs gathered for a speech by the King. Every day, carpenters bustled up and down the steps, while caterers delivered food for the feast.

But that year King James's advisers were worried, for his minister, Robert Cecil, had received a letter warning him not to attend. He sent secret agents to investigate, and discovered the Catholic plot.

Anxiously he discussed what to do with the other advisers. "Killing the king and Parliament would bring total chaos!" he said.

"And that," said Thomas Howard, earl of Suffolk, "is exactly what the plotters want!"

They agreed that Howard should search the buildings around the House of Lords, and he set off that afternoon, knocking on doors and asking people to open up storerooms. At the apartment next to Parliament steps he met John Johnson, who politely showed him a cellar that ran right under the House of Lords. Piles of old wood and coal were stacked up against the walls.

"What do you keep in here?" Howard asked.

"Old stores," Johnson replied. "I keep meaning to clear it out!"

With only a few hours to go before Parliament opened, Howard went back to his office more anxious than ever. He imagined the lords and MPs packing the benches, the roll of drums as King James walked up the steps, the silence when he rose to speak – and then the thunderous roar of an explosion, windows shattering and walls collapsing as a column of smoke billowed up into the air above Westminster. It *mustn't* happen, he thought.

But where had the plotters hidden their bomb? He wondered where *he* would hide a bomb, if *he* wanted to blow up Parliament, and found himself picturing a cellar running right under the House of Lords, a cellar that seemed to be full of old wood and coal – but was that all it contained?

"Soldiers!" he shouted. "Follow me!"

He ran all the way back to Parliament, burst through the door of John Johnson's apartment and tumbled down the steps to the cellar. By the light of his lantern the soldiers pulled the coal and wood aside, and behind them found barrels full of gunpowder.

"John Johnson" was captured in the apartment, dressed in travelling clothes to make his getaway. He soon revealed who the other plotters were, and confessed his real name – Guy Fawkes.

When news spread that an attack had been averted, people lit fires to celebrate. And ever since, the day Guy Fawkes was caught – 5 November – has been Bonfire Night, when people set off fireworks to remember the day the government was nearly blown up.

❖ The Mayflower ❖

AFTER the Gunpowder Plot James tried harder than ever to make people join the Church of England, and persecuted Catholics and Puritans who refused. Eventually a group of Puritans decided to leave England altogether and found a colony in America where they could live and worship as they pleased.

There was already an American colony called Virginia, where the colonists had built a village, cut down trees and planted tobacco plants. They had often fought with the Native Americans, until one of them married a Native American princess called Pocahontas, who came to London and met King James.

The Puritans decided to start their own colony, so they hired a ship called the *Mayflower*, and paid its captain to sail them across the Atlantic Ocean.

The journey was hard. The *Mayflower* was blown north until the sea was cold, green and covered in mist. It was two months before they saw land, but by then it was winter and they had almost run out of food, so they stayed on the *Mayflower*, hungry and seasick, wondering if their colony would ever work. In spring they landed, and the Native Americans taught them how to fish and grow corn. When they gathered their first harvest, they held a Thanksgiving feast to thank God for saving them.

What none of them knew as they ate their feast was that one day the United States of America would be the most powerful country in the world. And one day millions of Americans would celebrate "Thanksgiving" each year to remember the arrival of the "Pilgrim Fathers".

❖ The Troubles of King Charles I ❖

KING James died in 1625. By then his eldest son had died, so his younger son, Charles, became king of England and Wales, Scotland and Ireland. Charles was good-looking and charming, but when people got to know him they realized he was stubborn, not very clever, and determined to have his own way. He soon became unpopular. Puritans hated him even more than they had hated James, because he married a Catholic princess from France, Henrietta Maria, and then appointed an archbishop of Canterbury called William Laud, who was Protestant but gave the Church of England new rituals which Puritans thought were just like Catholic ones.

Apart from religion, Charles argued with Parliament about how the kingdom ought to be governed. It had long been the custom in England and Scotland for kings to ask Parliament's approval of any new laws. King John had been made to sign Magna Carta because no one liked the idea of a king doing what he wanted. Simon de Montfort had first called Parliament, and Edward I had always asked Parliament to agree taxes. That was how the government of England worked, and Scotland was much the same.

In other kingdoms, though, parliaments were much less important. The king of France was so powerful he ruled all by himself. He believed God had made him king, and all the power in France belonged to him. Charles dreamed of having absolute power in his kingdom as well. Unfortunately he was very extravagant and needed money to fight wars, buy paintings (he persuaded the great Flemish painter Anthony Van Dyck to come and paint him), and build palaces like the Banqueting House in London. To raise money he needed taxes, and that meant calling Parliament.

But the House of Commons was full of Puritans who hated Charles's luxurious habits and Catholic wife, and knew he really wanted to govern without Parliament, like the king of France. So they sent him a letter called the Petition of Right, reminding him of their right to be consulted properly on all laws and taxes.

"How dare they!" Charles raged. "I'm king and will do what I like!"

So he ignored the Petition of Right, dismissed Parliament and, for eleven years, ruled his kingdoms by himself. To raise money his lawyers went through old history books and found taxes that didn't need Parliament's agreement. But old-fashioned taxes made people furious, and Puritans became even angrier when Archbishop Laud kept changing the Church of England.

"He wants us to worship like Catholics!" they complained.

The Scots were angrier still. When Laud told them to use a new prayer book from England, they refused, and drew up an agreement called the Covenant, telling Charles to leave their churches alone. Thousands of Scots signed the Covenant, queuing in marketplaces and walking for miles across mountains to add their names to it.

Charles was furious when he heard about the Covenanters' rebellion, but didn't have enough money to put it down. The first army he sent to Scotland was too small to fight a battle; the second was defeated by the Covenanters, who captured Newcastle and demanded a huge ransom for it. Since the king couldn't afford to pay the ransom, he had to call Parliament and ask for new taxes. But by then MPs were furious with Charles for trying to rule without them. They attacked him so fiercely that he dismissed them after only three weeks and called elections, hoping the new Parliament would be more helpful.

It wasn't. Its MPs were even angrier.

"He ignored our Petition of Right!" they bellowed from their benches. "He can't be trusted!"

When a rebellion broke out in Ireland and Charles asked them for an army to put it down, they refused.

"Give King Charles an army?" they roared. "Never! He'll use it against us!"

And five of the MPs wrote out a list of all the mistakes Charles had made, and everything wrong with how he ran Britain. Their leader, John Pym, called it the Grand Remonstrance.

"Treason!" shouted Charles, trembling with rage. And he decided to arrest them.

A few days into the new year, he set off down Whitehall with drawn sword and a troop of soldiers behind him. People hurried to watch. No king had ever attacked Parliament before. A crowd fell in behind the soldiers,

squeezed up Parliament steps, and pushed forward to see what would happen.

The House of Commons was full. MPs lined the benches on both sides. Most of them were grim-faced men dressed in Puritan black. When the king appeared in his court finery, he seemed like an exotic bird from a zoo. Charles unrolled a sheet of paper and read out the names of the five MPs, John Pym's among them.

"I have come to arrest these traitors!" he called.

First there was dead silence, then someone started to laugh. The king stared along the benches. Suddenly he realized that none of the five was there.

"I see the birds have flown," he muttered. And everyone jeered as Charles, mustering what dignity he could, turned and led his soldiers back to the palace.

There was no chance of peace after that. No one could agree how the country should be governed, or what the churches of England and Scotland should be like. On 22 August 1642 Charles went to Nottingham, unfurled his royal banner, and called his supporters to come and fight for him. He had declared war on his own subjects.

❖ The First Civil War ❖

CIVIL wars are even worse than wars between countries. Civil wars are fought between father and son, brother and brother. They tear apart families, towns and counties. They destroy everything that holds us together.

The king's most fervent supporters, who were called Cavaliers, wore rich clothes and kept their hair long, like the king and his nobles. Parliament's supporters dressed in sombre black and cut their hair short, so they were called Roundheads.

Most people didn't know which side to join. They hated fighting against their king, but didn't want him to have absolute power. They hated attacking Parliament, but didn't want to be ruled by Puritan religious fanatics who would make them give up dancing and music. On the whole, people in Wales and the west supported the king, while most of London and the east supported Parliament. Even so, there were Cavaliers and Roundheads everywhere, and no one knew whom to trust.

The first proper battle of the Civil War was at Edgehill in Warwickshire. Charles's nephew, Prince Rupert, who had learned how to fight during the war in Europe, led the king's cavalry in a charge that almost destroyed the army of Parliament. The Roundheads only just managed to escape without defeat.

For most of the time, though, there were no big battles, just skirmishes. Troops of soldiers attacked one another at crossroads, leaving a few dead in the dusty roadway. Soldiers besieged manor houses and set fire to them, then galloped away, leaving behind them a column of smoke and a family weeping over its wrecked home. Often it was hard to tell what was going on. People tried to follow by reading newspapers, for there were printing presses in many towns by now. Those who couldn't read clustered around the readers to hear the latest news.

Because London supported Parliament, King Charles set up his own headquarters at Oxford. Meanwhile Parliament made a deal with the Scottish Covenanters, called the Solemn League and Covenant, agreeing that if Parliament won the war it would make the Church of England Presbyterian, just as the Scots wanted. In return the Covenanters sent

an army to help. Thanks to them, the Roundheads won a battle at Marston Moor in Yorkshire. But winning one battle wasn't the same as winning the war, so the Roundhead leaders met to decide what to do next.

Oliver Cromwell, leader of the Roundhead cavalry, was determined to get rid of interfering politicians. Cromwell, who was one of the most fanatical of the Puritans, was rough and coarse-mannered, and a lot of MPs were afraid of him; but his cavalry, who were called the Ironsides because of their heavy armour and strict discipline, swept everything before them.

"What we need," he said, "is for politicians to stick to politics and fighters to stick to fighting." And he was the first to sign a "self-denying ordinance" saying he would give up politics until Charles was beaten.

"But we haven't beaten him yet," someone objected. "The Cavaliers are too brave."

"We need an army of godly soldiers to beat them," growled Cromwell.

So he made Parliament a new army, which he called the New Model Army. It was well organized and trained, and the soldiers were Puritans, who sang hymns as they marched and listened to sermons around their campfires.

"You are fighting for God!" their preachers shouted.

The New Model Army followed the king's army to Naseby in Northamptonshire. The night before the battle, Cavaliers heard its soldiers praying and singing hymns. This time, when the Royalists charged, they faced lines of soldiers in steel helmets, whose long, sharp pikes didn't waver. The fighting went on until the grass was wet with blood, and in the evening the Royalists fled.

From then on, Oliver Cromwell (who never gave up politics at all, whatever he had promised) won victory after victory with his New Model Army, and the soldiers gave thanks to God after each triumph. At last King Charles realized he couldn't fight any longer. He didn't want to surrender to Cromwell, so he disguised himself as a servant, travelled north towards Scotland, and gave himself up to the Covenanters.

The First Civil War was over.

THE CIVIL WAR BATTLES

X Battles

🏰 sieges

SCOTLAND

Edinburgh
Dunbar X

Drogheda 🏰
IRELAND

Wexford 🏰

Marston
Moor
X X York
Preston
ENGLAND

Edgehill
X X Naseby
Worcester
Oxford

WALES

London

❖ The Second Civil War ❖

THE king was a prisoner. Sometimes, in the Middle Ages, kings had been captured by their rivals, but never before had a king been jailed by his own people. The Covenanters didn't want to keep Charles prisoner, though, for they had problems of their own – while their army was in England helping Parliament, the marquis of Montrose had captured most of Scotland for the Royalists. So the Covenanters sold Charles to Parliament and went back to Scotland to fight Montrose.

The New Model Army seized Charles from Parliament, and locked him up in Carisbrooke Castle on the Isle of Wight. Charles sat in the castle brooding. He was very stubborn and believed that God had made him king and his subjects ought to obey him, so he refused Parliament's proposals. During the negotiations he made promises and then broke them, and Parliament soon learned not to trust him.

Meanwhile, Parliament's supporters started arguing among themselves, because a lot of MPs were afraid of Oliver Cromwell and his New Model Army.

"We don't want religious extremists in charge!" they said.

But the soldiers of the New Model Army became bolder, took control of London, and demanded that everything in England should change.

"Everyone's equal," they said. "And everyone should be allowed to vote!"

That seems fair today, but in those days only men who owned land were allowed to vote. Levellers, who said that everyone was equal, seemed new and dangerous. Nonetheless they forced Parliament to come and debate their ideas with them at Putney, just outside London.

Seeing how powerful they were, the Scottish Covenanters started to worry. Some of them, who became known as Engagers, decided it was better to trust King Charles than the New Model Army, so they sent messages offering to help him on condition that he made the churches of Scotland and England Presbyterian. Charles agreed, and that was how the Second Civil War began. Welsh Royalists raised an army for Charles, and the Engagers crossed the border and marched south to set him free.

Unfortunately they had all forgotten how skilful a general Oliver Cromwell was. First he beat the Welsh Royalists, then marched north to fight the Engagers. He found them near Preston in Lancashire, where he fought a battle that lasted for two days. By the end of it, two thousand Scots were dead.

Cromwell looked at them lying on the battlefield, while his soldiers kneeled in groups to thank God for their victory.

"This time we must deal with King Charles once and for all," he shouted. "It's no use bargaining with him – he always breaks his promises! There will be no peace as long as we have a king!"

By now MPs were more worried about Cromwell than King Charles. With his New Model Army, he could defeat anybody. Could they trust him? One day, as they met in the House of Commons, they were astonished to see the door burst open, and a friend of Cromwell's called Colonel Thomas Pride stride in. Pride marched up and down the benches, pointing at each member in turn.

"You get out!" he barked. "*You* can stay... Soldiers, take *that* man out as well!"

One by one, all Cromwell's opponents were driven from the House of Commons. Then his supporters voted to arrest King Charles and put him on trial.

❖ The King's Death ❖

THE king was charged with betraying his own country. Every day, looking pale and tired, he was brought to Westminster Hall, where his judges sat on long benches. People crowded into the public gallery to watch. Facing his enemies, Charles was far braver than he had ever been before. But at last he was found guilty and sentenced to death.

Puritans and soldiers of the New Model Army cheered, but most people were shocked, even if they had supported Parliament in the Civil War.

"Is it right to kill a king?" they whispered to one another. "Can a country manage without a king?"

On the day of the execution Whitehall was packed. Boys climbed railings to get a better view of the platform which carpenters had built outside the Banqueting House. It was draped in black cloth, and a block stood ominously in the middle of it. Soldiers were stationed around the platform to stop anyone rescuing the king.

"He deserves to be killed," some in the crowd muttered. "We'll be better off without him."

Even they fell silent, though, when the Banqueting House window opened and the king walked out between two guards.

No one had liked Charles, or trusted him. He had broken his word and caused a civil war. But at least he knew how to die like a king.

His head was bare and he wore a white shirt. In fact, he had secretly put on two shirts in case he shivered with cold and people thought he was scared. Fearlessly he walked to the middle of the platform, kneeled and prayed. When he laid his head on the block, some people turned away so they wouldn't have to watch. The executioner's axe rose up into the air. Afterwards one onlooker remembered there was no cheering. Instead, a terrible silence seemed to spread outwards from the platform. The axe lingered for a moment, then fell with a dreadful, final *thump*. And from the crowd, he wrote later, there arose *"such a groan as I never heard before, and desire I may never hear again."*

The king was dead.

❖ Britain Without a King ❖

IN a revolution, everything changes. There is no government, no one knows who's in charge or how to choose a new government, and the people who take over aren't usually the most sensible, but the most ruthless.

Puritans were determined to make everyone live under religious law, so they closed down theatres, banned dancing, and forced everyone to attend church, where preachers spoke for hours about sin and death. They went from village to village, driving out vicars who disagreed with them, and replacing them with Puritans. Because they hated cathedrals, they turned St Paul's into a stable, smashed the stained glass windows and hacked the faces off statues. Most people didn't agree with the Puritans, but were afraid to challenge them.

Levellers campaigned for everyone to be equal. "No more lords!" they shouted. "Ordinary people should decide what happens!"

Others, called Diggers, decided land should be shared equally, rather than owned by rich people. With the king dead, it seemed as if anything was possible, and nothing would ever be the same again.

But the most ruthless and determined person in the whole of Britain was Oliver Cromwell. And with the New Model Army behind him he could do whatever he wanted.

He began by subduing the rest of Britain and Ireland. First he invaded Ireland, and rode through the country burning villages. The people of Drogheda closed their gates, but Cromwell's Ironsides burst over the walls and slaughtered two thousand of the inhabitants. The same happened at Wexford, where hundreds of women and children tried to escape by swimming the river, and were drowned.

Having conquered Ireland, he went to Scotland, where the Covenanters had taken over and passed religious laws just like the Puritans in England. But after quarrelling with the English Parliament, they had invited Charles's son, who was also called Charles, to come to Scotland. Charles was young, handsome and brave. He loved parties and flirting with girls, but he got a shock when he arrived in Scotland.

"No luxury!" the Covenanters told him. "No wine, and no girls!"

He had to spend hours in church, dressed in sober black, and felt more like a prisoner than a king.

When Cromwell arrived, he defeated the Covenanters' army in a battle near Dunbar. Charles's only remaining hope was to find more support in England, so he gathered the remainder of his army and marched south. But Cromwell followed him and at Worcester, in another great battle, beat the Royalists once and for all.

Charles had to escape in disguise. WANTED! said notices stuck up in every town, A TALL, DARK MAN!

Soldiers raided houses where he might be hiding. Once, they searched a forest while Charles hid up an oak tree above their heads. But at last he escaped and reached France in safety.

So the civil wars came to an end, leaving Britain and Ireland at peace. They weren't at peace because everyone was content, though, but because no one dared challenge Oliver Cromwell. Cromwell went back to London and stormed into the House of Commons. Since Pride's Purge, the remaining part of Parliament had been known as the Rump. Cromwell dismissed them.

"You have sat here too long for any good you have been doing," he shouted. *"Depart, I say, and let us have done with you!"*

After that Cromwell became Lord Protector. Britain was ruled by a military dictator.

❖ Lord Protector ❖

DICTATORS often take their countries to war and Cromwell, who knew nothing but fighting, was no different. First he attacked the Dutch, who had once been Britain's allies but had become such successful traders that they rivalled the British. Cromwell's ships stopped Dutch convoys, and developed new tactics to beat the Dutch in sea battles. Next he began a war with Spain. When Christopher Columbus had reached America, the Spanish had taken over the Caribbean islands known as the West Indies. Cromwell sent his navy across the Atlantic Ocean to attack them. British sailors weren't used to the heat of the Caribbean, its deep blue sea, or jungles full of parrots. But they captured Jamaica, which stayed British for three hundred years, and where many British today have their roots.

Cromwell's victories were popular, but no one liked the taxes he raised to pay for them, or the Puritans' sermons and religious laws. And most people hated the new type of government. Cromwell tried putting army majors in charge of each region, but that didn't work. He tried a new House of Commons whose MPs were chosen by army officers, but no one took it seriously.

"It's not a proper parliament," people whispered. "It does whatever Cromwell tells it!"

Some generals suggested Cromwell be crowned as King Oliver I, but he refused.

"My soldiers didn't get rid of one king to make another," he said.

One important decision Cromwell made was to allow in Jews, who had been thrown out of England by Edward I. They returned to London, built a synagogue, and for the first time in three hundred and fifty years, a rabbi lit the seven candles of the menorah, and the sound of Sabbath prayers was heard again in England.

As Cromwell grew more unpopular, people started wondering how they could get rid of him. The Levellers tried to assassinate him because he behaved too much like a king. Cromwell caught the plotters and threw them into jail. Royalists began a secret organization called the Sealed Knot to start a rebellion in favour of Prince Charles, who was living in

exile in Holland. Cromwell discovered the Sealed Knot's plans, arrested its leaders and executed them.

No one loved Cromwell, but no one could remove him. And at least there were no civil wars while the lord protector ruled Britain and Ireland. But then Cromwell fell ill and died. His son Richard became lord protector, but Richard wasn't a great general like his father, and he couldn't command the New Model Army, whose soldiers laughed and called him Tumbledown Dick.

After only a few months the army threw him out, and Britain's troubles began again.

❖ The Year of Chaos ❖

THE year that followed was one of the most difficult in Britain's long history. A council of army officers called Parliament back. It hadn't been elected properly since before the civil wars started, so people called it the Long Parliament, and its leftover MPs were still known as the Rump. But the Rump didn't know how to govern Britain. The MPs drew up plan after plan and spent hours in pointless debate. In the end an army general called John Lambert drove them out and set up the Committee of Safety to run Britain.

"The army's taken over!" people shouted.

Boys lit bonfires and rioted in the streets of London to protest against the army takeover.

"Down with the army!" they chanted. "Down with the Committee of Safety!"

Panicking at the sight of so many protesters, soldiers fired at the crowd, killing some of the rioters. That made everyone even angrier. There is a moment in every revolution when people realize the army can't control them, and they have nothing to fear. The rioters in London became bolder every day. When the army's commander in Scotland, General Monck, saw what was happening, he gathered his soldiers and marched south to restore order. In every town he passed through, he heard people discussing what should happen next.

"The army can't run things. They're even fighting each other!"

"We don't want the religious fanatics back!"

"Parliament's no good. Their 'Rump' needs a good kick!"

And that, Monck soon realized, left him only one choice: to bring back the king.

❖ The Restoration ❖

ALL this time, Charles II had been living in exile, first in France, then Holland. He was very poor. His courtiers called him "Your Majesty", but his fine clothes turned to rags, and his "palace" was an ordinary house in Holland whose landlord shouted at him for missing the rent. Every time he heard news of a Sealed Knot plot failing, Charles wondered if he should give up. He seemed to have no chance of returning to Britain as king.

Then came the news that the New Model Army was fighting itself, the Rump had been kicked out, and people were talking about restoring the monarchy. Straight away Charles put out a declaration promising that if he was made king, he wouldn't be like his father but would rule fairly. In London General Monck called a convention to decide who should run Britain, and after reading Charles's declaration it asked him back as king.

Everyone in Charles's court cheered when the news arrived. The Convention sent a ship to carry him back to England. It came from Oliver Cromwell's navy, and had once been called *Naseby*, after Parliament's victory in the Civil War. The Convention could see how tactless that was and quickly renamed it the *Royal Charles*. On the voyage back to Britain, Charles told his companions his story of hiding in an oak tree after the Battle of Worcester. Most of them had heard it a hundred times before, but they didn't mind. The fugitive in the forest was about to be crowned king of England.

Crowds waited at Dover to cheer Charles's return, and at every stop on his journey to London, people flocked to see their king. They sang and waved flags, for at last the Puritans were gone and they could play music, dance and enjoy themselves. And everyone liked the look of the new king, who was more than six feet tall, with dark skin and thick brown hair. He didn't seem to take himself too seriously, but joked with everybody – and winked at every pretty girl in the crowd.

Meanwhile, jewellers were already making new Crown jewels, for the Puritans had melted down England's ancient crown and sceptre. And on the night Charles reached London, fireworks soared into the sky.

"Never was so joyful a day ever seen in this nation," wrote one of the people watching the royal procession. *"I stood in the Strand and beheld it, and blessed God."*

❖ Scientists ❖

IT seemed as if people had done nothing for years but argue about politics and religion. But of course they had been busy with other things as well, for life goes on even in troubled times. During the civil wars and the Interregnum (the time when Britain had no king), merchants went on trading, and authors went on writing books. And scientists made discoveries that completely changed how people thought about the world.

In those days people didn't think it was possible to find out more than they already knew, and that wasn't much. They didn't understand diseases and infections. They didn't know about molecules and atoms, planets and stars, why things fall when you drop them, what your lungs and liver do, or why acid burns. That was why doctors weren't much use when you fell sick, and why people still travelled on horseback, heated their houses by lighting fires, and went to bed at sunset because there were only candles to read by. They had no telephones, computers or TVs, no aeroplanes, cars or space rockets, no machine guns or tanks, no fridges and no electricity, because no one knew enough to invent them.

But towards the end of the Middle Ages, as the Renaissance and Reformation made everyone question their beliefs, some people started to look at the world around them more curiously. The Polish astronomer Copernicus watched the stars until he discovered that the earth and planets revolved around the sun, not the sun around the earth. Before then, most people believed the earth was the centre of everything (athough the ancient Greeks had discovered the truth, everyone had forgotten). An Italian called Galileo made the first telescope, and proved Copernicus right.

The Church was furious with Galileo. It worried that if people asked too many questions about the world, they would stop believing in God and going to church. They even made Galileo give up his experiments. But since the Reformation, the Catholic Church no longer controlled the whole of Europe, and it couldn't stop people elsewhere questioning things.

An Englishman called Sir Francis Bacon, who lived in the time of James I, loved asking questions.

"If you're not sure about something," he said, "you must carry out an experiment. If you want your experiment to work, you must measure things accurately. That's the only way to know if something is true."

Bacon lost his life doing an experiment. He wanted to know if keeping food cold would make it last longer, so he went out on a winter's night to stuff a chicken with snow. He proved that freezing preserves food, but caught cold and died.

Bacon's method of testing whether things were true was the start of science, although experimenters in those days didn't call themselves scientists but "experimental philosophers". People didn't have to guess any more. And the things they discovered by experiments were more wonderful than any story. William Harvey discovered the heart was a tiny pump that pushed blood round the body. John Flamsteed set up a telescope at Greenwich and made the first catalogue of the stars. An Irish scientist called Robert Boyle wondered whether air was "something" or "nothing", so he made a pump and connected it to a metal ball.

"What is inside the metal ball?" he asked the people watching.

"Nothing," someone replied.

"On the contrary," said Boyle. "The ball is full of air. If we take the air out, *then* it will be full of nothing."

He began to pump, a dent appeared in the ball, and suddenly it crumpled into a lump of twisted metal – he had made a vacuum. Thanks to Boyle, people began to understand about air and pressure.

When the king was restored and peace returned, people became more and more excited about science. Charles II, who loved experiments, started the Royal Society for scientists. It still exists today, and the most famous of all scientists, Isaac Newton, was one of its first members.

Newton had very odd habits. When he was working on an experiment, he became so absent-minded that he forgot to eat for days on end. At Cambridge, where he went to university, gardeners didn't smooth over any marks they saw on the gravel paths in case they were calculations Newton had made when he was out for a walk.

First, Newton discovered gravity. Before then, people took it for granted that things fell downwards when you dropped them, but Newton worked out why. He worked out why the planets move in the way they do and what holds the stars and planets together. Then he investigated light and discovered that white isn't the emptiest colour, as you'd expect, but the fullest, being made up of all the other colours put together.

Today we understand much more about the world and the universe than ever before, and scientists keep on discovering things. But Newton understood that the world is so vast and complex that there will always be more to find out. Just before he died, someone asked him about his wonderful discoveries. *"I seem to have been only like a boy playing on the seashore,"* he replied, *"and diverting myself in now and then finding a prettier shell than ordinary, whilst the great ocean of truth lay all undiscovered before me."*

❖ Plague ❖

TO start with, everything went well after the king was restored. Many people felt as if they were waking up from a nightmare. They were allowed to dance again, and go to the theatre. Noblemen dressed in the brightest colours they could find. Merchants imported rich silks and bought other fashions from China as well: wallpaper to decorate houses, and furniture far lighter and more elegant than people in Britain were used to. They imported coffee, and coffee houses opened all over London. People used to go there in the morning to read newspapers and meet their friends.

The king was among the first to adopt each new fashion. He put on Chinese clothes, then started to wear a wig, a fashion copied from France. Charles's court was a gay scene of parties and dances, while the prettiest women competed for the king's attention. But just when Britain seemed set for a new age of pleasure and prosperity, it was struck by a series of disasters – first plague, then fire, then war.

Hundreds of years before, the Black Death had killed a third of the people in Britain and Ireland. The plague had never been so bad since, though it had never quite gone away, so when doctors found one case in London, they weren't too worried – at first.

But then they found another. And another.

London was very dirty and crowded. The streets were made of mud and the buildings of wood. Houses jutted out so far that they almost touched each other, blocking all sunlight from the ground. Streets ended in crooked alleys where hundreds of people lived together, sleeping ten to a room. There were no toilets or drains. The whole town stank of horse dung and rotting food.

In such a dirty, crowded place diseases spread quickly, and there was nothing doctors could do to help. Today we know plague is spread by fleas carried on rats, but doctors in those days didn't know where it came from and had no medicines to cure it. Children watched their parents groaning, with eyes rolling and terrible black swellings erupting in their armpits, but all they could do was pray. The authorities sealed up every house where there was a case of plague and painted a red cross on the

door. The victims' families were sealed up with them, and passers-by, seeing faces peering out of the windows, knew most of them were doomed. Every week, newspapers published lists of how many had died. Soon the graveyards were full, so pits were dug on the outskirts of the city; and each morning, carts rumbled through the streets to pick up the bodies.

"Bring out your dead!" chanted the drivers.

Families loaded the corpses of their dead parents or children onto the carts, and they were taken away and thrown into the pits.

The rich left the city to escape the danger, while the poor watched from alleyways as their carriages rolled past. They couldn't escape – they had nowhere else to go. Markets were deserted, and shops boarded up, while the lists in the newspapers grew longer and longer. Only when winter came did the plague end. But by then thousands in London had died.

Other towns were struck by the plague as well. Norwich had an epidemic, and so did Portsmouth and Newcastle. The little village of Eyam, in Derbyshire, had its own attack of the plague, which came in a chest of infected cloth from London. When the women who unpacked the chest fell sick, the vicar of Eyam, William Mompesson, realized his village was doomed. He called a meeting, and the villagers bravely agreed that to stop the plague reaching the neighbouring villages, they would shut Eyam off from the world. No one would be allowed in or out.

For more than a year, nothing was heard from Eyam. It was as if the village no longer existed. Only when the plague was over did the church bells ring again, and people from neighbouring villages went down the road to see what had happened. They found William Mompesson praying in his church, but only a few villagers were left to pray with him.

Everyone else was dead.

❖ The Great Fire ❖

THE plague came to an end, but London's troubles were not over, for in the very next year it was destroyed by fire. The blaze started in a baker's shop in Pudding Lane, near London Bridge. Fires happened quite often in those days, because all the houses were made of wood, so when the lord mayor was told about it, he didn't even bother to get out of bed.

"Pish!" he said. *"A woman might piss it out!"*

But that night a strong wind was blowing. It plucked sparks from the flames and scattered them across the rest of the city. Soon two or three fires were burning. Because the buildings were close together, the fire easily jumped from one to the next. By the following morning, everyone who lived near Pudding Lane had to move out of their houses, while soldiers ran to and from the river with buckets of water to throw on the flames.

It didn't do any good. The fire spread further. A pall of smoke hung over London, and smuts fell on the Thames like black snowflakes. The roads out of the city were blocked with people pushing carts piled with chairs, chests and cooking pots. Scared-looking children ran alongside, carrying their pet cats and dogs. In the city itself, the roaring of flames was so loud that no one could hear the orders soldiers shouted. Burning roofs exploded in showers of sparks. Men and women shoved along the streets, trying to save their possessions before the fire devoured them.

Rumours spread along the alleyways.

"The fire's reached Shoreditch!"

"It's almost at St Paul's Cathedral!"

When night fell, the fire was still raging. London Bridge was in flames, and the river Thames glowed orange in its reflection. Some escaped in boats piled high with possessions – suitcases, tables, even musical instruments – and stared in horror at their burning city, above which St Paul's Cathedral blazed like a great candle.

After three days, the fire was stopped by blowing up the houses nearest the flames, so there was nothing for them to burn. But by then most Londoners had lost their homes and were living in refugee camps around the city. After the fire Samuel Pepys, who kept a diary, went for a walk

through London. The streets were still hot, and there were piles of charred wood everywhere. He climbed a church tower to see how much had been destroyed, and what lay before him almost made him weep. *"It was the saddest sight of desolation that I ever saw,"* he wrote in his diary.

In just three days, old London had disappeared.

❖ The Dutch Wars ❖

AFTER plague and fire, people hoped they were due for a run of good luck, but instead the disasters went on. The third was a war against the Dutch.

The Dutch, who had won their freedom from the Spanish, were the newest and strangest nation in Europe. They didn't have a king, allowed many different religions, and became rich not by fighting but by trade. In time, people in Britain would learn many lessons from the Dutch, who became their allies, but to start with they were furious that Dutch trade rivalled their own. Oliver Cromwell had fought a war against them, and Charles II fought two more.

When they had faced the Spanish Armada, the English had proved themselves the better sailors, but the Dutch, who were used to the sandbanks and tides of the North Sea, were just as skilful. The year after the Fire of London, Admiral de Ruyter led his ships up the Thames to the river Medway, where the English fleet was anchored. Before anyone could raise the alarm, he seized some of the English ships and sank the rest, then sailed back to Holland in triumph.

Never before had the English suffered so shameful a defeat at sea. They won victories against the Dutch as well, but even so, the wars gained little, and some people started to mutter that since the Restoration, Charles's kingdoms had known nothing but plague, fire and defeat.

"We shouldn't have called the king back!" they grumbled.

And all the old arguments about politics and religion started up again.

❖ The Exclusion Crisis ❖

WHEN Charles II became king he had ordered Oliver Cromwell's body to be dug up. He had executed the MPs who signed Charles I's death warrant. He had passed laws to make everyone join the Church of England and to stop Puritans getting jobs. He called Parliament for a few years, but then dismissed it and ruled alone.

"Charles II is turning out just like Charles I," Puritans grumbled.

Most people didn't mind at first, because they were so glad the wars were over. But when things went wrong, they started to complain. They grumbled about Charles's mistresses, his fine clothes and his extravagant habits. Charles, who was clever and charming but very lazy, preferred parties to running his kingdoms. They criticized him for not calling Parliament. And most of all, they complained about his friendship with the king of France.

The king of France, Louis XIV, was the most powerful ruler in Europe. He called himself the Sun King, because he was as mighty as the sun. He built a huge palace at Versailles, and had absolute power in France, never calling parliaments or asking for advice. Louis sent Charles money so he could do without taxes and avoid calling Parliament in England. People began to wonder whether Charles wanted to become an absolute monarch himself.

They didn't trust Louis' faith either, for he was a Catholic and Catholics were becoming more and more unpopular in Britain. People feared they were trying to take over the country (even though there were so few Catholics in England and Scotland that they had nothing to worry about). They even accused them of starting the Fire of London.

"Catholics care more about their faith than their country," they muttered. And they noticed how many of Charles's friends were Catholic – his wife, Catherine of Braganza; several of his mistresses; and his younger brother, James, who suddenly announced he was giving up the Church of England to become Catholic. Charles had no legitimate children (meaning children with his wife, the queen – he had plenty of children with his mistresses), so James was next in line for the throne when Charles died.

"We could end up with a Catholic king!" people said nervously.

So when rumours spread of a "popish" plot to kill Charles, crown James and make Britain Catholic again, many people believed them. To start with, Charles didn't take the plot seriously, for James was unpopular.

"Who'd kill me to make you king?" he joked.

But the rumours grew until he had to call Parliament. Parliament had split by now into two parties. Tories supported the king, saying his right to rule came from God, and no one could challenge him. Whigs (many of whom were Nonconformists, meaning they refused to join the Church of England) said the king had to obey the law like everyone else, that his power came from the people, and if the people didn't like the way he ruled, they could get rid of him.

Whigs began a campaign to have James excluded from the throne. Riots broke out in London, and it looked as if Charles's kingdoms were heading for another civil war. But although many disliked James and hated the thought of a Catholic king, they hated the idea of civil war even more. So when Charles dismissed Parliament after three years of arguing, most people supported him. Whigs were furious, though, and some began a plot to assassinate Charles and James at Rye House, on their way back from Newmarket races. When the plot failed, Charles executed its leaders and retaliated by passing laws against Nonconformists, who were no longer allowed to worship in their own way.

Then Charles, who is sometimes called the Merry Monarch because of his sense of humour, started to behave like a tyrant. Newspapers could only print what the king allowed. Many Whigs fled into exile in Holland. In Scotland the Covenanters started a revolt against him but were beaten, and many exiled or put to death. To Scots, the last years of Charles's reign became known as the Killing Time.

It was bad news for those who hoped Britain's civil wars were over, but what followed was worse. For when Charles died, not long afterwards, it turned out he had been a secret Catholic all along. And his brother, James, who was crowned king of England, Scotland and Ireland, became the first Catholic monarch since Bloody Mary.

❖ Huguenots ❖

EVERYONE feared James would try to make his kingdoms Catholic again, and rule as an absolute monarch, like king Louis of France. And in the very year he became king, Louis proved how cruel absolute monarchs could be by passing a law that everyone in France had to become Catholic or leave. There were still many Protestants in France, who were called Huguenots, and Louis sent soldiers to burn their churches and drive them out of their homes.

"Is that what James wants to do to us?" people in Britain whispered to each other.

Sadly the Huguenots packed up and left France. Some went to Holland, where people of all faiths were welcome, and many came to England.

You have to be very brave to leave everything you know and go to a new country to make a new life. Huguenots arrived on ships, carrying everything they owned. Most didn't speak English, so when they asked for directions people shrugged, or spoke so quickly they couldn't understand. Often Huguenots stuck together so they could speak their own language, worship with their friends and eat food they were used to. Some settled in Spitalfields, in the East End of London, and others in Soho.

Many Londoners were kind, helping them find jobs and homes, but there are always people who hate anyone different, and some treated the Huguenots badly, refusing to serve them in shops, or spitting on the pavement when they heard them speaking French. For a lot of the immigrants, the first years in England were frightening and difficult.

Fortunately many of them were skilled craftsmen: silk weavers, bankers, lawyers or silversmiths. Huguenots worked hard to build a new life and give something back to the country that had taken them in. And as time went by, people in Britain realized they could learn from them. They started to enjoy French food and to buy the fashions of the Huguenot silk-weavers. For their part, Huguenots learned English so they could talk to people around them.

And so Britain learned an important lesson about immigrants. By trying to make everyone the same, Louis XIV had made France weaker. Instead, the immigrants' energy and new ideas went to Britain, and, by welcoming them, Britain became stronger than ever.

❖ The Glorious Revolution ❖

TODAY, Protestants and Catholics believe much the same things, and no longer argue with each other, so it's hard to understand how they hated each other in those days. Each thought the other evil, and persecuted them whenever they got the chance. In Britain, there were Protestants of different kinds - Puritan and Church of England, Presbyterian and Church of Scotland - who often quarrelled; but they agreed about one thing: they hated Catholics even more than they hated each other.

Everyone wished Charles II had had a Protestant son who could be king instead of his Catholic brother, James. In fact, Charles did have a son, the duke of Monmouth. He was handsome, charming *and* Protestant, but unfortunately his mother was one of Charles's mistresses, so the duke of Monmouth was illegitimate and couldn't be king. When Charles died, Monmouth, who was living in Holland, decided to try to make himself king anyway. He declared his mother had married King Charles secretly so he wasn't illegitimate, landed at Lyme Regis in Dorset, and called all Whigs to help him.

But Monmouth's Rebellion didn't last long, because most people hated the idea of another civil war, and didn't believe the story about his mother. His army was beaten at Sedgemoor, in Somerset; Monmouth was taken to the Tower of London and executed; and James II was crowned king.

"Just wait!" warned the Whigs. "He'll put Catholics in charge, get rid of Parliament and run the country by himself!"

And that was exactly what happened. James fell out with Parliament and closed it down, while his lord chancellor declared the king had the right to change laws or ignore them just as he pleased. The lord chancellor, George Jeffreys, was hated and feared because he had judged the prisoners who were captured after Monmouth's Rebellion, and sentenced so many to death that the trial became known as the Bloody Assizes.

Then James quarrelled with the Church of England and passed a law to say people didn't have to belong to it, but could worship in any way they wanted.

"It *sounds* fair," said the Whigs. "But actually he just wants to help Catholics!"

And it was true that all James's closest friends and advisers were Catholics, and he kept trying to persuade courtiers to become Catholic too.

Things went from bad to worse. When Church of England bishops complained about what he was doing, James sent seven of them to the Tower of London, and riots broke out.

"Remember Bloody Mary!" people shouted. "The Catholics will take over and burn Protestants at the stake!"

At least James had no son to become king after him. His only children were two daughters by his first marriage, Mary and Anne, who were both Protestant. In fact, Mary, the elder daughter, was married to the most famous Protestant in Europe, the Dutch leader, Prince William of Orange, who had saved Holland when Louis XIV of France tried to attack it. But then James's second wife, an Italian called Mary of Modena, became pregnant and gave birth to a baby boy. That meant Britain's next king would be a Catholic like James.

"Impossible!" said the leaders of both the Whigs and the Tories. And some of them wrote to William of Orange asking him to come and help.

William wasn't sure what to do. What would everyone say if he drove his own father-in-law off the throne? But he was worried that if Britain turned Catholic, it would become an ally of France, and France would attack Holland again. William was a quiet man, small, moody and bad-tempered, but he was very determined. At last he decided to invade Britain.

When the Spanish Armada had tried to invade Britain, a hundred years before, it ended in disaster. William tried not to think of that. To make the invasion even more dangerous, it was autumn, and gales whistled across the North Sea. The first time the Dutch navy set sail it was driven back by a storm. But William didn't give up. He set sail again, and this time an east wind blew his fleet across the North Sea and down the Channel. The same wind trapped the British navy at Harwich, unable to get to sea.

William landed at Torbay. It was the first time an army had invaded Britain since the Norman Conquest. Sailors rowed the soldiers ashore, then went back for bundles of muskets and barrels of ammunition. Horses were lowered into the sea and swam through the waves. William's force was made up of Dutch soldiers and French Huguenots, English and Scottish exiles. Officers tried to sort everyone out, shouting orders in four different languages until the army was ready to set off towards London.

In London James had done nothing to prepare, because he didn't believe his son-in-law would dare invade. When he heard about William's arrival he panicked. Quickly, he tried to undo all the unpopular laws he had passed since coming to the throne, promising to change everything back to how it was before. But no one trusted James any more, and no one believed his promises. One by one, his supporters deserted him. Generals rode away from his army. Even his younger daughter, Anne, rode out of London to join William. James started to have nosebleeds and headaches. At night he lay awake imagining being executed like his father, Charles I. Eventually he decided to escape. He sent his wife and baby son to France, then disguised himself in a black wig and crept out of the palace with two friends.

When people in London realized James was gone, they rioted, smashing up Catholic chapels and houses. Then they sent letters to William, asking him to take over. William couldn't believe his luck. James had run away of his own accord, so he didn't have to drive him off the throne. He could win power without fighting a battle.

Unfortunately James's escape went wrong. His friends had arranged for a boat to meet him on the north coast of Kent and take him to France. But the boat got stuck on the mud, and before it could free itself, some fishermen arrived and arrested James and his companions. The fishermen didn't recognize the king to start with, and thought he was a Catholic priest trying to escape.

"Traitor!" shouted Harry Moon, one of the fishermen.

They made him take his trousers down to search him, then took him to a pub in Faversham as a prisoner. Only then did they realize who James was. The king begged the sailors to let him go, first threatening them then trying to bribe them, but they refused and sent him back to London.

That was the last thing William wanted. So in the middle of the night he sent two of his officers to wake James up and send him back to Kent. A few days later James escaped again and finally reached France.

Meanwhile, William and his army marched into London with crowds lining the streets. Some people waved oranges on sticks to greet the prince of Orange. "Liberators!" they shouted. "Thank you for coming to free us!"

But not everyone cheered. Others didn't like the sight of foreign soldiers marching in front of the king's carriage. "Invaders!" they muttered.

In fact, no one could quite decide what had happened – whether James had run away or been forced to leave, whether William was a friend or an enemy, and – most important of all – what ought to happen next.

William called a convention of politicians, who argued about it. Some Tories said James was the lawful king, and wanted to allow him back if he promised to behave better. But Whigs thought James had given up the right to be king by breaking the law, and wanted William and his wife, Mary, to take over as king and queen.

In the end even most Tories realized William was the only one strong enough to be king. But Whigs also wanted to make sure that from now on kings would obey the law, and never rule without Parliament. So they put forward a new law called the Bill of Rights.

"*Suspending laws without consent of Parliament is illegal,*" it said. "*Elections of Members of Parliament ought to be free. Freedom of speech in Parliament ought not to be questioned.*"

When everything was agreed, Mary sailed to England from her home in Holland. She went to the Banqueting House with William, where the Bill of Rights was read out and they became joint king and queen.

Of course, not everyone was happy with what had happened. The supporters of James, who'd gone to France as a guest of Louis XIV, said he was still the real king of Britain. They went on describing him as King James II, and called themselves Jacobites, from *Jacobus*, the Latin word for James.

James tried to win his kingdoms back. He went to Ireland, where he had a lot of supporters because most of the people there were Catholic. But the Protestants in Ulster supported William of Orange (indeed, some Ulster Protestants still call themselves Orangemen today) and fought back. William took his army to Ireland and confronted James at the river Boyne. James's Irish supporters fought bravely, but James himself ran away. After that the Irish called James *Seamus an chaca*, or "James who pooed himself". Some of the Irish kept on fighting under their leader, Patrick Sarsfield, but in the end they had to give in, and fled to France to join the French army, becoming known as the Wild Geese.

That was the end of Britain's civil wars and its last revolution, which is often called the Glorious Revolution. Since then Parliament has met every year, and kings and queens have obeyed the law. They have gradually become less important, so that now it is Parliament which runs Britain. Since then law courts have been free. And not long after the revolution, Parliament passed an Act to let people write whatever they liked, giving them "freedom of speech".

But there remained one important thing to settle: how to stop people quarrelling about religion.

❖ Toleration ❖

NONCONFORMISTS thought the Church of England, with its bishops, robes and ceremonies, was too like the Catholic Church. Scottish Presbyterians thought the Church of Scotland (which was sometimes called Episcopalian from the Latin word for bishop) was no better. They'd all been fighting for decades. How could everyone live together in peace?

Some thought people's beliefs ought to be up to them. Governments shouldn't interfere, they said, and people shouldn't interfere with each other. One of them was a philosopher called John Locke. Locke was a Whig who had spent many years in exile in Holland. There, people believed whatever they wanted, and Jews, Protestants and Catholics all lived peacefully together. John Locke thought Britain should be the same, so he wrote a book called *A Letter on Toleration*.

Ever since the Reformation, he wrote, the people of Europe had argued about religion, and thousands had been killed in wars. It was time to do things differently. For there would always be different faiths – Christian and Jew, Muslim and Hindu – and each would be divided – into Protestant and Catholic, or Sunni and Shiite. It was obvious people would never agree about faith. So instead of fighting and arguing, Locke said, they should agree to let everyone believe what they chose. And governments should stop telling people what to think, and let them worship in freedom.

After the Glorious Revolution, many could see he was right. "We can't go on fighting for ever," they said.

So Parliament passed a Toleration Act to let people worship how they wanted. It wasn't perfect, for the Church of England went on being the official religion in England (and still is today), while the Presbyterians became the official Church in Scotland. But Protestants who disagreed were allowed to worship in their own way.

After a century of fighting, the people of Britain had finally reached a conclusion: toleration is the only way everyone can live together in peace.

TIMELINE

❖ ❖ ❖ ❖ ❖ ❖ ❖

1605 ❖ The Gunpowder Plot: some Catholics try to blow up the king and Parliament.

1616 ❖ The pope bans Galileo from carrying out experiments. Dr Harvey proves that blood circulates through the body. Four years later, Francis Bacon writes a book about the scientific method of discovering things.

1618–48 ❖ The Thirty Years War in Europe.

1620 ❖ The *Mayflower* sails to America to start a colony.

1625 ❖ James I and VI dies and is replaced by his son Charles I.

1628 ❖ Parliament sends

Charles its Petition of Right.

1629–40 ❖ Charles rules without Parliament. William Laud, archbishop of Canterbury, changes the Church of England, and Puritans think he's making it too Catholic.

1638 ❖ Scots sign the Covenant, demanding their own kind of Church.

1639–40 ❖ The Bishops' Wars between Scotland and the king. When he is defeated, Charles calls the Short Parliament.

1642 ❖ Charles tries to arrest five MPs. The First Civil War begins, and the Battle of Edgehill is fought.

1643 ❖ Parliament and the Scottish Covenanters agree the Solemn League and Covenant.

1644 ❖ Parliament beats the Royalists at the Battle of Marston Moor. Oliver Cromwell suggests the Self-Denying Ordinance to keep politicians out of the war, and founds the New Model Army.

1645 ❖ Archbishop Laud is executed. Parliament wins the Battle of Naseby.

1646 ❖ King Charles surrenders. The New Model Army seizes him and sends him to the Isle of Wight.

1647–48 ❖ Scottish Engagers offer to help King Charles. The Second Civil War begins, but the Engagers are beaten at the Battle of Preston.

1649 ❖ King Charles I is beheaded by Parliament.

1650 ❖ Cromwell beats the Scots at the Battle of Dunbar.

1651 ❖ Prince Charles is defeated at Worcester and escapes, first to France, then Holland.

1652–54 ❖ The First Dutch War.

1655 ❖ Jamaica is seized from Spain.

1658 ✧ Oliver Cromwell dies. His son Richard becomes lord protector, but the next year the army takes over. As chaos threatens, General Monck takes control and invites the king back.

1660 ✧ Charles II is restored as king.

1665 ✧ The plague.

1666 ✧ The Great Fire of London.

1667 ✧ The Dutch defeat the English at the river Medway in the Second Dutch War.

1672–74 ✧ The Third Dutch War.

1678–79 ✧ Rumours of a "popish plot" to kill Charles and make his brother James king.

1679–81 ✧ Charles quarrels with Parliament. The Whigs try to stop his Catholic brother James becoming king in the Exclusion Crisis.

1683 ✧ Disappointed Whigs try to assassinate Charles and James in the Rye House Plot.

1685 ✧ Charles dies and James becomes King James II. The duke of Monmouth starts a rebellion but is defeated and executed.

1688 ✧ In the Glorious Revolution, James II is driven away by William of Orange, who becomes William III in 1689, while his wife, James's daughter, becomes Queen Mary. From now on, Parliament meets every year. The Toleration Act is passed in 1689.

1690 ✧ William defeats James at the Battle of the Boyne.

THE
GEORGIANS

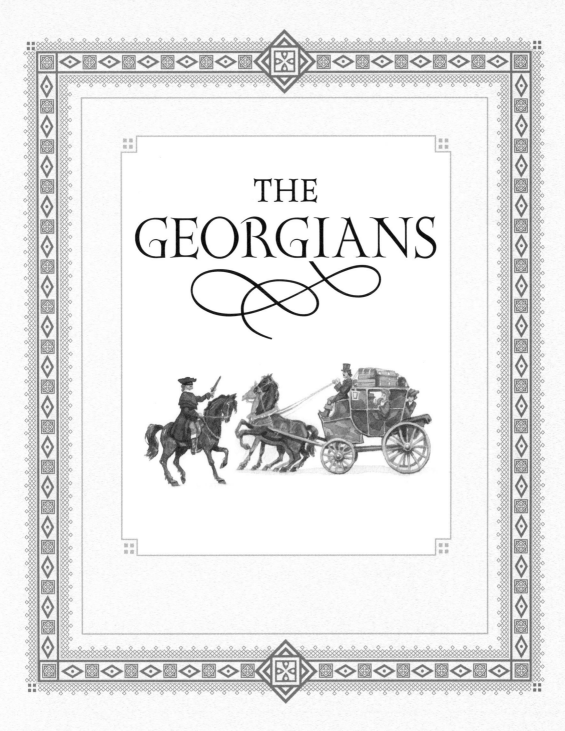

Ignatius Sancho

❖ ❖ ❖ ❖ ❖ ❖ ❖ ❖

BORN A
SLAVE

Bonnie Prince Charlie

❖ ❖ ❖ ❖ ❖ ❖ ❖ ❖

LED A REBELLION

William Pitt

❖ ❖ ❖ ❖ ❖ ❖ ❖ ❖

BUILT AN EMPIRE

James Cook

❖ ❖ ❖ ❖ ❖ ❖ ❖

EXPLORED
THE OCEAN

George III

❖ ❖ ❖ ❖ ❖ ❖ ❖

MAD KING

Wolfe Tone
❖❖❖❖❖❖❖

FOUGHT FOR
IRELAND

Horatio Nelson
❖❖❖❖❖❖❖

DIED IN VICTORY

Duke of Wellington
❖❖❖❖❖❖❖

DEFEATED
THE FRENCH

Lord Byron
❖❖❖❖❖❖❖

MAD, BAD AND
DANGEROUS
TO KNOW

ADMIRAL NELSON AT THE BATTLE OF TRAFALGAR

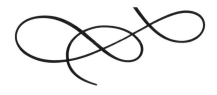

❖ Slavery ❖

DESPITE all the arguments it had caused, the people of Britain were proud of their revolution. Their law courts were fair, and they chose the politicians who made their laws.

"We can say what we want and think what we please!" they boasted.

That may have been true, but in fact not everyone was allowed to vote in elections. Men had to own land or a house, and women weren't allowed to vote at all. But even those who couldn't vote joined in by cheering their favourite and booing their opponent.

"In other countries everyone does what the king tells them," the British said. "But we're free!"

So it was all the more sad that just when the British won their own freedom, they turned other people into slaves.

Slaves have no freedom at all. If you're a slave, you belong to someone else, and your owner can starve or whip you just as he chooses. He can kill you if he wants, and no one will say a thing, because his slaves belong to him, just like sheep or cows. If he wants more slaves, he buys them. If he wants fewer, he sells them.

The Caribbean islands that the British took from the Spanish were perfect for growing sugar, which people in Britain wanted to put in their tea and sweeten their food. But there weren't enough men in the Caribbean to work on the sugar farms, because the islands' original people, the Caribs, were killed when the Spanish came, or died of disease. So the British went to Africa and took Africans to the Caribbean as slaves.

When slave ships appeared off the African coast, everyone who lived there ran to hide in the forest. Every village had a story of a father, a wife or a son disappearing and never being seen again, and rumours went round about what happened when the slave traders found you.

"They chain your hands and make you walk for days through the jungle. Then they put you on a ship and take you far away across the sea."

"What happens across the sea?" people asked.

No one knew, for none of the slaves ever came back.

When West African kings fought one another, they sold their prisoners to the British as slaves. Realizing how much gold the British would pay for a slave, they raided neighbouring towns and captured the strongest men and women. But if British slave traders arrived on the coast and there weren't any slaves to buy, the slavers loaded their guns and set off into the forest to hunt them. They seized women who had gone to the river to fetch water, and dragged away men who were herding cattle. They threw boys and girls into sacks. Then they loaded their new slaves onto their ships, and when the ships were full, set sail for the Caribbean.

The journey across the ocean was called the Middle Passage. Each ship had a deck where the slaves were forced to lie down in rows with chains fastened around their necks and ankles. They were packed so tight together that they couldn't move. When the ship swooped over the waves, the slaves were seasick. They were given hardly any food or water, there was no light or air, and the heat was stifling. Many died. The survivors closed their eyes and tried not to think of their children and families, and the homes they had been taken from. Often they wished they could die as well.

When they reached Jamaica, they were taken to the slave market. The sugar farmers, who came to the market to buy them, held handkerchiefs over their noses to keep out the smell. They paid most for the strongest men and prettiest girls. Sugar farmers were very rich and their houses were like palaces, so some of the slaves were washed and put to work as servants. But most of them worked in the fields. No one looked after them. They toiled for as long as their owner told them, and were whipped until their backs were bloody.

When the sugar was harvested, they helped load it onto ships.

"Where are the ships going?" they asked.

"To Britain," they were told.

And they remembered Britain was the island where the slave ships came from, and wondered what sort of devils the British were, who liked

SLAVERY

N. AMERICA

EUROPE

SUGAR TO BRITAIN

GOODS TO AFRICA

AFRICA

THE CARIBBEAN

Slave Coast

THE MIDDLE PASSAGE

S. AMERICA

N

eating sugar, and bought and sold men as if they were cattle.

We all want to be proud of our country, and the people of our islands have a lot to be proud of. We made ourselves free and helped free others as well. Our discoveries and inventions have made the world much better. But the slave trade was a shameful evil that we should never forget. Millions of families were destroyed by slavery, and millions of African men and women killed.

It would be more than a hundred years before the British realized that the freedom they loved so much should belong to everyone, not just them.

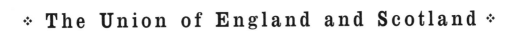

❖ The Union of England and Scotland ❖

WHEN the Glorious Revolution was over, England, Wales, Scotland and Ireland all had the same king and queen – William and Mary – but they were still separate kingdoms. And even though a Scottish king had first brought Scotland and England together, the Scots often complained they were treated unfairly.

"The king does what's best for England," they grumbled. "He doesn't care about us."

It was true. King William let his ministers in Scotland do what they wanted. The result was the terrible massacre of Glencoe.

The Scottish Parliament passed a law to say that every Scottish clan chief had to swear allegiance to the new king, but many of the Highland chieftains preferred James II.

"At least he's a Stuart," they said, "and a Scotsman at heart, even if he's a Catholic and a fool."

The chief of the Glencoe Macdonalds put off swearing the oath of allegiance until the very last minute; then a blizzard held him up, so he swore it late.

"This is my chance to deal with them," muttered John Dalrymple, the king's Scottish minister, who had always hated the Macdonalds, and he got the king to sign an order to let him punish them as he chose.

A few weeks later, the Macdonalds saw a column of Campbell soldiers winding down the path into Glencoe. The Campbell and Macdonald clans had always been enemies, but under the Scottish laws of hospitality every stranger was welcomed and given a bed for the night, so the Macdonalds let the soldiers into their cottages. Some days passed. Then, one night, when it was freezing cold and snow was falling, the Macdonalds banked up their fires and said goodnight, while the soldiers lay down on the floor with their muskets beside them. But the soldiers did not go to sleep. In the middle of the night they got up and attacked their hosts.

Woken by the screams of women and children, the Macdonalds struggled to escape. Soldiers ran after the children as flames leaped from burning cottages and stained the snow blood red. The Macdonalds fled up into the bare hills, stumbling through snowdrifts, until the cold numbed

their legs and they sank down to die on the bare hillside of Glencoe.

Afterwards William said he signed his order to John Dalrymple without knowing what would happen. He didn't understand Scotland and its different clans. But that just showed the Scots how little the government in London cared about them.

Not long after William died, an even more serious argument blew up between Scotland and England about who should be king next. William and Mary had no children, so when both of them died, Mary's younger sister, Anne, became queen. Anne's seventeen children all died young (which was quite common in those days before proper medicine), so there was no one left to rule after her.

James II was still alive. His supporters, the Jacobites, wanted him to be king; and when he died, they wanted his son to become James III. But James was a Catholic, and most people didn't want to make him king as if the revolution had never happened. They called him the Pretender and began searching for an alternative. Lawyers dug out a family tree of the Stuarts and searched through it until they found a Protestant who could become king. He was a distant German cousin of Anne's called George, and Parliament passed a law to say that when Anne died he should become King George I of England, Wales, Ireland and Scotland.

No one in Scotland liked being bossed about by the English. "We're a separate kingdom!" raged Scottish MPs. "It's not up to the English to say who'll be king of Scotland!"

All the same, a lot of Scots preferred George to the Pretender, and many thought it was time England and Scotland stopped quarrelling.

"It doesn't make sense for us to have different kings," they said. "We trade together; we fight together; we've been ruled together for a hundred years. We shouldn't just share a king - we should turn England and Scotland into one country. We should form a Union."

"Have you gone mad?" other Scots shouted. "The English are our enemies! Have you forgotten Robert Bruce and William Wallace?"

"It's time we looked beyond our own borders," replied the Unionists. "A Union will let us trade freely with England and grow rich. We'll keep our Scottish law and Scottish religion - and have MPs in London too!"

So Scottish and English politicians prepared a treaty to abolish the

Scottish government and turn Scotland and England into one country. For all their arguments, though, they still couldn't persuade everyone that joining England was a good idea.

"Traitors!" people chanted as the politicians went to Parliament to debate the Union.

Rumours began to circulate that MPs were being bribed to vote for the Union. It was said the duke of Argyll, the Unionist leader, had been promised lands in England and given a chest of gold to reward anyone who supported him. And at last the Scottish Parliament voted in favour of it.

"This Parliament is now over," said the lord chancellor, and even though he supported the Union, he felt a moment of sadness. *"And there,"* he added, *"is the end of an auld song."*

The Scottish Parliament wouldn't meet again for three hundred years.

So Scotland, England and Wales became a new country called Great Britain, and a new flag called the Union Jack was created by mixing together the Scottish saltire and the cross of St George (there was no room in it for a symbol of Wales, which many people still think wrong). No one could be sure whether Scottish MPs had voted for the Union because of the benefits it would bring or because they had been bribed, but most Scots were furious at what had happened. No one had listened to them! And they were sure that from now on the English would run Britain for their own advantage, never thinking about the good of Scotland.

❖ Marlborough's War ❖

AT just that time, though, the British showed how much they could achieve if they only worked together.

Louis XIV, France's Sun King, didn't like Britain's Glorious Revolution because James II was a friend of his, while William of Orange was his deadliest enemy; so for most of William's reign, Britain and France were at war. But although the war went on for nine years, Louis couldn't beat the English and Scots, and another war started after Anne became queen. It began with an argument over who should be the next king of Spain, so it was called the War of the Spanish Succession.

"This is our chance to smash the British once and for all!" roared Louis as he ordered his generals to get ready.

But Britain was allied with Austria (which was a huge empire in those days) and had a brilliant general to lead its army – John Churchill.

Churchill had realized that the most successful armies weren't always the largest, or even the bravest, but the ones who were commanded most cleverly. He was skilled at getting his soldiers into just the right position for a battle, and surprising his enemies by attacking when they least expected it.

He first beat the French at the Battle of Blenheim, in southern Germany. Thinking he was far away, the French had attacked Austria, but Churchill marched his soldiers two hundred miles, took them by surprise and defeated them.

After that, he beat the French again and again, at the battles of Oudenarde, Ramillies and Malplaquet. To thank him for all his victories, the government made him duke of Marlborough, and built him a mansion outside Oxford called Blenheim Palace.

Not long before, Europeans had joked that Britain was *the land of revolutions*. But in the War of the Spanish Succession the British showed they could defeat the strongest country in the world.

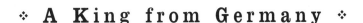

❖ A King from Germany ❖

DESPITE the victory against France, many Scots were still angry about the way English politicians had treated them, and hated being part of the Union. When Queen Anne died and King George I arrived from Germany, they grew even angrier.

George had never been to Britain before. All he had done was run a small town called Hanover. He was bad-tempered, middle-aged, and spoke no English. His ship was delayed by a storm, so when he landed no one was there to welcome him. It wasn't a good start.

Some Scots began a rebellion to make the Pretender king instead. "He's a Stuart," they declared. "At least he's one of us!"

Their leader, the earl of Mar, gathered an army in Scotland and called all Jacobites to join him. Unfortunately the rebellion went wrong from the very start. The Pretender, who arrived from France, turned out to be just as foreign as George of Hanover. He had lived all his life abroad and hardly spoke English. Apart from that, he was as stubborn, bossy and slow-witted as his father, James II. And when some Highland chieftains led their clans to join the rebellion, a lot of Lowland Scots were put off.

"Do we want our country to be like that?" they whispered as they saw the fierce-looking highlanders in their tartans. And they decided to support George instead.

For his part, George of Hanover turned out to be a much better leader than anyone expected. He got an army ready and beat the Jacobites at the Battle of Sheriffmuir. The Pretender ran away to France, and the rebellion of 1715, which came to be known as the '15, came to an end.

So King George I kept his throne, and his successors – George II, George III and George IV – were kings for the next hundred years. That is why people of the eighteenth century are often known as Georgians. And with the war against France won and the Pretender out of the way, the Georgians settled down to get rich.

❖ The South Sea Bubble ❖

ONCE, the best way to be rich was to own land. Lords were rich because of their land; and kings, who owned the most land, were the richest of all. Merchants became wealthy too. They owned no land, but by buying and selling things they earned gold, which they locked away in strong chests.

However, not many people were landowners or merchants. Most stayed poor, working on the land and eating what they could grow. They often went hungry, and that was how things had always been. There had always been rich and poor. No one thought the whole country could get richer.

Yet after the Glorious Revolution, it did.

Britain became rich by copying ideas from Holland. The Dutch had made themselves richer without owning any land at all – a lot of their country was water – and they weren't that interested in gold either.

"Money's no good locked up in chests," they said. "You have to use it if you want to get rich!"

In the Dutch capital, Amsterdam, there was a bank that lent money to merchants, who paid interest to make the bank richer, and used the bank's money to make themselves richer. Thanks to their bank, far more trade happened in Holland than anywhere else, and the whole country became wealthy.

Then the Dutch found other ways to get rich. Groups of merchants started companies to trade together. If they needed more money to build ships, they divided the company into shares and sold them. In that way, ordinary people could buy a share in a trading company and make money. The cost of shares in the company went up or down depending on how well the company's trade was going, so people got rich by buying and selling the shares as well.

And that was when the Dutch realized that *everything* could be bought and sold. It wasn't just food and clothes, beds and chairs, tables and candles and pans. It wasn't just houses, fields, sheep, eggs, paintings, books and shoes. You could buy and sell money. You could buy and sell shares. You could buy and sell the chance of a house burning down or a ship being sunk at sea. Everything had a price, and the price wasn't fixed.

You could even make a fortune betting on whether the price of something would go up or down.

The British soon copied the Dutch. Not long after the Glorious Revolution, a Bank of England was founded in London by William Paterson, a Scot, and John Houblon, a Huguenot (the Bank of England is still in charge of Britain's money today), and the British started companies and began trading in shares.

As they became richer, people spent the money they made on new clothes and houses, shopping and fashion. They turned London into one of Europe's most exciting cities, where you could buy luxuries from all over the world. At night you could visit theatres and concerts, or go to pleasure gardens where bands played and waiters hurried through the crowds with trays of food and bottles of wine. Irish, Scots and Welsh, black people, Jews, French Protestants and English all jostled one another in the streets. Religion didn't seem so important any more. All people cared about was how to become rich.

The only problem with the new way of making money was that it was very risky. People could make fortunes buying and selling shares, but they could lose them as well.

One day, a rumour went round the City of London that a business called the South Sea Company was making a lot of money.

"What does the South Sea Company do?" some asked.

No one was quite sure, but people were so eager to get rich that no one cared. They all hurried to invest in it, and the price of South Sea Company shares shot up.

"If we invest a hundred pounds," men told their wives, "by the end of the month we'll have a thousand! We never need to work again!"

So families invested all they had. Carpenters sold their tools, merchants sold their ships, and rich ladies drove to the City in carriages to invest their jewels. None of them saw the danger they were in. The South Sea Company didn't actually do anything, and wasn't worth anything. It only looked big because so many people had put their money into it. It expanded like a bubble – and one day the bubble burst.

A rumour went round that the directors of the South Sea Company were cheats. People started to sell their shares, so the share price began to go

down instead of up. Suddenly, instead of getting richer, investors found they were getting poorer. They hurried to the City to sell their shares, but met crowds so thick they couldn't get through. South Sea shares fell faster and faster, until they were worth less than people had paid for them. Then they were worth nothing at all.

"Ruined!" whispered the carpenters, merchants and rich ladies. They had sold everything to invest in the company, and now they had nothing left. All they could do was stand in the street and whisper, "Ruined!"

Daniel Defoe was a writer who lived near where the shares were bought and sold, and saw the investors walking home to tell their families what had happened. *"I'll remember a man with a South Sea face for as long as I live,"* he wrote.

Today people still invest in shares, and still make fortunes. London has become one of the great financial centres of the world, with share traders working in huge tower blocks in Canary Wharf and the City. But shares still crash sometimes, and when they do, there are pictures in the papers of traders sitting in front of their computers with their heads in their hands – and you can see what Daniel Defoe meant by *"a man with a South Sea face"*.

❖ Aristocrats ❖

AFTER the Glorious Revolution, ordinary people were sure things would get better. "From now on, Parliament will meet every year," they told each other. "We'll have more of a say in things!"

And it was true that the law courts worked better, people could go to church where they wanted, and many became richer (so long as they hadn't put their money in the South Sea Company). But although Britain was free, it didn't become more fair. If anything, it became less so, because while the richest people got richer, the poorest stayed hungry.

Aristocrats – the dukes, earls and barons who sat in the House of Lords – were the richest of all. The House of Lords was half of Parliament, so when Parliament became more important, the lords became more important too. They even started to take over the House of Commons, for a lot of MPs were the younger brothers of lords, and the rest were gentlemen, which was the next rank down from a lord. Besides, aristocrats owned so much land that they could get their favourite candidates elected by their tenants.

Once they were in control of Parliament, the aristocrats passed laws to make themselves even richer. They took away the common land where country people used to graze their cows and sheep, enclosing it with hedges to make farms for themselves. They invented jobs paid by the government, and gave them to their families and friends. Politicians became more and more dishonest, and it became harder to get rid of them because aristocrats passed a law to stop elections happening too often. In fact, a lot of MPs were simply chosen by the local lord, so it was hardly worth voting anyway.

As they became richer, aristocrats used their money to build palaces, which they decorated with columns and filled with paintings and statues. Around them they laid out parks with fountains and lakes, and around the parks built high walls to keep everyone else out. Today we can all visit stately homes, and walk through the grand rooms where aristocrats held their parties, but at the time, no one was allowed in. Poor men who were caught climbing the walls to hunt rabbits were hanged as thieves.

For the poor, life seemed to be getting harder just as everyone else was getting rich. So it wasn't surprising that some of them turned to crime.

❖ Stand and Deliver! ❖

IN London, poor people didn't have anywhere to live, so they slept in doorways and alleys, or crammed into slums where ten strangers had to share a bed. In those days governments didn't think it was their business to look after the poor, so there were no doctors to treat them when they grew sick, no schools to educate their children, and if a man had an accident and couldn't work, his family starved.

Because London was said to be rich, people flocked there from all over the country to make their fortunes. They sailed across the sea from Ireland, tramped down the highways from Glasgow and Cardiff, and left villages where they had lived all their lives. But there was nothing for them in London. All they could do was walk along the streets and gaze in shop windows full of gold watches, jewels, silk handkerchiefs and fine clothes that cost more than they would earn in their whole lives.

Being poor was worse when everyone else was getting richer, so some people started to steal. As pickpockets pushed through crowds, hoping to take a gentleman's purse or silk handkerchief, the city became more and more dangerous, particularly at night. There were no street lights. Anyone crossing an alley might be set upon and robbed.

"We must punish thieves more harshly," the politicians decided.

In those days murderers and thieves were killed by the government. They were taken to Tyburn, near Marble Arch, where nooses were put round their necks and they were hanged. Crowds turned up to watch, and cheered as they do at football matches today.

To start with only the worst criminals were killed, but as politicians became more worried about crime, they executed less serious criminals too. A mother who stole bread for her children could be hanged; so could a boy of ten who stole a biscuit. Everyone could see that wasn't fair. And because the law was unfair, people stopped respecting it. They cheered criminals as if they were heroes, and told stories about their favourites.

Some stories were about pirates like Blackbeard and Captain Kidd, who sailed to the Caribbean to attack ships, stealing their cargo and drowning the sailors. Pirates didn't have any law to live by or aristocrats to sneer at them, but did as they pleased. Others were about the highwaymen who

stopped carriages on lonely roads out of London to steal money and jewels from the passengers.

In these stories highwaymen weren't villains, but "gentlemen of the road" who fought bravely, and treated their victims with courtesy. And the most famous of all was Dick Turpin, who robbed travellers on the road through Epping Forest.

One day Dick Turpin stopped a gentleman riding a fine black racehorse. "I'll swap your horse for mine," he said, and rode away on Black Bess, the fastest horse in England. Soon afterwards, when he was ambushed at Whitechapel, he leaped onto Black Bess, rode out of London, and – so the story went – galloped all the way to York in just fifteen hours.

When he was finally captured and sentenced to death, Dick Turpin spent his last money on fine clothes so he could hold parties in his prison cell. A huge crowd came to cheer him when he was hanged. And even after his death, travellers in Epping Forest still peered nervously out of their carriage windows and shouted at their coachmen to whip the horses harder. They could still imagine Dick Turpin galloping out of the trees on Black Bess to shout the highwayman's cry: *"Stand and deliver!"*

❖ Bonnie Prince Charlie ❖

LONG after the 1715 rebellion had failed, Jacobites kept dreaming they could bring back the Pretender, who went on living abroad as King James III. By now he had a son called Charles, so James became known as the Old Pretender, while his son was called the Young Pretender. Gradually, though, most people stopped worrying about the Jacobites. George I died, and his son, George II, became king, but there was no Jacobite rebellion.

"It's ancient history," everyone said. "We ought to look forward, not back."

But just when they least expected it, the Young Pretender started a rebellion in Scotland that almost drove the Georges off their throne. It happened in 1745 and became known as the '45.

The Jacobite plan was for Charles to land in Scotland with a French army, beat the British, and proclaim the Old Pretender king. The French never sent their army, but the Young Pretender sailed to Scotland and began the rebellion anyway.

Charles was young and handsome – so handsome that the Scots called him Bonnie Prince Charlie – and Scottish Jacobites hurried to join him. Bonnie Prince Charlie led his little force into Edinburgh and crowds cheered as he rode up the Royal Mile, smiling and waving his hat in the sunshine. Soon afterwards he beat the British army at the Battle of Prestonpans.

"When we invade England," he told his generals, "all the Jacobites will join us and we will ride into London in triumph!"

So he led the Scottish Jacobites across the hills into England. Most of his army came from the Highlands, wore Highland clothes and carried the old Highland weapons of sword and shield. They captured Carlisle, and then Manchester. When they reached Derby, news came that everyone in London was panicking, lords and ladies were fleeing the city, and the Bank of England had closed down.

But Bonnie Prince Charlie's generals were becoming worried, for no English Jacobites had joined them. In fact, there didn't seem to be any English Jacobites left. They had hoped the Irish would rebel when they

heard of the Young Pretender's landing, but nothing happened in Ireland either. Besides, although Scots had cheered when the Jacobites captured Edinburgh, the generals knew many Scots liked the Union, and wanted to keep King George. They also knew the British army was far bigger than their little band of Highland fighters, and had discovered, by now, that Bonnie Prince Charlie was not the great leader Jacobites had longed for.

"He's always drunk," they whispered. "And he behaves like a spoiled child! He has tantrums if he doesn't get his way!"

So they told the Young Pretender they had no choice but to return to safety in Scotland. He was furious, but his generals insisted, and they set off north with Bonnie Prince Charlie sulking in his carriage.

No one cheered as they marched back into Edinburgh. People were tired of Bonnie Prince Charlie's adventure, and many Lowland Scots had joined the British army that was pursuing the Jacobites. There were even some highlanders among them. The army was led by King George II's second son, the duke of Cumberland, and instead of swords and shields it had muskets and cannon. One by one, Bonnie Prince Charlie's supporters left to go home. And when the remaining soldiers marched north into the Highlands, the British army followed them.

The two armies camped north of Inverness.

"We'll take them by surprise!" shouted the prince, who was drunk – as usual – and he ordered a night attack.

In darkness the Jacobites set off towards the British army. It began to rain, the moorland grew boggy and they lost their way. Exhausted, frozen and soaked to the bone, they went back to where they started. They were so tired they lay down to sleep in the rain, and, when the trumpets blew at dawn, could barely get to their feet. They had had nothing to eat since the morning before.

On the other side of the moor, they watched the British army form a line with bugles blaring and flags flying.

"What is the name of this place?" asked Bonnie Prince Charlie.

"Culloden Moor," said his generals.

The tired and hungry highlanders were as brave as ever. When they were ordered to charge, they waved their swords and ran across the heather towards the British guns. But the battle didn't last long. By mid-morning

Culloden Moor was covered with dead Jacobites, while gun smoke drifted along the lines of British soldiers.

"What shall we do with the prisoners, Your Grace?" a British officer asked the duke of Cumberland.

The duke smiled grimly. "Kill them," he said. "And destroy their lands."

Jacobite prisoners were lined up against walls and shot. They were herded into barns and burnt alive. Their villages were set on fire, and their families driven off their farms. Because of his cruel order, the duke was known afterwards as "Butcher" Cumberland.

Many Scots had fought against Bonnie Prince Charlie, and it was completely unfair to punish the whole of Scotland for what the Jacobites had done. But laws were passed to ban highlanders from wearing tartan or playing the bagpipes, and soldiers marched along the glens, building forts and destroying villages.

The Highlands were never the same again. To make things worse, the Highland chiefs turned on their own people soon afterwards. They wanted to be like English lords, with palaces and huge estates, so they drove their followers out of their cottages, set fire to villages, and put up fences around their land. Barefoot and hungry, the highlanders walked west, carrying their children and their few possessions with them. They walked to the sea, because there was nowhere else for them to go. And when they reached it, since they had no other choice, they crossed it to find a new life in America, where their descendants still live today.

And what of Bonnie Prince Charlie?

He escaped from Culloden. Keeping well hidden, he travelled west until he reached the coast. There he met a young woman called Flora Macdonald, who took one look at his handsome face and fell in love with him. She rowed him to the Isle of Skye, and disguised him as a girl until a French ship came to take him away.

Flora Macdonald never saw Bonnie Prince Charlie again. Nor did Scotland. He went to live in Italy and died drunk, and neither he nor his father, the Old Pretender, ever uttered a word of regret about the ruin they had brought on Scotland.

❖ Rule, Britannia! ❖

FROM then on, there were no more Jacobite rebellions. The British became strong and successful together. They grew to love their Union Jack, made of the linked flags of England and Scotland, and their favourite songs, "God Save the King" and "Rule, Britannia".

> *Rule, Britannia! Britannia rules the waves!*
> *Britons never, never, never shall be slaves.*

And it wasn't long before a new war with France gave them the chance to show how strong their country was. It became known as the Seven Years War, because it lasted for exactly seven years, and it turned Britain into the most powerful country on earth.

By this time, thanks to their great ships and guns, European countries were taking over the rest of the world. The Spanish and Portuguese ran South America; the British and French had colonies in North America; while the British, French and Dutch owned trading towns in India and China. No one else had fleets so powerful; no one could defeat European armies. But wherever they met, Europeans attacked one another's ships, colonies and trading towns, so the Seven Years War was fought all over the world.

The war started with disaster for Great Britain. The French attacked the island of Minorca, which the British owned. They sent a fleet to the rescue, but its admiral, John Byng, arrived too late to help. He was sentenced to death for cowardice, and shot on the deck of his own ship.

Then, in India, a prince called Siraj ud-Daulah attacked the British town of Calcutta (which is now called Kolkata). After capturing it, he ordered all the British prisoners to be locked in a cell, so men, women and children were forced together into a single tiny room. Children were crushed underfoot, people screamed as they were squeezed against the walls, and there was only one small window, so no one could breathe properly. By morning, only twenty-three of the one hundred and forty-six prisoners were still alive. Afterwards the survivors called their prison the Black Hole of Calcutta.

Finally, Britain and Prussia (Britain's German ally) were beaten by the French in a battle in Europe.

Angry and confused, the British gathered in the streets of Edinburgh, Cardiff, Dublin and London. Politicians argued in Parliament, and at last chose a new leader called William Pitt. He wasn't a lord, so people called him The Great Commoner, but William Pitt turned out to be a brilliant leader. While he was in charge, Britain won its greatest victories yet. First the British and Prussians beat the French at the Battle of Minden. Next, Admiral Hawke destroyed the entire French fleet at the Battle of Quiberon Bay. Then the British captured most of the French islands in the Caribbean.

The most spectacular victory of all was in North America. Much of Canada belonged to the French, and its biggest town was Quebec, which stood on a high cliff. Everyone said it couldn't be captured, but General James Wolfe came up with a plan. At dead of night, his soldiers climbed the cliff, moving carefully so their weapons didn't make a sound. At dawn they fell on the French, and although James Wolfe himself was killed, Quebec was captured and all of North America became British.

The year 1759 was known as Britain's "year of victories", or, in Latin, "annus mirabilis". All over the country, people waved flags and sang songs. Once, Britain and Ireland had been two small, distant islands; after the Seven Years War they were at the very centre of the world. Ships of the Royal Navy commanded every ocean. Soldiers from Scotland, Ireland, England and Wales marched over European plains and through American forests.

And they marched across Asia as well. For one of Britain's most important victories in the Seven Years War took place in India, where the British defeated Siraj ud-Daulah and founded an empire that lasted for the next two hundred years.

❖ India ❖

CENTURIES before, India had been conquered by the Mughals, who came from the north. But the empire of the Mughals had grown weaker, and they couldn't stop Britain and France setting up trading towns where merchants of the British East India Company went to buy tea, silks and spices. The merchants loved India for its ancient palaces and temples, its elegance, luxury and learning. Many of them married Indian women and dressed in the Indian way.

As the East India Company grew richer, it became more powerful. It hired soldiers to protect its trading towns, fought wars with the French towns near by, and joined in quarrels between Indian princes. That was why Siraj ud-Daulah attacked the British town of Calcutta.

The British were determined to have their revenge, so the East India Company sent its best general, Robert Clive, to win Calcutta back. Clive, who had been so wild as a boy that his family sent him to India to get him out of the way, turned out to be a brilliant soldier. With only a small army he defeated Siraj ud-Daulah at the Battle of Plassey, then beat the French and drove them out of India.

That left the British the most powerful people in India, and the East India Company richer than ever. But Clive wanted more, so he approached the Mughal emperor and offered to buy the whole of Bengal. Indians couldn't believe the East India Company could actually buy part of their country. *"The transaction was done and finished,"* one of them wrote sadly, *"in less time than would have been taken up in the sale of a jackass!"* But from then on, the British took over more and more land until they ruled the whole of India.

Many Hindu Indians were glad to see the Mughals go, because they were Muslim. As for the East India Company, it didn't seem to believe in anything except money. Robert Clive became rich, and hundreds of merchants from Britain arrived in India to make themselves fortunes. The Indians watched them building houses and offices. They watched the East India Company's soldiers marching across the plains, and its sailors loading ships with cargoes to take back to Britain. They found that some Britons loved India, learned its languages and became their friends, while

others treated them cruelly, as if they were inferior.

What neither they nor the British realized was that they would be part of each other's stories for the next two hundred years, and that by the time the British left India, each would have changed the other for ever.

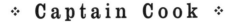

❖ Captain Cook ❖

INDIA wasn't the only country the British took over after the Seven Years War. They also became masters of a huge new continent in the south which no European had reached before.

People in Europe often wondered if there were any lands they hadn't found yet. What if there was another America to be discovered, with people they had never met, and animals they had never seen?

"If there's a missing continent anywhere, it will be in the south," they agreed. "Few European ships have ever been to the far south."

So the Royal Society sent an expedition to see. As captain, they chose a sailor called James Cook, whose father was Scottish and whose mother came from Yorkshire. He grew up on a farm, but went to sea and became expert at navigating and making charts. He told his friends he wanted to travel not only *"farther than any man has been before me, but as far as I think it is possible for a man to go."*

As Captain Cook's ship, the *Endeavour*, sailed across the Southern Ocean, blue waves reached as high as the mast, and albatrosses flew alongside. Cook kept watching for land. He had read that Dutch captains sailing to China had found land to the south, and hoped it might be the top of an unknown continent.

First Cook found the country we now call New Zealand. It was too small to be a new continent, but he mapped its two islands and sailed on. Then, one morning, the lookout reported land ahead. Cook climbed the mast with his telescope, and saw trees stretching from one end of the horizon to the other. When they drew closer, he saw a beach and people waving, and realized he had found the new continent.

The *Endeavour* sailed into a bay and Cook rowed ashore with his plant expert, Sir Joseph Banks. They jumped out onto the sand and looked around in wonder, for the trees were nothing like trees in Europe, and the animals, which bounced around on two enormous hind legs, were nothing like European animals. The British called the animals kangaroos, and the bay where they landed Botany Bay. They named the new continent Southern Land or Australia. Before leaving, Captain Cook tied the Union Jack to a tree and declared Australia part of the British Empire.

After that, many British men and women went to Australia, some as settlers, who cleared trees, built houses and began farms; others as criminals sent there as a punishment. When their sentence was over, they often stayed, rather than sail all the way back to Britain.

With Australia, India and America all flying the Union Jack, Britain owned the biggest empire the world had ever seen.

❖ The American Revolution ❖

BUT some people wondered if it was right for a small island in the Atlantic to rule so many other countries. Shouldn't they rule themselves? And indeed, it wasn't long before some in the empire started to protest.

"What right do the British have to govern us?" the Americans asked. And they pointed out how the British had got rid of kings who refused them a say in Parliament. "*We* don't have a say in Parliament either," they said, "but we still have to obey Parliament's laws and pay its taxes. It isn't fair."

The tax that annoyed Americans most was on tea. Americans loved tea as much as the British did, and couldn't see why they had to pay an extra tax. One morning, hundreds of men attacked the harbour at Boston, where ships full of tea arrived from Britain. Disguised as Native Americans, they smashed open crates and poured tea into the water until the whole town smelled of it.

"If we can't vote for Parliament, we won't pay its taxes," they shouted. *"No taxation without representation!"*

When it heard about the Boston Tea Party, the British government was furious, and passed laws saying the colonists should stop complaining and do as they were told. Americans found that intolerable, and, enraged by the Intolerable Acts, called a meeting of all the colonies at Philadelphia.

The British politicians couldn't see how unfair they were being. Too much power always makes people unfeeling, and with an empire all over the world, the British government had far too much power. Instead of trying to come to an agreement with the Americans, they sent soldiers to subdue them. The soldiers shot at rebels who had gathered at Lexington and Concord, in Massachusetts. But the rebels had guns of their own and drove them off. Britain found itself at war with its own colony.

The British had more money and weapons, but the Americans knew every hill and valley they were fighting for. Most of all, they knew they were in the right. On 4 July 1776 the American leaders, Thomas Jefferson and George Washington, announced they wanted America to be an independent country, based on principles they were ready to die for. Their announcement was called the Declaration of Independence. It started:

"We hold these truths to be self-evident, that all men are created equal, that they are endowed with certain unalienable Rights, that among these are Life, Liberty and the pursuit of Happiness."

Americans have been rightly proud of those principles ever since.

The war went on for seven years. The French sent money and soldiers to help the Americans, and George Washington turned out to be a skilful general. He defeated the British first at the Battle of Saratoga, then at Yorktown, where the British army surrendered. Canada stayed in the British Empire, but the rest of the American colonies became a new country with a new name: the United States of America.

The British liked to talk about freedom and fairness, so they shouldn't have been surprised that some people in their empire wanted freedom and fairness too. And perhaps they should have known that one day every man and woman in the empire, from slaves in Jamaica to villagers in India, would demand the same rights for themselves.

❖ The Scottish Enlightenment ❖

AT about this time, some important new ideas changed the way people thought about the world, much as the Renaissance had changed things at the end of the Middle Ages, and the ideas of scientists had brought change during the seventeenth century. By using the scientists' principle of believing things only when they had been properly tested, people found they could explain things that had always puzzled them, and disprove beliefs they had clung to for centuries. The change in thinking was called the Enlightenment. And a lot of the best new ideas came from Scotland.

Scotland had become more prosperous and successful than ever before. However much Scots had disliked the Union to start with, they quickly saw how much the British Empire could benefit them, as Scottish merchants traded all over the world, Scottish engineers built roads and harbours in America, and Scottish clerks worked in Indian offices, managing the new lands of the East India Company. With the money Scots made, they turned Edinburgh into one of the most exciting cities in the world, with its beautiful New Town of wide streets and stone houses, and a university famous for its learning. *"Here I stand at the Cross of Edinburgh,"* one visitor wrote, *"and can, in a few minutes, take fifty men of genius and learning by the hand."*

An Edinburgh economist called Adam Smith wondered how it was that people, towns and countries kept getting richer. Could they go on getting richer for ever? They could, he decided, so long as trade kept growing. And he wrote a book called *The Wealth of Nations* to explain his ideas.

A philosopher called David Hume wondered how we know things. Newborn babies know nothing, he pointed out, so how do people learn things as they grow up? And how can they be sure that what they learn is right? He decided the best way to understand things is to study them, come up with theories, and then test those theories by experiment. The best ideas come not from believing everything we're told, Hume insisted, but by questioning things and challenging them.

"We should use our reason," he said.

And many Scottish thinkers did just that. James Hutton was the first

to explain how rocks are formed. Joseph Black, a chemist, investigated how heat worked; and his pupil James Watt helped invent the steam engine. People didn't have to go on believing the same old things, the Scots showed, but could make the world better – if only they used their reason.

The strange thing was that just when so many in Britain were starting to use their reason, the most important person in the country lost his. King George III went mad.

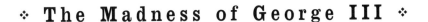

❖ The Madness of George III ❖

THE king shouted at his courtiers, howled like a wolf when anyone approached him, and fought off servants who tried to help. Some said he went mad because of losing his empire in America; others, because kings weren't as important as in the old days.

"He wants to rule like a king in the Middle Ages," they said, "but the politicians won't let him."

It was true that at the start of his reign George III had tried to take back some of the power kings had in the past. He dismissed the government, appointed his own advisers, and made a friend of his, Lord Bute, prime minister. MPs were so angry they held a special debate in the House of Commons. They agreed that *the influence of the crown has increased, is increasing, and ought to be diminished!"*

When George III heard about it, people said he was so enraged that he foamed at the mouth and went mad.

In the king's bedroom, doctors stood around him, arguing about what to do.

"A nervous excitement," said one.

"An inflammation of the brain," said another.

"He will recover."

"He will *not* recover."

The poor king thrashed about on his bed with eyes bulging. He bit his lips until they bled, and didn't even recognize the queen. The doctors took off his rings in case he cut himself, removed his fine gown and wrapped him in a madman's straitjacket with strings to bind his arms behind his back.

Meanwhile, MPs discussed what to do next.

"We run the country now," one said daringly. "Kings are less important than they used to be."

Indeed, all through the Georgian years, Parliament had become more important and the king less so. Sir Robert Walpole had been the first prime minister who ran the government almost as he pleased. But no one wanted to get rid of the king altogether. So eventually they agreed to make the king's son Regent while he was ill.

The king's son was a fat boy, also called George, who spent his time on clothes, horses - and pretty girls who only liked him because he was a prince. He didn't get on with his father and, to annoy him, had made friends with Charles Fox, the politician who criticized the king the most.

"Send for George," sighed the MPs.

And while the king howled in his bedroom at Windsor Castle, the prince regent held parties for his friends in the palace in London.

Sometimes the king's madness lifted for a short while. "What happened to me?" he would say, shaking his tired head. But his recoveries never lasted long. He would go mad again, and his crown would be taken away and his arms tied.

And so the time of kings drew to a close. For the very year after the king of Britain went mad, the king of France, who was even more powerful, was driven from his throne by a revolution that changed Europe for ever.

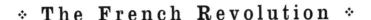

❖ The French Revolution ❖

A hundred years before, Louis XIV, the Sun King, had made France the richest and strongest country in the whole of Europe. His nobles were so afraid of Louis that they did whatever he told them. There was no parliament in France, and nothing happened unless the king wanted it. The kings who followed him, Louis XV and Louis XVI, were the same.

Meanwhile, the people of France grew poorer and poorer. They ate roots instead of meat, lived in hovels, and walked barefoot while aristocrats passed them in carriages decorated with gold. They couldn't pay tax, because they had no money. That meant, eventually, that the king ran out of money himself, and the day came when his treasury was empty.

"You must call representatives of the people," suggested his advisers.

So invitations were sent out, and representatives arrived from all over France - lords, priests, lawyers and merchants. But when the representatives made suggestions about how to govern France better, Louis XVI flew into a rage.

"No one tells the king what to do!" he shouted, and sent soldiers to drive them away.

But the representatives refused to leave. People in Britain and America had a parliament, they complained. And they gathered in the biggest room they could find, an indoor tennis court.

"It's time the king stopped running everything!" they shouted. "It's time we governed ourselves."

That was how the French Revolution started. When people heard of the meeting in the tennis court, a crowd gathered in Paris, attacked the king's prison, the Bastille, let out the prisoners and set it on fire. While it burned, they danced, cheered and waved a new red, white and blue flag called the *tricolore.*

"Liberty!" they yelled. *"Equality! Brotherhood!"*

To start with, most people in France agreed with the revolution. They liked the idea of having more say in their lives. But revolutions can quickly go wrong, because in the excitement people listen to wild ideas they'd usually ignore - and many revolutionaries had wild ideas.

Some of them wanted to kill all priests. "Religion is old-fashioned!" they shouted.

Some wanted to kill the king. A crowd of women set off from Paris to the king's palace at Versailles, broke into his bedroom, and took him back to Paris.

The revolutionaries became more and more violent. "Get rid of lords!" they screamed. "Abolish the Church! Kill the royal family!"

They broke into mansions, smashed mirrors and hacked furniture to pieces. In the middle of Paris they set up a guillotine, a machine for cutting off heads. Lords, their fine clothes crumpled by nights in prison, were taken to the guillotine and killed while old women sat knitting beneath it, singing, "Let's water our fields with their dirty blood!"

"We will make France perfect," declared the leader of the revolutionaries, Maximilien Robespierre, "by killing everyone who is not perfect."

And so the revolutionaries killed the king and queen, the bishops, counts and dukes. They killed everyone who stood up to them, then killed Maximilien Robespierre as well. It looked as if the guillotine would go on cutting off heads, and the old women would go on singing, until there was no one left in France but old women and executioners.

❖ The Irish Rebellion ❖

UNTIL the killing began, most people in Britain welcomed the French Revolution. "Why shouldn't the French be free, like us?" they said. It even made them wonder if their life was quite as good as they thought. After all, Britain might be free, but everyone knew it wasn't fair. Aristocrats were more in control than ever, and politicians more dishonest. Elections happened less and less often.

Life was most unfair in Ireland. After William of Orange had beaten James II at the Battle of the Boyne, English landowners had taken over Irish land and ruled the island so cruelly that the Irish became like slaves in their own country. They grew poor and hungry, and, as Catholics, weren't even allowed to vote or worship freely.

The French Revolution seemed to wake the Irish up, as if they suddenly saw how unfairly they were treated and realized they didn't have to put up with it. A Protestant from Dublin called Wolfe Tone founded a "Society of United Irishmen", which wanted Catholics and Protestants to stop quarrelling and work together until everyone in Ireland could vote, govern themselves, and worship as they pleased. When the British government refused to listen, the United Irishmen began their own revolution and asked the French to help.

But things went wrong from the start. The French couldn't reach Ireland because of a storm. Meanwhile, the British government got Protestants on their side by telling them the rebels wanted to make Ireland Catholic, and persuaded the Catholic Church to help by offering to open a Catholic school. Soon the United Irishmen had no friends left.

One by one the rebel armies were defeated and their leaders arrested. The last rebels, in Wexford, south of Dublin, retreated from the British until they were surrounded at a place called Vinegar Hill. They had their wives and children with them, but that didn't stop the British bombarding their camp. Soon the Irish rebellion was over and Wolfe Tone committed suicide.

The British government realized it wasn't fair to let English landlords go on doing as they liked in Ireland, but instead of making Ireland free, they made it part of Britain. Just like Scotland a hundred years before,

Ireland joined the United Kingdom; the red diagonal cross of St Patrick, patron saint of Ireland, was added to the Union Jack; and Irish MPs joined the House of Commons. But only Protestants were allowed to vote for them. The rest of the Irish had no say in their own lives, and grew more bitter than ever. From now on, Irishmen would never stop campaigning and fighting until Ireland was free.

❖ Napoleon Bonaparte ❖

REVOLUTIONS nearly always go wrong. They start with high hopes but end in confusion and fear; and when everything has fallen into chaos, people turn to the strongest man they can find to rescue them. That was what happened after the civil wars in Britain, when Oliver Cromwell took control. And when the French Revolution ended in terror and death, the French turned to an army general called Napoleon Bonaparte.

Napoleon came from the island of Corsica, in the Mediterranean. He was small, ruthless and determined, and gradually made himself the most powerful man in France.

Other governments in Europe were terrified by the French Revolution. "What if a revolution starts here?" they said. "What if they arrest *our* king, and guillotine *us*?"

They sent armies to defeat the French, but the French, who were proud of their tricolore flag and revolution, fought back. Napoleon, a brilliant general, beat the Austrians and Prussians; and when the Russians entered the war, he beat them as well. The British joined the wars against Napoleon, but didn't send an army to Europe to fight him. Instead the Royal Navy attacked the French fleet, and it was they who defeated Napoleon for the first time.

Napoleon decided to invade Egypt and set sail along the Mediterranean. The British sent their youngest, most skilful admiral, Horatio Nelson, to chase him. Nelson found the French anchored in Aboukir Bay, near the mouth of the river Nile, with their guns pointing out to sea, ready for battle. Ignoring warnings that the water was too shallow, Nelson ordered his ships to sail behind the French fleet and attack from the land side, where their guns weren't ready. After a few hours' fighting, most of the French ships were sunk, and their flagship blown up.

Napoleon returned to France. The defeat at the Battle of the Nile didn't stop him wanting power. On the contrary, he seemed to want it even more. He had himself crowned Emperor Napoleon I, and went to war against Britain again.

Britain's prime minister at this time was William Pitt, son of the Great

Commoner who had won Britain so many victories in the Seven Years War (to avoid confusion, the son is often called Pitt the Younger, and his father, Pitt the Elder). Pitt made alliances against Napoleon, and sent the kings of Europe money, but Napoleon beat them, and the Austrians, Prussians and Russians fled. Britain seemed unable to stop him.

As his empire grew, Napoleon made one of his brothers king of Holland and another king of Spain, married the Austrian emperor's daughter, and made friends with the Russian czar. It looked as if he would end up ruling the whole of Europe. He dreamed of invading Britain as well, and stood on the heights of northern France, staring at the white cliffs of Dover and picturing his armies marching into London.

Fortunately Britain went on beating him at sea. The Royal Navy's sailors came from all over the world, mixing English, Scots, Irish and Welsh, black sailors from the Caribbean, and Asians from India and China. Their officers were skilful navigators and fighters, promoted not just because they were aristocrats, but for their ability. In battle after battle the Royal Navy beat the French, until their ships didn't dare leave harbour at all. Day and night, summer and winter, the British stood guard, stopping any ship from getting in or out of France.

But one day a storm blew the British ships far out to sea and the French escaped, joined up with their Spanish allies, and sailed towards Britain.

Horatio Nelson was sent to fight them. He knew how important the battle would be: if he lost, the French would invade, and Napoleon become emperor of Britain. He pursued them all the way across the Atlantic Ocean and back before catching up with them near Cape Trafalgar in southern Spain. As the two fleets drew closer, Nelson ordered signal flags to be hoisted to the mast of his flagship, HMS *Victory*. His signal read: *"England expects that every man will do his duty."*

As always, Nelson had thought up a new tactic for the battle. Instead of fighting the line of French and Spanish ships side by side, he attacked it at right angles in two columns, with HMS *Victory* leading one column, and HMS *Royal Sovereign* the other. The sailors cheered as they drew closer. When *Victory* reached the French line, her three rows of cannon roared out. As her sailors heaved at ropes to get the guns ready again, *Victory* broke through the line and turned behind it, where the

French were unprepared. Nelson had already ordered another signal to be hoisted: *"Engage the enemy more closely."*

Victory herself could not have got any closer. The gunfire was deafening, and smoke coiled so thickly about the deck that the French could barely be seen. Men screamed, wood splintered and masts fell. But the British, who had spent so long at sea and fought so many battles, fired faster, and gradually the cannon fire from the French grew weaker. When the smoke eddied, burning ships drifted into view, their masts gone and rigging trailing over their sides. Soon the victory was complete, with two thirds of the French and Spanish ships destroyed or captured.

But the British had suffered a terrible loss as well: Horatio Nelson was killed. All through the battle he had worn his best admiral's uniform, even though his friend Captain Hardy urged him to put on an ordinary coat so the French sailors wouldn't notice him. And as he and Hardy walked up and down the deck of *Victory*, a French sniper caught sight of him and shot him.

Nelson was carried below. Hardy and the other officers drew round as he grew weaker, but he was still conscious when news of victory was brought.

"Thank God I have done my duty," he said.

And then he died.

❖ Napoleon's Mistake ❖

TRAFALGAR was a great victory. Unfortunately battles at sea don't win wars, and on land Napoleon still couldn't be defeated. In the same year as the Battle of Trafalgar, he had his greatest triumph so far by beating the Austrians and Russians at the Battle of Austerlitz. And Napoleon might have gone on winning, if he hadn't made a terrible mistake. He decided to invade Russia.

Russia is enormous. From the eastern edge of Europe it stretches thousands of miles to the Ural Mountains, and thousands of miles further across Siberian forests, where there are more wolves than people and lakes remain frozen half the year round. Only a madman would try to conquer such a place, but perhaps Napoleon was a little mad. No one had ever defeated him on land, and he thought he could conquer the whole world.

At first the invasion seemed easy enough. As the French soldiers marched eastwards, the Russians fell back. They fought battles and the Russians fell back again. As they approached Moscow, the Russian capital, they felt sure the Russians would give in.

But the Russian czar simply retreated further east. For each army the French beat, he summoned another. Rather than let the French take Moscow, the Russians set fire to it. Napoleon's soldiers groaned: they had been expecting to find food there. Their legs ached, they were sick of fighting, and thousands of miles of Russia still stretched before them.

Emperor Napoleon realized the task of conquering Russia was impossible. Abandoning his army, he climbed into a coach and drove back home. The French soldiers were left to follow him as best they could. They had nothing to eat, so they shot their horses and ate them. They ate the mules that carried their guns and ammunition – then they had to leave their guns behind. Meanwhile, the Russians pursued them, attacking at night like wolves. Winter – the Russian winter, colder than anything we know in the west of Europe – fell on Napoleon's doomed army. Men woke in the morning to find their friends frozen to death. Snow buried the roads, and soldiers sank into snowdrifts, unable to march any further. By the time the French reached the border of Russia, there was hardly anything left of Napoleon's great army.

When they saw that Napoleon had been defeated, the kings and emperors of Europe joined together to finish him off. All this time, a British army led by General Arthur Wellesley had been fighting the French in Spain, gradually forcing them back towards the borders of France. Napoleon's enemies converged from all sides, until at last he surrendered.

The war had gone on for ten years, and everyone cheered when it came to an end. Napoleon was sent to the island of Elba, off the coast of Italy, and peace returned to Europe.

But peace did not last long.

❖ The Battle of Waterloo ❖

KING Louis XVI's brother was made king of France, and the French soon began to complain. Under Napoleon they had become the strongest country in Europe, and they hated the thought that their great days were over. When news came that Napoleon had escaped from Elba, they ran excitedly out into the streets.

"Have you heard? The emperor's returning to France!"

Tricolore flags were waved in Paris. The king ran away and old soldiers hurried to sign up to Napoleon's army. Napoleon led them to Belgium, where the British were camped under the command of General Wellesley, who had just been made duke of Wellington.

Wellington had beaten every one of Napoleon's generals, but had never fought Napoleon himself. His army was small, and he knew he couldn't win without help. As his Prussian allies were still far away, he ordered his soldiers to gather at the Belgian capital, Brussels.

Brussels was full of aristocrats who were accompanying the army. The duchess of Richmond decided to hold a party for them, and since Wellington didn't want anyone to panic, he agreed to attend as well, as if nothing was wrong. But in the middle of the party he was sent a message that Napoleon's soldiers were crossing the border. Wellington pretended it wasn't important, but sent word round all the officers to slip out quietly and go back to the army.

"How odd!" said the duchess of Richmond just after midnight. "There are no men to dance with! Where have all the officers gone?"

By then they were desperately galloping south to join their soldiers. The next day they fought the French at the Battle of Quatre Bras, but were forced to retreat to the village of Waterloo where Wellington decided to make his stand. At dawn he ordered his men to take up position along a ridge. He hoped he could hold out until the Prussians arrived, but when he looked at the French army through his telescope, he wondered if it would be possible. Blue French uniforms filled the whole plain. Artillerymen were preparing their guns, and cavalry officers galloping to and fro, while columns of infantrymen – Napoleon's famous Old Guard – cheered as the emperor's carriage drove past.

Wellington knew Napoleon would start by bombarding his army with cannonballs, so he ordered his men to lie down behind the ridge. When the French opened fire, their cannonballs flew harmlessly overhead.

Then he saw the French cavalry getting ready to charge. "Form into squares!" he ordered.

That was the best way for footsoldiers to fight cavalry. All along the ridge, men in red uniforms hurried to form into squares bristling with guns and bayonets.

"Here they come," they whispered.

The French cavalry charged again and again, breaking in waves against the red squares, only to be beaten back down the slope with bodies and wounded horses left behind. As the day wore on, the air grew heavy with the stench of blood, but Wellington kept his telescope trained on a column of dust to the east. He knew it was the Prussian army, marching to rescue him.

Napoleon saw the dust too. He realized he hadn't much time left, so he ordered his best soldiers, the Old Guard, to attack.

The Old Guard had never been defeated. Four abreast, they marched up the slope towards the British.

"Form a line!" ordered Wellington, and the squares broke up as his soldiers hurried to obey. A thin red line stretched out along the ridge.

"Fire!" shouted the sergeants.

The men were tired and scared, but they knew this was their final chance. Desperately they fired, reloaded, and fired again. And from the back of the French column a terrible groan went up: *The Old Guard are retreating!*

Just then the Prussians arrived. The French hesitated for one more moment, then turned and fled. Napoleon could do nothing to stop the panic. Gunners ran from their cannon. Cavalrymen leaped onto their horses and galloped away. Wellington saw the confusion through his telescope and knew he had won a great victory. He lifted his hat and waved it to give the order to advance.

The Battle of Waterloo finally ended the wars which had begun with the French Revolution. Napoleon was captured and sent to the distant island of St Helena in the south Atlantic – too far away for him ever to

escape to France again – while the French king was put back on his throne. Wellington became a hero, and Waterloo is still remembered as a great British victory.

But it was won at a terrible cost. Thousands died in the battle, the last that the French and British would ever fight. As night fell, the moon shone on their silent bodies, the dead of both sides mingled together. By then the duke of Wellington was riding back across the battlefield to his headquarters.

"Next to a battle lost," he said afterwards, *"the greatest misery is a battle gained."*

And as he looked about him, his officers saw that, in the moonlight, his cheeks were wet with tears.

❖ The End of the Slave Trade ❖

WARS change things. Men leave home to fight and women take over their work. Everything is thrown into disorder.

"And afterwards?" people ask each other. "What will the world be like afterwards? Will things go back to how they were before?"

During the wars, those who wanted Britain to be made fairer had been forced to stop protesting. William Pitt thought it too dangerous to talk of changing things when the country was fighting for its life. But when the war ended, everyone felt restless. People didn't want things to go on in the same way. First America had made itself free, and then France. Why couldn't the whole world be free? Why couldn't *everyone* be free? And that included the Africans Britain had turned into slaves.

The terrible crime of slavery had continued all through the Georgian years. Slave ships still appeared off the coast of West Africa. Men and women were still captured, sold like cattle, and forced onto ships for the Middle Passage. Chains still bit into their legs and they still died of thirst in the darkness of the ships' holds.

Through those years, the ports the ships sailed from, like Bristol and Liverpool, became rich, and so did landowners in the Caribbean. Meanwhile, hundreds of thousands of black men and women worked on their plantations, whipped and starved, and had children who were born slaves, never knowing what it was like to be free.

But more and more people began to realize how stupid it was to think black people any different from whites. When they were allowed a proper education, black people did just as well. Francis Williams, a black poet, went to Cambridge University. Ignatius Sancho, who was born on a slave ship, and whose father committed suicide rather than live as a slave, escaped slavery to become a musician and writer.

An MP called William Wilberforce believed passionately that as long as slavery existed, the British could not call themselves civilized. So he began a campaign to ban the slave trade.

Many tried to stop him. "You can't end slavery," they said. "Businesses will suffer. Sailors will be put out of work. The sugar farmers will lose money."

William Wilberforce ignored them. He and his friend Thomas Clarkson collected evidence about the cruelty of slave owners, and described the horror slaves suffered on the voyage from Africa to the Caribbean.

"Never, never will we desist," he told the House of Commons, *"till we have extinguished every trace of this bloody traffic, of which our posterity, looking back to the history of these enlightened times, will scarce believe that it has been suffered to exist so long a disgrace and dishonour to this country."*

In 1807 William Wilberforce got his law passed, and although it was a little longer before keeping a slave was banned, the evil traffic of the slave ships came to an end. Families in West Africa could sleep in peace. And the black men and women of the Caribbean islands knew that their children would be born free.

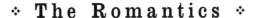

❖ The Romantics ❖

EVERYTHING seemed different after the slave trade was abolished. Freedom was in the air, like the smoke from a bonfire that spreads from street to street to make people all over town raise their heads. Everyone sensed something new. If the slave trade had been abolished, what else could change?

Mary Wollstonecraft wrote a book arguing that it was time to stop treating women as second best. In those days women didn't do proper jobs, and men talked about them as if they were only good for marrying and having children. That was a kind of slavery, Mary Wollstonecraft said, and if women could only be educated, everyone would see how their talents had been wasted.

Inspired by the idea of freedom, musicians composed music that was wilder and more passionate than ever before (Ludwig van Beethoven, a German, was the most famous). Writers wrote poetry about youth, love and freedom – poetry so powerful and uncontrolled that some people thought them mad. John Keats wrote poems day and night, and died young in Rome, still dreaming of all the verses he hadn't been able to write. Percy Shelley, who imagined a world with no rules, drowned at sea trying to sail his boat through a storm. William Wordsworth went to Paris to see the French Revolution for himself. Afterwards he wrote:

Bliss was it in that dawn to be alive,
But to be young was very heaven!

The wildest of the Romantic poets was Lord Byron, who was handsome, listened to no one, and behaved exactly as he pleased. People shook their heads when they heard stories of what he did.

"Mad," they said. "Mad, bad, and dangerous to know."

But the poets weren't mad. They were writing a new kind of poetry for a new kind of age – an age when kings were killed and slaves set free.

An age when no one knew what was going to happen next.

TIMELINE

❖ ❖ ❖ ❖ ❖ ❖ ❖

1692 ❖ The Macdonald clan is attacked by the Campbells in the Massacre of Glencoe.

1702 ❖ William dies (Mary died earlier, in 1694), and Mary's sister Anne becomes queen.

1704 ❖ During the War of the Spanish Succession, John Churchill, later duke of Marlborough, beats the French at the Battle of Blenheim.

1707 ❖ The Act of Union turns Scotland and England into one country.

1714 ❖ Queen Anne dies and, through the Protestant Succession, a distant relative, George of Hanover, becomes King George I.

1715 ❖ Jacobites rebel in favour of the Old Pretender, but are stopped at the Battle of Sheriffmuir.

1720 ❖ Investors lose fortunes in the South Sea Bubble.

1721 ❖ Sir Robert Walpole becomes Britain's first prime minister.

1739 ❖ The highwayman Dick Turpin is hanged at York.

1745 ❖ Bonnie Prince Charlie leads a Jacobite rebellion in Scotland. He is beaten next year at the Battle of Culloden.

1756–1763 ❖ The Seven Years War makes Britain the most powerful country in the world. 1759 is her *annus mirabilis*, with the victories of Minden, Quebec and Quiberon Bay.

1765 ❖ Clive of India, who won the Battle of Plassey in 1757, buys Bengal for the East India Company.

1768–1771 ❖ On Captain Cook's first voyage he discovers the east coast of Australia.

1775–1783 ❖ Americans win freedom from Britain in the American Revolution, or War of American Independence.

1788 ❖ George III goes mad. He recovers, but only for a time. His son is made Prince Regent in 1811.

1789 ❖ The French Revolution begins. The king of France, Louis XVI, is guillotined in 1793.

1793 ❖ Britain joins the war against the French. Apart from a short peace in 1802, the war continues until

Napoleon is defeated in 1814.

1798 ❖ Nelson defeats Napoleon at the Battle of the Nile.

1798 ❖ The United Irishmen, led by Wolfe Tone, start an Irish Rebellion, but the rebellion ends at the Battle of Vinegar Hill.

1805 ❖ Admiral Nelson beats the French and Spanish at the Battle of Trafalgar.

1807 ❖ William Wilberforce gets the slave trade abolished.

1814 ❖ After failing to conquer Russia, Napoleon surrenders and is sent to the island of Elba.

1815 ❖ Napoleon escapes and returns, but Wellington defeats him at the Battle of Waterloo.

THE
VICTORIANS

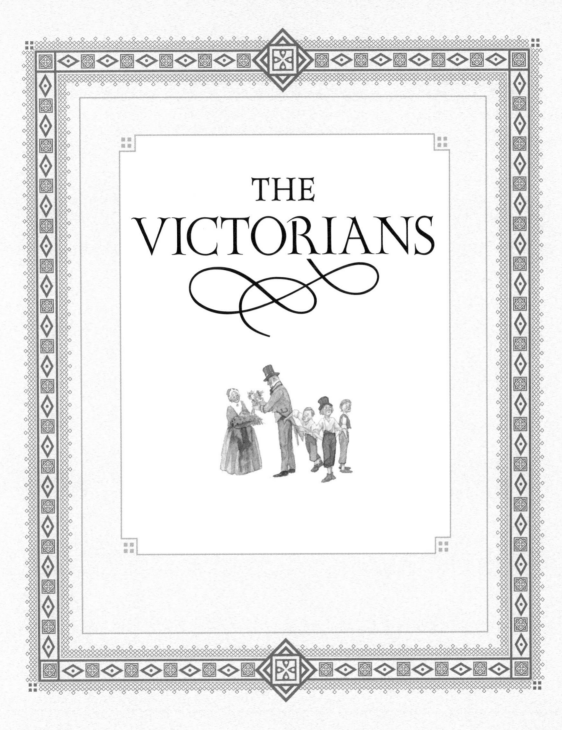

Daniel O'Connell
THE LIBERATOR

Mary Seacole
NURSED THE DYING

Isambard Kingdom Brunel
BUILT THE RAILWAYS

Victoria

❖ ❖ ❖ ❖ ❖ ❖ ❖

EMPRESS
OF INDIA

Benjamin
Disraeli

❖ ❖ ❖ ❖ ❖ ❖ ❖

THE QUEEN'S
FRIEND

William
Gladstone

❖ ❖ ❖ ❖ ❖ ❖ ❖

FOUR TIMES
PRIME MINISTER

Emmeline
Pankhurst

❖ ❖ ❖ ❖ ❖ ❖ ❖

CAMPAIGNED
FOR WOMEN

STEPHENSON'S ROCKET

❖ Being British ❖

B Y beating Napoleon, the British showed how strong they were when they worked together. Welsh, Scottish, Irish and English soldiers had fought side by side in Wellington's army, while sailors from all over Britain's empire had made the Royal Navy the best in the world.

Scottish soldiers had fought as hard as anyone, for many Scots had decided it was time to forget about the Jacobite rebellions.

"We can be Scottish *and* British," they said. "We can be proud of both!"

The famous author Walter Scott agreed. His books described the Scottish mountains and lochs, and the old life of the Highlands; some of them told stories about Jacobites. He was as proud of being Scottish as anyone. But he was also proud to be British. Scott decided it was time for the king to visit Edinburgh and show he wasn't just English, but king of all Britain.

The king was George IV (who had been prince regent while his father was mad). George was even fatter than before, and when Walter Scott saw him dressed in a huge tartan plaid he could hardly stop himself laughing. He was afraid the crowds would laugh too, but he needn't have worried. When the king appeared, the Union Jack and the Scottish saltire waved together over Edinburgh, and cheers echoed from Arthur's Seat.

The Scots showed that because Britain was made up of four nations, being British wasn't simple, like being French or German. British people could be proud of more than one thing – they could be British *and* something else.

❖ The Peterloo Massacre ❖

Britain should have been happy after its great victory at Waterloo, and the British should have been content. But they were not, because although freedom was in the air they didn't feel free. The aristocrats were still in control.

Aristocrats still ran Parliament and cheated in elections. There were two parties, the Whigs and the Tories, but there didn't seem much difference between them. Both Whig and Tory politicians invented government jobs and gave them to their friends. Aristocrats still had all the money and all the power. No one had changed Parliament since the Glorious Revolution, more than a hundred years before. Since then, some towns had shrunk to tiny villages but still sent an MP to London, while others had grown into huge cities but didn't have an MP at all.

Most people still weren't allowed to vote. In America all men could vote, but aristocrats thought that far too dangerous for Britain.

"We can't have a government chosen by *ordinary* people," they said. "There are more of *them* than there are of *us*. They'd take over the country and start running it themselves!"

No one was allowed to protest during the war against Napoleon, but when it was over, people became more and more determined to win change, or "reform". Some reformers in Manchester decided to hold a demonstration at St Peter's Fields, a meadow not far from town, and invited a well-known reformer, Henry Hunt, to make a speech. Hunt, who always wore a white top hat, was so famous for his fiery speeches that he was called "Orator" Hunt. When the day of the meeting came, thousands of people streamed into Manchester from the surrounding villages.

Everything had been carefully planned.

"We don't want any violence," the organizers insisted. "This will be a peaceful demonstration."

But to the magistrates of Manchester, who were sitting in a house over-looking the fields, the sight of such a big crowd was terrifying.

"There's going to be a revolution," they whispered, staring at each other in horror. "They're going to cut off our heads, just like they did in France!"

In those days there was no police force, so they called the army.

"Dirty rebels!" snarled an army officer, glaring out of the window, and he pulled his sword from its scabbard.

In the middle of St Peter's Fields, Orator Hunt stood up on a wagon to make his speech to the eighty thousand people around him.

"We're all equal!" he shouted. "And we all deserve the vote!"

The crowd couldn't hear much, but they saw his white top hat and cheered as loudly as they could.

"The revolution has started!" whimpered the magistrates. "Arrest the speaker before it goes too far!"

So soldiers set off through the crowd towards the wagon. The crowd was packed so thick that they began to hack a path with their swords. People screamed and tried to get away, but to the panicking magistrates it looked as if they were attacking the soldiers. At their orders, hundreds of cavalrymen appeared along the edge of St Peter's Fields. Horses tossed their heads, and soldiers drew their swords.

"Charge!" shouted an officer.

Four years before, the same cavalry had charged the French army at Waterloo. Now they attacked an unarmed crowd of British men and women. People desperately tried to get away from the trampling hooves, but there was nowhere to run to. Women slipped and fell in the mud; children lost their parents. Ten minutes later, St Peter's Fields was nearly empty. The spectators had fled, leaving behind broken banners, bodies lying on the ground, dazed people sitting on the grass, and children crying as they looked for someone they knew.

Afterwards the magistrates said they had to send in the soldiers to keep law and order. But when they heard about the massacre in St Peter's Fields, most people were furious.

"How brave of the soldiers to fight women and children!" they scoffed. "First we had the Battle of Waterloo, now we've got the Battle of Peterloo!" And from that moment on, they became even more determined to change the way things in Britain were done.

Unfortunately the government was just as determined to stop them.

"The country is in a dangerous state of revolution!" declared MPs, who sent Orator Hunt to jail, cancelled reformers' meetings and banned books calling for change.

The Whigs wanted reform, but only so long as aristocrats stayed in charge; the Tories didn't want anything to change at all.

"Britain's fine as it is," insisted the Tory prime minister, Lord Liverpool. "Change is dangerous. Look at France!"

After Lord Liverpool retired, one of the next prime ministers was the duke of Wellington, who had beaten Napoleon at Waterloo, but since then had turned into a stern old man who thought everything should stay as it was. He refused all demands for change; it looked as if the country was deadlocked.

In fact, change might never have come to Britain at all, if it wasn't for an Irish politician called Daniel O'Connell.

❖ Daniel O'Connell ❖

LIKE most Irish, Daniel O'Connell was Catholic, so he wasn't allowed to vote. More than a hundred years had passed since the Catholic king, James II, was thrown out, but Catholics were still distrusted. They weren't allowed to be MPs or hold important jobs. In Ireland, where English Protestants owned the land and made all the decisions, they couldn't even build Catholic churches in their own villages. Everyone in Ireland longed for an Irishman who would stand up to Britain.

Daniel O'Connell was the answer to their prayers, for he was bold, brash and feared no one. He started a campaign to have the laws against Catholics changed. Thousands joined his Catholic Association, and for the first time since the Irish rebellion, felt proud to be Irish again. Some of his followers wanted to attack English landowners and set fire to English houses, but O'Connell stopped them, for he was determined not to use violence.

"Liberty totters when it is cemented with blood," he said. "We're in the right because of what we believe. If we hurt people, we put ourselves in the wrong."

When an election was called in County Clare, he put forward his name.

"But he's a Catholic!" the duke of Wellington's government protested. "He isn't allowed!"

"I'm not allowed to be an MP," O'Connell answered, "but you can't stop people voting for me!"

And the people of County Clare did just that. Daniel O'Connell won, and bonfires were lit all over Ireland.

In his house at Hyde Park Corner, the duke of Wellington gathered his advisers together. "Britain is a Protestant nation," he said. "If we let in people of other faiths, then the country will fall apart."

"If we keep them out," said his advisers nervously, "people of other faiths will never feel British."

In the end even the duke of Wellington agreed it was too dangerous to ignore Daniel O'Connell. So Parliament passed a law allowing Catholics to vote and become MPs just like everyone else. And it turned out that the duke of Wellington was wrong. Britain didn't fall apart; it grew stronger

because more people felt part of it, rather than thinking Britain didn't want them.

Meanwhile, O'Connell, whom the Irish called the Liberator, became a hero in Ireland. And reformers all over Britain, seeing how he had ended the law against Catholics, realized that with one more effort they could change how Britain worked.

❖ The Great Reform Act ❖

THE duke of Wellington resigned, and the new prime minister, a Whig called Lord Grey, told the king it was time to reform Parliament. By now George IV had died, and his younger brother William had become king.

"Why do things need to change?" William complained. "Change is dangerous."

Indeed, only that summer news had come from France of another revolution in which the king had been driven from his throne. William didn't want that to happen to him.

"Change may be dangerous," replied Lord John Russell, one of Grey's ministers, "but sometimes it is even more dangerous *not* to change things." And he handed the king reports from all over the country of meetings, protests and campaigns for reform. "What we need," he said, "is a Reform Act that satisfies the reformers once and for all, so nothing need ever change again."

Unfortunately, when Lord John Russell put forward his Reform Act, the Tories voted against it, and there weren't enough Whigs to pass it by themselves. The Whigs called an election and won, so they had enough MPs for the House of Commons to pass the Act. But there were more Tories than Whigs in the House of Lords, so the Tory lords voted against it, and defeated it again.

When they heard the Reform Act had been turned down a second time, people were furious. All over Britain they gathered outside town halls, chanting and booing. A crowd rampaged through the middle of Bristol, breaking windows and hurling stones at the great houses of the aristocrats.

"If the lords won't let us vote," they shouted, "then we'll throw stones. There's no other way to show what we think!"

In London crowds even attacked the duke of Wellington's house, throwing bricks and smashing the windows.

"But what can *I* do?" King William complained when he heard about the riots. "It isn't *my* fault the Lords refused the Reform Act."

Then Lord John Russell came up with a plan. He persuaded the king to

create new Whig lords so the Whigs had a majority in the House of Lords as well as the House of Commons. And in that way the Great Reform Act was passed.

The Great Reform Act changed most of the bad old ways. Many more men were allowed to vote than before. Big towns that had never been represented, like Manchester, Leeds and Sheffield, were given MPs, and a lot of the cheating in elections came to an end. Politics after the Reform Act seemed much fairer than before.

Even so, many said the Act didn't go far enough, for aristocrats were still much more powerful than anybody else. And if Russell thought everything could stay the same from now on, he was in for a shock. For in fact, Britain was changing faster than ever. There were changes in how people lived and how they worked. A kind of revolution was taking place – today we call it the industrial revolution – and it altered the country for ever.

❖ The Industrial Revolution ❖

IN the old days everything was made by hand. Each family had a trade – joiners made tables and chairs; cobblers made shoes – and people often got their names from the trades they followed. Men called Smith were blacksmiths who made fire grates and railings; those called Cooper made barrels.

Making things by hand took a long time. To make cloth, first someone had to spin thread; then a weaver, working at home in his cottage, wove it, thread by thread, into a length of fabric.

"Too slow!" thought an inventor called James Hargreaves. And he invented a new kind of spindle called the Spinning Jenny that let one man spin several reels of thread at once.

Then Richard Arkwright came up with a spinning frame that could make thread even faster, and John Kay invented something he called the Flying Shuttle, which rattled from one side of a loom to the other, weaving cloth far quicker than anyone could by hand.

Once people had started inventing, they saw how many things could be made quicker by machines. Machines were made of iron, which was expensive, so inventors came up with better ways of making that too. At Coalbrookdale, in Shropshire, Abraham Darby built a new type of furnace that blazed day and night, producing iron far more cheaply and quickly than before.

Once they had bought machines, businessmen realized it didn't make sense for tradesmen to work by themselves in their own cottages, so they built factories where hundreds could work together. They divided what the men did into separate tasks. In chair factories, instead of one man making a whole chair, they found it was quicker to have one cut the wood, another shape the legs, and a third fit everything together.

To drive all the machines in a big factory, they needed a new kind of power – something stronger than men or horses, stronger even than the wind that had been used to turn windmills for centuries. That power came from steam engines.

If you heat a kettle until it boils, a jet of steam will hiss out of the spout. If the kettle is enormous, then the jet will be powerful enough to turn a

wheel. Connect the wheel to machines by pulleys and belts, and the steam engine will drive the machines.

So businessmen set up factories wherever there was iron underground to make machines, and coal to heat boilers. Many factories were built in the north of England or Scotland. And many more appeared in the peaceful valleys of South Wales, which were changed by the industrial revolution for ever.

Once, the valleys had belonged to shepherds, but when factory owners realized there was coal under the grass and iron in the mountains, they drove away the sheep and closed the farms. They dug mines and built ironworks, and as their factories grew, advertised for people to work in them. From all over Wales, families walked to Merthyr Tydfil and the Rhondda, leaving behind their villages to become miners and factory workers.

New towns appeared, chimneys rose into the sky, and brick streets climbed the hillsides. The valleys filled with the clatter of machinery instead of birdsong, and coal dust instead of clean mountain air. Every morning, columns of men marched up to the mines, and returned at night black with coal. Their hands grew calloused and hard, and their skins pale from working underground.

Visitors who came to look at the new ironworks marvelled at their size. "They're bigger than cathedrals!" they gasped. They marvelled at the machinery inside them, at the steam engines belching smoke, the roar of wheels and the rows of men bent over their work. And they marvelled at the money they made.

Thanks to the industrial revolution, Welsh iron and coal were exported all over the world. In other parts of Britain things changed too. Scottish ships sailed every ocean, Lancashire cotton factories made more cloth in a week than a hundred weavers could have made in a year, and sleepy little towns like Manchester grew into huge cities.

Britain had invented a new way of making things, and the world would never be the same again.

❖ Railways ❖

THE industrial revolution didn't only change how people worked, but how they got around as well.

Two engineers from Northumberland, George and Robert Stephenson, invented a way of putting a steam engine on wheels. It ran on iron rails, dragging a tender of coal to heat its boiler, and was strong enough to pull carriages behind it.

The Stephensons built a railway from Stockton to Darlington, the first in the world. Then they built one from Liverpool to Manchester. On the day it opened, crowds gathered to watch. The Stephensons' locomotive engine, the *Rocket*, had a tall chimney like a boiler house, and pulled a tender of coal and two trucks for the passengers. Robert Stephenson had painted it yellow to make it look less frightening, but the roar of the engine made everyone cover their ears.

"What a peculiar machine," said William Huskisson, MP for Liverpool. "I must take a closer look."

"Watch out!" shouted Robert, and the *Rocket's* engineer slammed on the brakes, but it was too late.

"I could have told you," hissed the old duke of Wellington. "Change is dangerous!"

But it wasn't long before everyone was talking about railways. Factories echoed to the din of hammering as mechanics constructed bigger and stronger locomotives, while in offices in the City of London, businessmen started railway companies and planned lines from London to Birmingham, Leeds and even Edinburgh. Surveyors set out routes, and engineers designed bridges and tunnels. The most famous of the engineers was Isambard Kingdom Brunel, who built Clifton Suspension Bridge over a gorge at Bristol, and constructed soaring viaducts to carry the Great Western Railway to Exeter.

Before the railways came, travelling was so difficult that most people never left the area where they were born. Boys grew up to become farmers, while girls married farmers from the next village. The most exciting thing to do was walk to the nearest town, where you could see coaches stopping on their journey to London. It took days to reach London by

horse-drawn carriage, so most people never bothered to go there.

Railways changed everything.

Often, the first sign of the railway arriving was the roar of an explosion as engineers blasted the hillside to make a tunnel. Next, shining rails were laid in place; and a few months later, the villagers would see a column of black smoke above the trees, the ground would shake, and a gleaming train would rush by, with passengers waving from the carriage windows. The villagers would stare after it open-mouthed, wondering where the rails led. By train they could get from Birmingham to London in just five hours. They could reach towns and cities their parents had never visited. They could see London – or even the sea!

After the railways came, no one wanted to travel by horse any more. Coaching inns fell into ruins, and weeds grew up through the roads. People didn't want to stay in their villages – they wanted to go further and travel faster. So the slow, calm way of life in the country came to an end as, one by one, villagers packed their bags and went to the new industrial towns to find work in factories.

❖ Life in the Factories ❖

PEOPLE soon discovered that life in the new factories was far harder than they expected. For a start, it was very dangerous. Dust entered workers' lungs and made them cough blood. Machinery crushed their fingers. No one worried about health and safety, so a lot of people were killed in accidents.

Most factory owners didn't care about the men and women who worked for them; they didn't think it their responsibility. Their business was to pay them as little as possible and make them work as hard as they could.

"If they don't like it, they can go somewhere else," they said.

When factory owners realized it was cheaper to employ children than grown-ups, they put children to work as well. Boys of four were sent down mines, while young girls spent hours working at cotton looms until their arms ached and their heads spun with the clatter of machinery.

They weren't given any holiday, but worked every day, starting early and finishing late. Factory owners grew rich and built great houses, but the people who worked for them lived in damp basements or draughty attics, shared beds with their families and lived in single rooms where windows were boarded over and the air was choked with coal fumes. Factory workers never had enough to eat, couldn't afford new clothes, and had no toys or books. Children's only pleasure, after a day of hard toil, was to fall asleep and dream – until the factory bells rang again, and their mothers woke them to go back to work.

No one looked after workers when they grew old or sick, and no one tried to make factories safer. Some MPs suggested a law to stop people working so hard, but the factory owners soon persuaded them against it.

"If they worked less hard, we'd have to close our factories!" they said.

Some MPs wanted a law to stop children working, but the factory owners complained about that as well.

"We need children to clean our factory chimneys!"

The only thing worse than work was having no work, for then the factory owners closed their gates and sent everyone home. To start with, it was a relief to have some time off, but at the end of the day there was no money, so the workers had no food to eat, and their families starved.

Some workers thought factories shouldn't be allowed. They called themselves Luddites and went round destroying machines and smashing factory windows. But others saw that factories were here to stay. And as their lives grew harder, they realized that no one else would help them – so they decided to stand up for themselves.

❖ Unions ❖

"WE need to stick together," the factory workers agreed. "If the owners do something unfair, then we'll *all* stop work, and they'll have to close their factories. That'll make them listen!" So the workers formed societies they called unions. If a boss sacked someone unfairly, the union called a strike, everyone stopped work and the boss had nothing to sell.

The factory owners were furious. "Damned rogues," they growled. "We need to show them who's in charge!"

When some workers at Tolpuddle, in Dorset, started a union, their boss had them arrested. In those days murderers and burglars weren't jailed, but loaded onto ships and sent to Australia. And the six men from Tolpuddle were sentenced to be transported as well. When one of them, George Loveless, was told he was to be punished like a common criminal, he wrote a poem in protest:

> *We raise the watchword liberty,*
> *We will, we will, we will be free!*

So many people thought it unfair to treat the six men like criminals that at last the government gave in and allowed the Tolpuddle Martyrs to come home.

After that, more and more workers joined unions. They campaigned to have the working day made shorter, to stop children being put to work, and to make food cheaper. The factory owners hated unions, sacked anyone who joined one, and had union leaders arrested, but the workers were determined not to give in. They knew they deserved something better than the misery of life in the factory towns.

And they discovered that more and more people agreed with them.

❖ Better Lives ❖

WELL-TO-DO people were shocked when they visited the new towns and discovered how factory workers lived. Walking along the streets, they saw little children begging and women shivering in doorways.

"Surely it's wrong," they said, "that people live like that in Britain, the richest country in the world!"

London was the most shocking city of all. It had grown so much in the industrial revolution that it was less like a town than a smoking, foggy monster which ate up the fields and villages around it, and belched a plume of soot across the whole of southern England. People miles away in the countryside sniffed the reek of London and called it the Big Smoke.

Under its smoke, London was a jungle of roads and alleyways where children roamed in gangs, living on the streets by day and hiding in basements at night. The writer Charles Dickens knew just what it was like to be a poor child in London because he had been poor himself. When he was only a boy, his father lost the family's money and went to jail, and Charles Dickens was sent to work in a factory.

Dickens wanted more people to know what poverty felt like, so he wrote stories about the children who lived on the streets and slept in basements. One of the most famous was *Oliver Twist*, about a boy who was forced to work as a pickpocket. People were scared of the rough-looking children they saw on the streets of London, but Dickens showed them street children had feelings just like theirs. He described London so well that his readers felt as if they were walking through it, and visiting the kind of places where the poor lived: *"a villainous street, undrained, unventilated, deep in black mud and corrupt water ... and reeking with such smells and sights that he, who has lived in London all his life, can scarce believe his senses"*.

Other writers also taught people about the lives of the poor. Elizabeth Gaskell wrote about families in factory towns in the north of England, and Charles Kingsley explained what it felt like to be a poor boy put to work cleaning chimneys. People started to collect money for those who had no work, and set up charities to look after the sick who couldn't afford doctors. Some factory owners built better houses for their workers.

"But shouldn't the government do more?" everyone asked.

In the old days MPs didn't think it was their business to care for ordinary people, but now so many were suffering that they changed their minds. They passed laws to stop employees working too many hours each day, and to stop young children being put to work. A politician called Robert Peel started a police force to make London safer.

Cities were still very unhealthy, though, and became more so when cholera, a terrible new disease, appeared. During cholera epidemics it felt as if the Great Plague had returned. Then a doctor called John Snow discovered it was caused by drinking bad water. Poor people had nothing else to drink, because their houses had no proper toilets or water pipes. Thousands died and everyone agreed that something had to be done. So Parliament set up a committee to find out just how bad life was for the poor.

As the head of the committee, Edwin Chadwick, visited people's homes, he became more and more worried. Because there were no proper sewers, sewage flowed into the rivers until they were thick, black and stinking – but people went on drinking from them because there was no other water. The air was dense with smoke, and yellow fog filled the streets for days on end. Babies were born small and died young. Thousands of people died because they couldn't breathe properly. Chadwick described it all in his report:

"The annual loss of life from filth and bad ventilation are greater than the loss from death or wounds in any wars in which the country has been engaged."

It was time to make life better, not just for the rich, but for everyone. So Joseph Bazalgette designed London a proper sewage system, and Parliament passed laws to bring water to town in clean pipes. Later, MPs voted to build schools, so that children could learn how to read and write instead of being forced to work.

Thanks to its factories, Britain had become the richest country in the world. But the British couldn't feel proud until the men and women who worked in them had food to eat and clean water to drink – and lived the way the people of a great country deserved.

❖ The Great Exhibition ❖

K ING William IV didn't have any legitimate children, and his brothers and sisters were all dead, so when he died, the crown passed to his niece, Victoria. She was queen for longer than any other monarch, and because of her the people of the nineteenth century are often called Victorians.

Victoria was only eighteen when she inherited the throne. She described how it happened in her diary:

> *I was awoke at 6 o'clock by Mamma, who told me the Archbishop of Canterbury and Lord Conyngham were here, and wished to see me. I got out of bed and went into my sitting-room (only in my dressing-gown), and saw them. Lord Conyngham then acquainted me that my poor Uncle, the King, had expired at 12 minutes past 2 this morning, and consequently that I am Queen.*

Victoria was shy and knew nothing about politics, but soon after becoming queen she married her German cousin Albert, who helped advise her as Britain changed from a country of fields and farmers to one of factories and towns.

Albert loved factories and inventions. "Machines don't *have* to make life worse for people," he told Victoria. He thought the British should be proud of the new world they were making, and of their great empire. So he decided to stage an exhibition of everything new and spectacular in Britain and Ireland, and everything exotic in the empire.

A competition was held to design a hall for the Great Exhibition in Hyde Park, London. The winner was a gardener called Joseph Paxton.

"The hall should be novel, like everything in the exhibition," said Paxton. "I will build a palace made entirely of iron and glass!"

No one had ever done that before, but he wanted to show that machines could even change what buildings looked like. So he made columns of iron and sent them to Hyde Park to be put together, then had thousands of sheets of glass lifted into position. When Londoners saw Paxton's glass hall glinting in the sunlight, they called it the Crystal Palace.

The Crystal Palace was so big that the trees of Hyde Park went on growing inside. Its stalls displayed carpets and cutlery, statues and pottery, fabrics, lights and machines. Locked cabinets contained caskets of diamonds and pearls. Water spilled from marble fountains, and visitors climbed galleries to look down on the wonders below.

Princes came to the Great Exhibition from as far away as India, and ambassadors arrived from every country in the world. When Queen Victoria declared it open, bands played, flags waved, and millions of visitors queued in Hyde Park to see what was in the Crystal Palace.

One of them was the writer Charlotte Brontë, who could hardly find words to describe what she saw. *"It seems as if only magic could have gathered this mass of wealth from all the ends of the earth!"* she wrote.

When they visited the Great Exhibition, the British saw how their country had changed, and how rich it had become. And just as Prince Albert had hoped, they realized how much they had to be proud of.

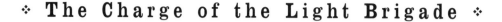

❖ The Charge of the Light Brigade ❖

BUT people soon had something more serious than the Great Exhibition to talk about, for not long afterwards, Britain went to war again. The war was against Russia, and the British were allied with the French. Some of the old generals who remembered fighting France when they were young got muddled and shouted, "Attack the French!" as they went into battle. That showed how long it was since the British had fought a war. The army wasn't ready – the soldiers didn't have enough bullets, and the generals didn't have proper maps – and things went wrong from the very start.

The British and French decided to invade a peninsula called the Crimea in the south of Russia. They thought it was so far south it would always be hot, so they didn't take thick coats or boots. In fact, winter in the Crimea was freezing cold and it rained so hard that carts full of supplies got stuck in the mud. The soldiers shivered in their tents without any blankets, and soon fell sick.

Things went wrong in battle as well. Today officers in the army are carefully trained, but in those days officers were chosen simply because they were aristocrats. They thought they could beat the Russians easily, but kept making mistakes. In fact, the most famous attack in the Crimean War was a mistake. It was called the Charge of the Light Brigade.

The Light Brigade was a regiment of six hundred lightly-armed soldiers who fought on horseback. During the Battle of Balaclava the British general, Lord Raglan, saw a small group of Russian artillerymen and ordered the Light Brigade to attack them. But his message got muddled, and by mistake the Light Brigade charged straight at the main Russian guns.

The Russian gunners couldn't believe horsemen would dare charge guns. They started to fire, but the horsemen didn't retreat – instead they broke into a gallop. Cannonballs tore gaps in their ranks and soldier after soldier fell from his horse, but the others simply drew together and charged on, while smoke blocked everything from view. It only cleared when the horsemen reached the guns and saw the gunners running away up the hillside. By sheer bravery the Light Brigade had captured their target.

Unfortunately it was the wrong target – and there were only a few of the Light Brigade left alive.

Afterwards the poet Alfred Tennyson wrote a poem about their courage:

> *Half a league, half a league,*
> *Half a league onward,*
> *All in the valley of death*
> *Rode the six hundred.*

Florence Nightingale and Mary Seacole

THE British learned all about the mistakes in the Crimean War because, for the first time, journalists travelled with the soldiers and wrote reports for people to read in newspapers at home. They could learn from pictures as well, for photography had been invented not long before. A photographer who went to the Crimea sent back images of the men who survived the Charge of the Light Brigade.

When they read about soldiers falling sick and running out of bullets, people in Britain were furious. And when a woman called Florence Nightingale read about wounded men dying in hospital because no one looked after them properly, she decided to go out to the Crimea to help.

At first the army tried to discourage her. "A war is no place for a girl!" the generals protested.

Fortunately Florence Nightingale's father was very influential, and Florence herself very determined. She argued with the generals until they let her visit one of the army hospitals.

She was horrified by what she saw. Sick and wounded soldiers lay together, so the wounded caught the diseases of the sick. There were no proper toilets, bloodstained bandages covered the floor, and the stink was appalling. Everything was filthy. Doctors didn't have enough medicine, and there were no nurses. Florence soon discovered that more soldiers died in hospital than were killed in battle.

On the very day she visited the hospital Florence Nightingale took charge. The doctors protested, but she ignored them. She made them keep the hospital clean, and provide fresh air and clothing for the soldiers. She made them change dirty bandages and separate the sick from the wounded. At night soldiers saw her moving from bed to bed with her lantern, and called her the Lady with the Lamp.

With Florence Nightingale in charge, far fewer soldiers died, and people realized how important cleanliness is to staying healthy. Later, when she returned to England, Florence started a school of nursing that changed British hospitals for ever.

But Florence Nightingale wasn't the only woman who went to the war to help sick soldiers. A Jamaican nurse called Mary Seacole also set off for the Crimea. Mary Seacole wasn't rich or well-connected like Florence Nightingale, and instead of working in the hospital, she decided to help soldiers in their camps and on the battlefield. She built a shed out of scrap wood where men could recover after they had been ill. Whenever she heard there was going to be a battle, Mary Seacole packed her bag of medicines and followed the soldiers. She often risked her life to help the wounded, for it made no difference to her whether they were British, French or Russian. Many soldiers lying in pain after a battle knew help had come when they saw "Mother" Seacole walking slowly across the hill, stooping to bandage wounds and bring them comfort.

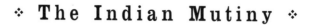

❖ The Indian Mutiny ❖

ONE of the reasons Britain went to war with Russia was to protect India, which was such a valuable part of the empire that it was called the "jewel in Britain's crown". The British often worried the Russians would invade India from the north – so often that sometimes they sent armies into Afghanistan, the country that lay between. Afghanistan was a mountainous place, full of warlike tribes, and it was madness to think it could be easily conquered. The first time the British invaded it, twenty thousand men set off into the mountains with elephants, horses and carts carrying ammunition. Three years later, a single horseman rode into a fortress in the mountains north of India, so badly wounded that he could barely stay in the saddle. When the soldiers revived him, he explained that he had been a doctor with the army that invaded Afghanistan.

"And what happened to the others?" the soldiers asked.

The doctor closed his eyes. "All dead," he whispered.

Despite such disasters, the British Empire kept growing. The countries Britain fought didn't have modern guns, so they couldn't defend themselves; and besides, the soldiers of the British army – Scottish, English, Welsh and Irish – were brave and well-disciplined, while the ships of the British navy ruled every ocean in the world.

It was a strange kind of empire, though, for it grew almost by accident as merchants looked for trade and the army followed to protect them. In fact, there were still a lot of people in Britain who didn't think the empire was a good idea at all.

"Is it right for us to run other countries?" they asked. "*We* want to be free. Why shouldn't *they*?"

All the same, the British became more and more proud of their empire, and at the Great Exhibition the biggest crowds of all gathered around cocoa beans from the Caribbean and furs from Canada, ivory from Africa and India's Koh-i-noor diamond, the biggest jewel in the world.

As the years passed, the British took over more and more of India (which included the countries we now call Pakistan and Bangladesh). The first merchants and soldiers who went there fell in love with the place, many of them taking on Indian ways and marrying Indian wives. But as the British grew more powerful, they became arrogant. They started to believe they must be better than the people they conquered. And instead of leaving Indians to live in their own way, Christian missionaries tried to make them give up being Hindu, Muslim or Sikh, and become Christian instead.

The Indians began to hate the British, and not long after the Crimean War they rebelled, just as the Americans had done in their War of Independence.

The British army in India had many regiments of Indian soldiers, known as sepoys. They were proud soldiers who fought bravely, and at first their British officers didn't notice some of them were grumbling. The problem was a new kind of bullet they had been given, whose cartridge – which they had to bite open to load their rifles – was greased with animal fat. To Muslims pig fat is unholy, while Hindus can't touch the grease of cows. So the idea that they were touching pig or cow grease every time they loaded their rifles made the soldiers furious.

"Trust the British not to care what we believe in!" they raged.

And before the officers realized what was happening, three sepoy regiments mutinied, killed all the British they could find, and seized the city of Delhi. In the Red Fort in Delhi they found the last of the old Mughal emperors, Bahadur Shah, living in retirement, and made him their emperor.

"India for the Indians!" they chanted. "Drive the invaders back to the islands they came from!"

Next they laid siege to Cawnpore and Lucknow, towns where British women and children lived alongside the soldiers. At Cawnpore the British retreated until they were crammed into a few small buildings. Fever broke out, and when they realized they couldn't hold out any longer, they made a truce with the Indians, who agreed the survivors could take a boat down the river to safety. But as they climbed on board, the British noticed soldiers watching them from the bank, and no sooner had they cast off than the soldiers started shooting. Children screamed as bullets smashed through the thin sides of the boat. Their mothers were shot trying to protect them, while those who flung themselves into the water to escape were hacked to death. Not one of the British made it out of Cawnpore alive.

In Lucknow things were almost as bad during the siege. There was little food for the desperate British trapped in the fort, and hardly any water. A soldier volunteered to break through the Indian lines and go for help, but it was months before the sound of bagpipes was heard and a Scottish regiment marched across the plain to rescue them.

Unfortunately for the Indians, they had no proper leaders, for before the British came they had been ruled by the Mughals. Besides, a lot of Indian families were afraid of what would happen if India turned to war. So before long, the mutineers were defeated, and the authorities won control again.

After the mutiny the British changed the way they ruled India, setting up a proper government instead of leaving everything to the East India Company. But they forgot that many Indians had helped end the mutiny, and began to treat all Indians with suspicion. From now on, British India would never be a contented place. Like Ireland, it had two separate races, subjects and masters, and – like the Irish – the Indians would one day rise up to challenge their conquerors again.

❖ Queen Empress ❖

TOO much power spoils people, and the British had too much power. They no longer wondered what their subjects in the empire thought of them, and were too busy enjoying themselves to care about those they governed. Every time news came of a victory in Africa or Afghanistan, they held a parade, waved flags and sang songs about how great Britain had become.

"We've got the greatest empire the world has ever known!" they boasted.

Not everything went their way. When they attacked the kingdom of the Zulus, in South Africa, the British were defeated. The survivors escaped to a ford called Rorke's Drift, where they held out all day against the whole Zulu army. Only when reinforcements arrived did their better weapons enable them to beat the Zulu king, Cetewayo, and take over his country. Later on, they were challenged by the Boers, Dutch settlers in South Africa, who didn't want to be part of the British Empire either.

But still the empire went on growing. An Englishman called Cecil Rhodes took over the old capital of Harare in East Africa, and called the new country after himself – Rhodesia. It was as if Cetewayo had conquered Britain and renamed it Cetewayoland. When maps were unrolled in schoolrooms, a third of the world was marked red, the colour of the British Empire, and one in four people on earth was a subject of Queen Victoria.

"The greatest empire the world has ever known," the British repeated proudly.

"And an empire," said the new prime minister, Benjamin Disraeli, "needs an empress."

So he made Queen Victoria Empress of India.

After her husband, Prince Albert, died, the queen was so grief-stricken that for years she didn't appear in public. It was Disraeli who persuaded her to go out again, and when he suggested she become empress of India, she agreed at once.

Victoria could not go to India to be crowned, but she sent a Viceroy to Delhi instead, and her advisers planned a lavish ceremony. Dressed in silk and covered in jewels, the Indian princes arrived on elephants to swear

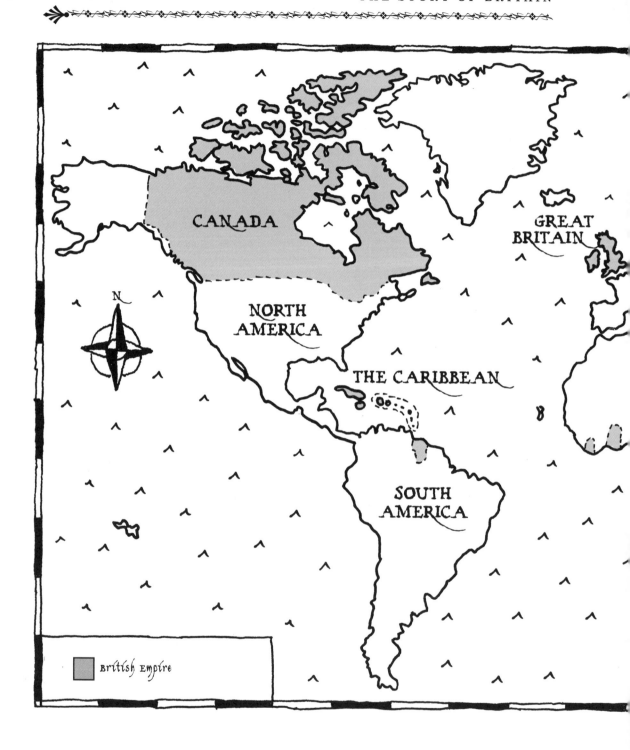

British Empire

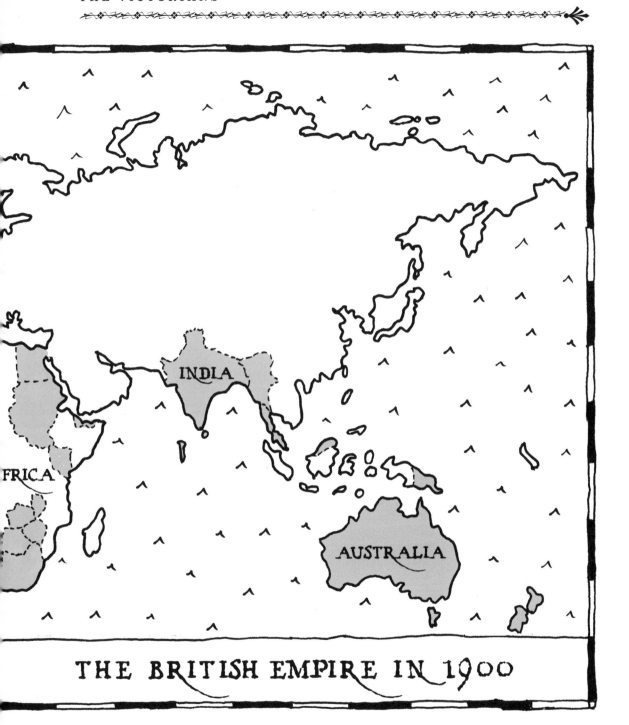

THE BRITISH EMPIRE IN 1900

their oath of loyalty, while Indian regiments marched past, bands played, and the Union Jack waved in the burning heat. To the spectators, it seemed as if the British Empire really was the greatest the world had ever known.

"And the most civilized as well," they boasted.

And it was true that the British built roads, railways and bridges in the countries they governed, set up schools, introduced medicine and established law courts in places that had never had them.

Yet they could also be terribly cruel. No one knew that better than the Irish, for when disaster struck Ireland one terrible summer, the British did nothing to help.

❖ The Irish Famine ❖

IRELAND was still as poor as ever. Despite Dublin's elegant streets and squares, the stink of its slums hung over the river Liffey, while in the countryside families lived in mud shacks, scraping a living out of the bogs. They didn't have enough land to plant wheat or vegetables, or keep sheep. All they could grow were potatoes, so the Irish grew them year after year and ate them every day – potatoes for breakfast and dinner, potatoes morning and night. And when the potato crop failed, the Irish starved.

Plants can catch diseases, just like people, and the potato disease arrived without warning. The plants came up healthily enough, but their leaves turned yellow, and whole fields began to rot as if they had been cursed. Fathers went out to fetch dinner and came back empty-handed. Children scrabbled in the mud, searching for healthy potatoes to eat, but found none. The first day they felt hungry, and the second, worse; but the plants went on dying and their hunger grew.

Today, people in Britain and Ireland don't know what it is like to starve. We don't know how it feels to have an aching belly at dinner time, but no dinner to eat, so the ache grows into a pain. We don't know what it is like to wake in the morning and find the pain still there, sharper and crueller. Children don't know what it is like to ask their parents for food and be given nothing.

Sometimes on television we see pictures of children starving in Africa. But the Irish famine wasn't happening in Africa – it was only a few hundred miles from London. And the government did little to help.

"The Irish never were good farmers," sighed one minister.

"Can't they buy bread instead?" asked another.

And they passed a law to make bread cheaper. But the Irish had no money for bread. Some of the English landowners gave them work so they could buy food, but most of the landowners never went to Ireland, didn't know about the famine, and didn't care what happened to the men, women and children who lived on their land.

The famine continued until the stink of death hung over the whole island. Fields reeked of decaying potatoes; people collapsed in the street, too weak to reach home; and crows flapped over bodies lying by the roadside.

When the famine had been going on for months and thousands had died, a group of starving villagers decided to walk to Dublin to ask the governor for help. When he looked out of the window of Dublin Castle, the governor thought he was having a nightmare, and an army of skeletons was invading the city. But as they came closer, he realized the skeletons were living people, so stooped they could hardly walk, so thin the bones cut through their flesh. And in horror he watched them sink down and die on the pavements of Dublin.

By the time the potato famine was over, a million Irish had died of hunger. A million more had decided they didn't want to live in a country where there was no food to eat and no chance of changing how things were run. So they walked west to the Atlantic shore, just as the Scottish high-landers had done when they were driven from their land. Crammed into leaking ships, still dying of hunger and disease, they sailed across the ocean to America in search of a better life.

Meanwhile, the Irish who stayed behind became more determined than ever to get rid of the British and govern themselves.

❖ Home Rule for Ireland ❖

THERE seemed little chance of Ireland governing itself, even though Irish MPs did what they could to win "Home Rule". The most determined of them was Charles Stewart Parnell. Parnell was a rich man, but he hated the way the poor suffered; he was a Protestant, but he wanted to help Catholics. He came from one of the English families who ruled Ireland – the Anglo-Irish – but longed for Irish freedom more than anyone.

Parnell knew there weren't enough Irish MPs to win a vote for Home Rule, so he came up with a new tactic: to disrupt the House of Commons so it wouldn't be able to pass laws or do any other work until it agreed. He and the other Irish MPs did that by talking. Under the rules of the House of Commons, you weren't allowed to interrupt an MP making a speech. So they talked for hour after hour, and no one could interrupt them or talk about anything except Irish Home Rule.

At the same time, Parnell persuaded the Irish to campaign against unfair English landlords. One of the landlords had an agent, Charles Boycott, who wouldn't pay decent wages, so all the Irish in the district stopped talking to him. When Boycott went into shops, people ignored him. When he shouted orders, they stared through him as if he wasn't there. They went on "boycotting" his estate until it was bankrupt, and the landlord had to give in.

Normally, if you want to change something, you persuade people to agree with you, campaign, write articles and make speeches until Parliament changes the law. But what if you live in a country that doesn't have a parliament – a country where the law is unfair and the government won't let you write what you believe? In that case, some people think they have no choice but to break the law, because if they don't, nothing will ever change.

Parnell wanted freedom for Ireland without breaking the law, but more and more Irish thought there was no chance of that.

"If we wait for Parliament to free us," they muttered, "we'll wait for ever!"

And a few went even further and turned to violence.

One evening, the governor of Ireland was waiting in his house in

Phoenix Park for two British officials to arrive for dinner. But as he stood by the window he heard a scream and saw two men running off into the trees. He went out into the park to investigate, and found the two officials' bodies. Terrorists had murdered them.

Violence always makes things worse. It poisons understanding, destroys trust and spreads fear. When they heard about the murders in Phoenix Park, people in Britain were so angry that they swore never to give Ireland freedom. Many in Ireland were just as outraged.

"We want freedom," they said, "but not through murder!"

Parnell condemned the killings, and went on trying to win Home Rule by persuasion, not violence. At last he persuaded the prime minister, William Gladstone, to agree. Some people found Gladstone pompous, but he was passionate about freedom. He hated Disraeli bragging about the empire, because he thought everyone had the right to rule themselves – and that included the Irish.

Unfortunately MPs in Britain were so angry about the Phoenix Park murders that even when Parnell and Gladstone proposed Home Rule together, they shouted them down.

"We'd have to give the Indians their own parliament too!" they protested. "And then the Africans!"

However stubbornly Gladstone and Parnell argued, they were defeated. And then Parnell got into trouble. A story came out that he had fallen in love with a woman called Kitty O'Shea, who was married to someone else. In those days people thought marriages should never be broken, so Parnell's career was ruined.

Because of Parnell's affair and the murders in Phoenix Park, the last chance of freeing Ireland peacefully was lost. From now on, the story of Irish independence would be written not in words, but in blood.

❖ Chartists and Communists ❖

ALTHOUGH the British were better off than the Irish, they were still angry they didn't have more say in their own lives. The Great Reform Act had made things fairer, but Britain still wasn't a democracy, where everyone had an equal share in choosing the government. Most men weren't allowed to vote, while women couldn't vote at all.

People didn't mind so much in good years, but they became angry when the price of food went up so they couldn't feed their families. Everyone knew politicians kept the price high on purpose. Because most MPs were landowners, they had passed Corn Laws (corn meant wheat and barley, from which flour was made) to stop bread being sold too cheaply. Working men joined a campaign to get the Corn Laws changed, and eventually forced Parliament to give in.

"But it would be even better," they said, "if we could choose the MPs who make laws in the first place."

So they signed a petition demanding that all men should be given the vote, poor men should be allowed to become MPs, and MPs should be divided fairly between towns. They called it the People's Charter, to remind people of Magna Carta, and the men who signed became known as Chartists. However, when the Chartists sent their petition to Parliament, it was ignored.

Today we're so used to the idea that everyone should be allowed to vote that we don't even think about it, but in those days aristocrats still thought it was dangerous to give a poor factory worker as much say in running the country as a lord – and others agreed. The Chartists rioted, went on strike, and prepared another charter, which three and a half million signed. Parliament ignored that as well. A third charter was drawn up, and the Chartists held a great meeting on Kennington Common in London before presenting it to Parliament. Thousands came to listen to speeches demanding the right to vote; but once again, Parliament refused to listen.

When the charter was refused for the third time, some workers decided the only way to free themselves was by a revolution. And just then, two Germans, Friedrich Engels and Karl Marx, came up with a revolutionary

new way of thinking, which they called communism.

Engels, who lived in England, made a study of the terrible conditions working people suffered in Manchester. It couldn't be right, he thought, that factory owners became rich just by investing their money, or capital, while the men who actually did the work starved. Marx and Engels called that capitalism, and said it would be better if workers ran the factories themselves. They urged workers to start revolutions, get rid of aristocrats, abolish religion and private property, and make everyone equal. They wrote a book about their ideas called *The Communist Manifesto*.

"Workers have nothing to lose but their chains," it ended. *"They have a world to win. Workers of the world, unite!"*

The idea of sharing everything sounded fair. The trouble with communism was that it meant no one would have anything that was really *theirs*. The government – the state – would own everything, and tell everyone what to do.

All the same, politicians could see how angry people in the industrial towns were becoming. What if they start a revolution? they thought.

So they agreed that, to placate them, they would pass a second Reform Act.

❖ "Change Is Inevitable" ❖

THE two most important politicians of the time were Benjamin Disraeli and William Gladstone. They couldn't have been more different. Disraeli was a Conservative (as the Tories were now called), and Gladstone was a Liberal (the new name for the Whigs). Disraeli loved the empire, while Gladstone thought countries should rule themselves. Disraeli was funny and Gladstone solemn; Disraeli showed off, while Gladstone read books. Not surprisingly, they hated each other.

For twenty years they took it in turns to be prime minister, and each day quarrelled in the House of Commons. Disraeli passed the second Reform Act, which gave more MPs to industrial towns, and allowed better-off workers to vote.

"Change is inevitable," he said. *"In a progressive country change is constant."*

But Gladstone thought Disraeli had set out to make sure the new voters would mostly be Conservatives, so at the next election he went around his constituency in Scotland making speeches to argue for a third Reform Act. Thousands came to listen, for the more people were allowed to vote, the more they took part in politics; and despite his seriousness, everyone admired Gladstone's passion and love of freedom.

Gladstone won the election and passed a new Reform Act that allowed more than half the men in Britain to vote. Poor men were still banned, and so were women, but from now on, Britain didn't just belong to aristocrats – it belonged to everyone.

In that case, people said, everyone should be allowed to become an MP. Politicians shouldn't just be rich men; they should be like the families they represented. By now, far more men and women in Britain worked in factories than on farms, and towns like Glasgow, Manchester, Birmingham and Leeds had become great cities. James Keir Hardie, a Scottish miner, decided to stand for election. At first people laughed at him for thinking a coal miner could sit in Parliment with a lord, but Hardie didn't care. He won in West Ham, and founded a new party called the Independent Labour Party to get more working men elected to the House of Commons. Then he moved to Wales and stood for election in Merthyr Tydfil. Welsh voters had

never had the chance to elect an ordinary miner before. They all supported Keir Hardie and sent him to Westminster as their Labour MP.

After that, more and more ordinary people were elected to Parliament. The most successful was a Welshman called David Lloyd George. In Wales a lot of people went to church at Methodist chapels, where preachers gave long sermons every Sunday. By listening to their sermons, Lloyd George learned how powerful words were, and became a great speaker himself. He joined the Liberal Party and was elected an MP, but never forgot the poor people he had grown up with. When he became chancellor of the Exchequer, he brought in pensions so that old people would have enough money to live on, free school meals for children, and National Insurance so that those who were sick or out of work wouldn't starve. Thanks to Lloyd George, poor people in Britain no longer needed to fear old age and sickness.

Some opposed him, of course, just as some had opposed the end of slavery. The House of Lords tried to stop Lloyd George's changes, so a law was passed that from now on the House of Commons was the more important part of Parliament. That showed how lords were becoming weaker, and ordinary people more powerful. Britain was becoming fairer at last.

In one way, however, Britain still wasn't fair at all. Although most men could vote, women could hardly do anything.

❖ Suffragettes ❖

WOMEN couldn't be MPs or judges, vicars, lawyers or journalists. Elizabeth Garrett Anderson qualified as a doctor and started a hospital, but she had to fight and argue for years to get her way. Most women who worked ended up in factories, or as servants to the rich – and they were always paid less than men who did the same jobs. And yet women were just as clever as men, just as hard-working, and just as able to come up with new ideas. Half of the country's talent was going to waste.

Millicent Fawcett, Elizabeth Garrett Anderson's sister, started a campaign to have the law changed so that women could vote.

"Women have to *obey* the law," she said. "Why shouldn't we help *make* the law?"

Most people laughed at the idea of women's suffrage (which meant the right to vote), but more and more women joined suffrage societies. In the north of England factory girls campaigned for the vote, attending meetings and singing suffragist songs – even though their husbands and bosses tried to stop them.

Emmeline Pankhurst and her daughters, Christabel and Sylvia, joined a suffrage society in Manchester, but soon got frustrated at how little the meetings and rallies achieved.

"None of the politicians listen to us!" they complained.

Like the Irish, women wondered how they could change things when they didn't have any rights. It was all very well to say they should obey the law, but the law was made by men. It was all very well to say they should work for change through Parliament, but Parliament didn't have any women in it.

"We need *deeds, not words*!" the Pankhursts said.

So they started a new organization, the Women's Social and Political Union. Women in the WSPU ignored the law. They smashed shop windows, disrupted politicians' meetings, and chained themselves to railings so the police couldn't take them away. Many suffragists hated the idea of breaking the law, but at least the newspapers noticed.

"See what the *suffragettes* are doing now!" they exclaimed.

The government arrested suffragettes, and sent Emmeline and

Christabel Pankhurst to jail. In prison, suffragettes went on hunger strike to protest against being treated like common criminals, but doctors tied them down and forced food down their throats. Once people had treated women's suffrage as a joke; now they realized how serious women were about winning equal rights.

"They will have to choose between giving us freedom or giving us death," Emmeline Pankhurst declared.

And one of the suffragettes, Emily Davison, proved she meant it. One morning, she joined the crowds to watch the most important horse race of the year, the Derby. She pushed her way through the spectators until she reached the railing at the edge of the racecourse, just by the winning post. That year, everyone expected the king's horse to win. People started to cheer as the thunder of horses' hooves came closer. And then the cheers turned to gasps and screams when Emily Davison, wrapped in the flag of the WSPU, ducked under the railing and ran right into the path of the king's horse.

She died that night in hospital.

To suffragettes Emily was a heroine. Others said her death didn't help women, for many were so shocked they stopped supporting the WSPU. But one thing was certain. From now on, everyone realized women were deadly serious about getting the vote.

❖ The Edwardians ❖

BY then Queen Victoria had died, after reigning for sixty-three years – longer than any king or queen before. You had to be very old to remember singing "God Save the King" instead of "God Save the Queen", and to younger people it seemed as if Victoria had been queen for ever.

Her son was crowned King Edward VII of Britain and emperor of India, and his coronation was celebrated all over the empire. In London flags were hung along Whitehall, there was a grand parade of soldiers and horsemen, and the archbishop of Canterbury led a service in Westminster Abbey. In other towns people put out bunting, set tables down the middle of the street and prepared feasts. In Trenchtown, Jamaica, there was a cricket match and all the children were given new school uniforms. In Johannesburg, South Africa, there were speeches in English and Zulu; and in Australia and Canada the governors general addressed Parliament.

But the greatest festivities of all took place in India, at the grand durbar (or festival) to celebrate the new emperor's reign. Outside Delhi, workmen built a city of tents with its own railway to carry visitors, its own police force, and strings of electric lights. Indian princes came to the durbar dressed in their finest jewels. The British viceroy, Lord Curzon, arrived on an elephant; the Indian army paraded with bands and flags; and the celebrations ended with sports, fireworks and a special ball.

To everyone who read about the durbar, it seemed as if the British Empire was as strong as always. "It will last for ever!" the British said.

But though it seemed as if nothing could possibly go wrong, the empire was already near its end.

Two years after Edward VII's son became King George V, the shipyard of Harland and Wolff, in Belfast, launched the largest passenger ship in the world. It could carry more than two thousand people, cross from England to America faster than any other ship, and the shipyard claimed it was unsinkable. They called it *Titanic*.

People rushed to buy tickets for *Titanic's* first voyage. The kitchens were stocked with oysters and champagne, an orchestra played in the ballroom, and passengers held parties in the cabins. When *Titanic* was

halfway across the Atlantic Ocean, fog descended. The captain received a warning there were icebergs near by, but kept steaming at full speed, while *Titanic's* lights blazed from a thousand portholes. What could go wrong with a ship so big?

"Iceberg!" screamed the lookout.

A horrible scraping sound came from one side, and the ship shuddered. To start with, no one realized anything was wrong. The engines were still throbbing, the lights were on, and passengers were still dancing in the ballroom. But tons of freezing water were pouring through great holes in *Titanic's* side, and gradually the decks began to tilt.

No ship is unsinkable; things can always go wrong. Seven hundred passengers crammed into the lifeboats, and watched as the great liner tipped up into the sky and dived under the waters of the Atlantic, drowning everyone left on board.

In the first years of the twentieth century, Great Britain was a bit like *Titanic*. It was the greatest nation on earth, with the biggest empire the world had ever seen. It was more elegant and modern than any other country. Surely it was unsinkable!

But things can always go wrong. Had the British not noticed they were no longer the only country with factories and machines? The United States of America had suffered a terrible civil war, but since then had become even richer than Britain. Germany, which had once been a collection of smaller countries, had united, and was having its own industrial revolution. The things the British made were no longer better than anyone else's.

Hadn't they noticed that the empire cost more than they could afford? In the old days, merchants started it to import tea, silk, copper, sugar and diamonds. Yet when the British fell in love with the idea of empire for its own sake, they invaded countries that made them no money, yet still had to pay for armies and officials to run them.

Besides, didn't they realize there was something wrong with the whole idea of the empire? They kept telling the Indians that British rule meant freedom and equality. How long could it be before the Indians demanded the same freedom and equality for themselves?

Didn't the British see they couldn't go on treating Ireland so badly?

Didn't they realize how many arguments in their own country were still

undecided, from women's votes to decent pay for workers in factories?

Didn't they worry about the new ideas of the communists?

The British were enjoying themselves too much to notice anything was wrong. They were unsinkable! Nothing could possibly happen!

"News! Important news!"

"Let me see your paper – what's the headline?"

GREAT WAR BEGINS IN EUROPE!

GREAT BRITAIN DECLARES WAR ON GERMANY!

TIMELINE

1812–1827 ❖ Lord Liverpool, the Tory prime minister, refuses all demands for reform.

1819 ❖ Soldiers attack a crowd calling for reform in the Peterloo Massacre.

1825 ❖ George Stephenson opens the Stockton to Darlington railway.

1829 ❖ Daniel O'Connell forces the duke of Wellington to allow Catholic Emancipation, letting Catholics vote and worship freely. In the same year, Robert Peel founds the Metropolitan Police.

1832 ❖ The Great Reform Act is passed.

1834 ❖ The Tolpuddle Martyrs, who try to form a union, are transported to Australia.

1837 ❖ Victoria becomes queen.

1845–1850 ❖ The potato famine in Ireland kills a million people. A million more emigrate to America.

1846 ❖ Parliament gets rid of the Corn Laws to allow food to become cheaper.

1848 ❖ The Chartists present their final petition to Parliament after two previous Charters, in 1838 and 1842. It is rejected. Karl Marx and Friedrich Engels publish *The Communist Manifesto*.

1851 ❖ Prince Albert holds the Great Exhibition in Joseph Paxton's Crystal Palace in Hyde Park.

1853–1856 ❖ Britain and France attack Russia in the Crimean War. They suffer disasters like the Charge of the Light Brigade, but Florence Nightingale helps by improving hospitals for soldiers.

1854 ❖ Dr John Snow discovers cholera is caused by bad drinking water.

1857–1858 ❖ Indians rebel against British rule in the Indian Mutiny, which Indians call the First War of Independence.

1867 ❖ Disraeli passes the second Reform Act.

1870 ❖ The Education Act introduces free schools. Ten years later, school is made compulsory.

1879 ❖ The Zulus beat a British army at the Battle of Isandlhwana, but are soon afterwards defeated.

1882 ❖ Irish terrorists kill two British officials in Phoenix Park, Dublin.

1884 ❖ William Gladstone passes the third Reform Act.

1889–1896 ❖ Cecil Rhodes seizes part of Southern Africa, which he calls Rhodesia. Today it is called Zimbabwe.

1893 ❖ Keir Hardie starts the Labour Party and becomes the first Labour MP.

1897 ❖ Women who want the vote form the National Union of Women's Suffrage Societies.

1901 ❖ Queen Victoria dies and her son becomes King Edward VII.

1903 ❖ Emmeline Pankhurst and her daughters start the Women's Social and Political Union, the "suffragettes", who campaign for the next ten years.

1908–1915 ❖ Lloyd George, as chancellor of the Exchequer, introduces pensions and National Insurance to help the poor, old and sick.

1912 ❖ *Titanic* sinks on her maiden voyage.

1914 ❖ The Great War begins between Britain, France, Russia, Austria and Germany.

THE
TWENTIETH
CENTURY

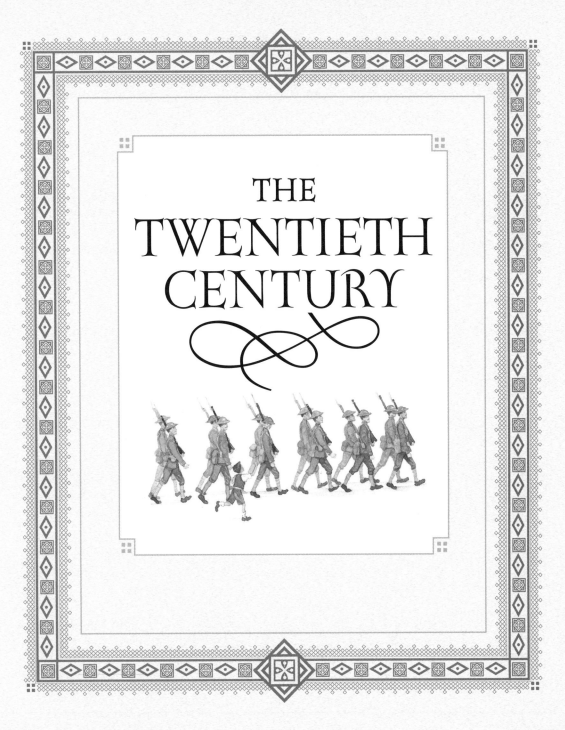

Nye Bevan

❖ ❖ ❖ ❖ ❖ ❖ ❖

BUILT THE
HEALTH SERVICE

Winston
Churchill

❖ ❖ ❖ ❖ ❖ ❖ ❖

LED BRITAIN
TO VICTORY

Gandhi

❖ ❖ ❖ ❖ ❖ ❖ ❖

MAN OF PEACE

Elizabeth II

❖ ❖ ❖ ❖ ❖ ❖ ❖

QUEEN OF NEW
BEGINNINGS

Tim
Berners-Lee

CONNECTED
THE WORLD

Margaret
Thatcher

THE IRON LADY

The Beatles

PLAYED SONGS
FOR EVERYBODY

THE BLITZ

❖ Germany ❖

G ERMANY had once been divided into small, peaceful countries, but towards the end of Victoria's reign a politician called Otto von Bismarck united it under an emperor or "kaiser", and the Germans turned to war. They attacked the French and beat them. The French emperor resigned, and Paris, the French capital, was taken over by working people who turned it into a commune, just as communists had always dreamed. Although the Paris Commune didn't last long, it took years for the French to recover.

After that victory, the Germans grew even more warlike. "France and Britain are finished!" they crowed. "It's *our* turn to have an empire!"

And the countries of Europe got ready for war.

The British didn't need to become involved, for they had an empire of their own, and didn't much care what happened in the rest of Europe. But when Germany started building a navy to rival their Royal Navy, they were furious.

"No one challenges us at sea!" they said.

The Royal Navy had ruled the oceans ever since the Battle of Trafalgar, and British ships could sail into any harbour in the world. *"Rule, Britannia!"* their sailors sang. *"Britannia rules the waves!"*

By this time, battleships were nothing like Nelson's sailing ships. They were made of steel, driven by huge steam engines, and instead of rows of cannon had guns that could blow up enemy ships fifteen miles away. When he saw the German navy growing, the head of the Royal Navy, Jacky Fisher, designed a new battleship called *HMS Dreadnought*, which was faster and more powerful than any other afloat. Then the Germans started building Dreadnoughts of their own, and a race began to see who could build ships fastest.

The other countries watched Germany and Britain arguing like two children in the playground who everyone knows are going to have a fight. France and Russia took Britain's side; Austria took Germany's.

"It's time the British were cut down to size!" growled the Germans.

"It's time the Germans were taught a lesson!" spluttered the British.

Often the quarrel that starts a fight doesn't itself seem very important. It was like that in 1914. That summer, in the town of Sarajevo, in Serbia, a terrorist shot the heir to the Austrian throne. The Austrians blamed the Serbs, the Serbs asked Russia for help, and Russia called on Britain and France. One shot by a terrorist was enough to start the whole of Europe fighting.

"War!" shouted newspaper sellers in London, Dublin, Cardiff and Edinburgh.

"War!" they shouted in Berlin, the German capital.

To start with, many actually welcomed the idea of a war. "Hurrah!" they yelled, and hurried to join their armies.

Only a few understood that this war would be more terrible than any before, that it would last for years, and that after it nothing would ever be the same again. One of them was the British foreign minister, Edward Grey.

"The lamps are going out all over Europe," he sighed as the soldiers marched off to France. *"We shall not see them lit again in our lifetime."*

❖ The Great War ❖

GERMAN soldiers marched west to invade France and east to invade Russia. German guns bellowed, and little towns shook as shells crashed onto their roofs.

Britain sent its army to help the French, and fought a battle against the Germans near the town of Ypres. They stopped the Germans advancing, but couldn't drive them back. The Germans marched north to get round them, so the British headed north as well, until both armies reached the sea. Then the Germans tried attacking in the south, but the French army was waiting to stop them. For hundreds of miles, from the North Sea to the Alps, huge armies faced each other. Neither could win, so they stayed where they were and began digging fortifications.

Soldiers dug lines of trenches in the earth, strengthened them with sandbags and barbed wire, and set up their great guns behind. The trenches zigzagged for hundreds of miles across fields and up hills. Sometimes they were only fifty metres apart, and the British could hear German soldiers singing, and officers giving orders. The land between the two lines of trenches was called no-man's-land, because it belonged to no one, and no one could cross it without being killed.

And that was the start of the most terrible war Europe had ever known. Afterwards, people called it the Great War. The Great War wasn't like other wars. It was fought by machines. Machine guns fired bullets so fast that soldiers running across no-man's-land were mown down in seconds. Aeroplanes flew over the trenches dropping bombs; cannon hurled shells from twenty miles away; and poison gas was released from canisters to choke soldiers, blind them and burn their skin.

Millions of British, French, German and Russian soldiers were killed in the Great War. They were buried in mud, for after a few months not a tree or a blade of grass remained in no-man's-land. The only flowers that grew were poppies, red as blood, which came up every spring. And still, every year, we wear poppies to remember the dead of the Great War.

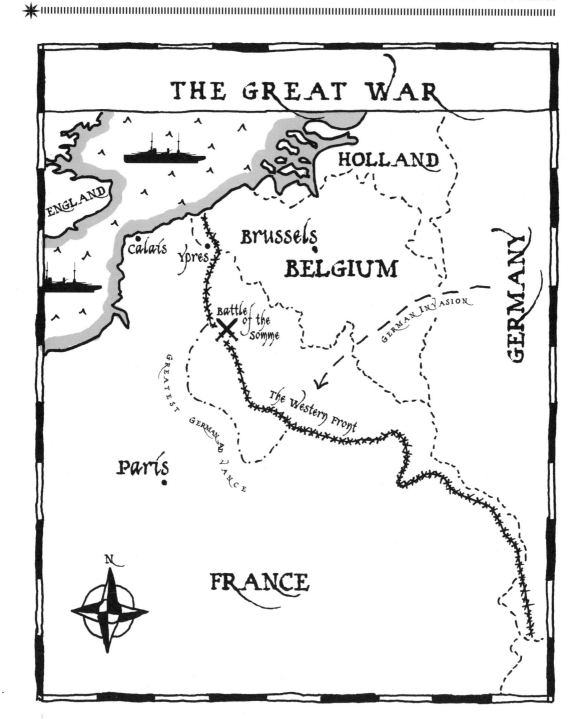

THE GREAT WAR

ENGLAND

HOLLAND

Calais

Ypres

Brussels

BELGIUM

GERMANY

Battle of the Somme

GERMAN INVASION

GREATEST GERMAN ADVANCE

The Western Front

Paris

N

FRANCE

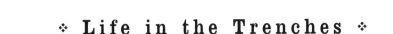

❖ Life in the Trenches ❖

SUCH a huge war needed more and more soldiers to fight it, so recruiting posters were stuck up all over Britain and Ireland. *"Your country needs you!"* they said.

"If you join the army," the recruiting sergeants told boys who gathered to read the posters, "you can fight together. We'll give you a regiment of your own."

And so new regiments were invented with names like the Accrington Pals and the Grimsby Chums.

"We'll soon beat the kaiser!" the friends joked as they put on their new uniforms.

At Waterloo Station in London, they saw wounded soldiers being carried off a hospital train. Some of them had lost legs or arms, and others had bandages over their eyes.

"It won't happen to us," the friends said.

At Dover they heard a rumbling sound. "Is there thunder at sea?" they asked the sailors.

The sailors just laughed. "Those are the guns firing in France," they said.

And the friends looked at each other nervously.

When they got to France, they were told to march along a trench to "the front". Long before they reached it, the noise of guns became deafening. When shells landed near by, the whole earth shook and they flung themselves to the ground. Even though it was night, the sky was lit up by the flashes of exploding shells.

The front was the trench right opposite the Germans.

"That's no-man's-land," the sergeant told them. "There's nothing out there but barbed wire and machine guns!"

The friends were given tea which tasted of mud and sandwiches which tasted of mud, and told they were going "over the top" at dawn. Going over the top meant climbing out of the trench and charging across no-man's-land towards the Germans.

"But what about the barbed wire?" the friends whispered to each other. "What about the machine guns?"

No one slept. They spent the night thinking about school and their friends at home. At dawn, the officer blew his whistle and they scrambled up the side of the trench. But they couldn't run across no-man's-land because it was choked with barbed wire; and they couldn't stay in line because of craters left by the shells. Then the German machine guns started firing and one by one they saw their friends killed.

At home, postmen got used to delivering the official telegrams the army sent families when their sons died. Sometimes, after an attack, they would have to deliver a telegram to every family in the district. People dreaded the sight of the postman, because he so often brought bad news.

Wilfred Owen, a poet who fought in the trenches, described marching back from the front:

> Bent double, like old beggars under sacks,
> Knock-kneed, coughing like hags, we cursed through sludge.

Life in the trenches was just as bad for the German soldiers. Their trenches were just as muddy, and the British and French had machine guns and barbed wire of their own. Sometimes all the soldiers – German, British, French and Russian – thought about the men they were trying to kill, and who were trying to kill them, and wondered what they were like. On Christmas Day in the first winter of the war no one wanted to fight. Gradually everyone stopped shooting, then soldiers from both armies climbed cautiously out of their trenches and approached each other across no-man's-land.

"What's your name?"

"Dominik. I'm from Hamburg. Yours?"

"Euan. I'm from Glasgow."

The soldiers swapped cigarettes and photographs. Some of them began games of football. Then the officers blew their whistles and ordered everyone back into the trenches. A gun went off, and then another, and the war started up again. After that the soldiers were ordered never to talk to their enemies again, in case they made friends and refused to kill them.

Meanwhile, in their headquarters, the generals tried to think up new ways to win the war.

"One big attack will do it," said a British general called Haig. "First our guns will batter the Germans for weeks. Then thousands of soldiers will attack at once. The Germans won't stand a chance."

He decided to make his attack near the river Somme. The British soldiers were soon deafened by the sound of shells whistling overhead and explosions in the German trenches.

"They'll be dead before we attack," their officers told them.

When the day of the attack came, the men climbed out of the trenches at dawn and marched towards the German lines. But the Germans had not all been killed, for their trenches were deep enough to keep them safe. Quickly, they ran to their machine guns and started firing. In one day almost sixty thousand British soldiers were killed or wounded.

The Battle of the Somme went on for months. By the time it ended, three hundred thousand soldiers were dead, and the British had only gained a few miles of ground.

Men from all over the empire were sent to join the army in France. Sikhs, Hindus, Muslims, Africans and fighters from the Caribbean arrived, and marched along the trenches under the thunder of gunfire. But they couldn't beat the Germans either. Because they couldn't win a victory in France, the British decided to attack somewhere else. The Turks were allies of the Germans, so they sent soldiers from New Zealand and Australia to attack Gallipoli in Turkey.

"The Germans may be unbeatable," the generals said, "but we'll easily defeat the Turks!"

The Turks proved brave fighters, however, and thousands of Australians and New Zealanders were killed.

Next the Germans tried to use their navy to defeat the British. Their battleships left harbour and steamed out into the North Sea. The British admiral John Jellicoe knew how important it was not to let the Germans win.

"He's the only man who could lose the war in a single afternoon," people said anxiously.

Unfortunately Jellicoe knew the German ships were better built than the British ones, so he didn't dare attack them head-on. For a day and a night the great steel battleships hurled their shells at each other. More British ships were sunk than German, but in the end it was the Germans who turned away, went back to port and never came out again.

It looked as if neither side could beat the other.

"This war's going to go on for ever," people said gloomily.

Week after week, year after year, trains set off from Waterloo Station carrying young men to France, and returned full of coffins. It seemed as if the war would go on until there were no young men left to fight it.

❖ The End of the War ❖

ONE morning, at dawn, two German soldiers heard a roaring sound coming from no-man's-land. "What is it?" they asked each other nervously.

They peered out of their trench. The noise grew louder. Before they could call for help, a huge steel shape appeared. The soldiers fired at it, but their bullets bounced off the sides. Another shape appeared, then another. The machines moved on caterpillar tracks, bristling with guns, and the Germans fled in terror as they rolled over the trench and opened fire.

The British called their new machines tanks. Neither machine guns nor barbed wire could stop them. At last they had found a way of getting through the German trenches.

They were only just in time. The Russians gave up the war, so all the German soldiers who had been fighting in Russia were sent west to fight the British and French, and it looked as if the Germans would win. Tanks helped stop them. Then the British and French found a new ally, the United States of America. Since becoming independent, the USA had grown into a rich, strong country whose factories were the biggest in the world. When thousands of American soldiers arrived in France to help, it wasn't long before the Germans surrendered.

At eleven o'clock on 11 November 1918 – the eleventh hour of the eleventh day of the eleventh month – the guns stopped shooting at last, and from one end of the trenches to the other a terrible silence fell.

"I can hear a bird singing," said a soldier. It was the first time he had heard birdsong in four years.

At last the Great War was over. No one had ever seen such terrible destruction before. Thirty-seven million soldiers had been killed or wounded. If you go into any church in Britain or France, in even the tiniest village, you will see a war memorial with rows of names carved on it. Those are the names of all the young men who were killed, and left sorrowing families behind them.

Even when the fighting ended, people didn't stop dying, for right after the war a terrible epidemic of influenza swept across the world, killing even more.

"We'll never forget the dead," everyone promised.

And to this day, the nearest Sunday to 11 November is still called Remembrance Sunday. We wear poppies to remember all those who have been killed in wars, and at the eleventh hour – eleven o'clock – we fall silent and pray that we never have to fight such a war again.

The countries of the world started a League of Nations to decide arguments between countries by discussion not war.

"There won't be another war like that," people said. "That was *the war to end all wars.*"

And everyone breathed a sigh of relief, and settled down to enjoy the peace.

❖ The Jazz Age ❖

"WE were good enough to die for our government," soldiers said as they came back home, "so we're good enough to *vote* for our government!"

"If we were good enough to work in factories making guns and ammunition when the men were fighting," said women, "we're good enough to vote as well!"

And so, straight after the war, a law was passed which let all men over the age of twenty-one vote in elections, and finally gave women the vote (although they had to be over thirty). Nancy Astor became the first woman MP, and Britain became a democracy where all adults had a say in choosing the government.

People felt different after that. They didn't have to look up to aristocrats as they had in the old days.

"What's so special about *lords*?" they asked. "We're all equal now!"

Nobody wanted to work as a servant any more, so the aristocrats had nobody to look after them, and one by one their palaces were closed down or sold off.

Just as they had after the Napoleonic Wars, people felt restless. They had travelled to France and met men and women from other countries. They didn't want to go back to the old ways.

"The world's changing!" they said. "And we want to change too!"

Wherever they looked, they saw new inventions to wonder at. For centuries people had used candles to light their homes at night. Because candles were dim, most families rose at dawn and went to bed at sunset to make the most of the daylight. But then Michael Faraday had discovered how electricity worked, and after the Great War more and more families lit their homes with electric lights.

For centuries people had dreamed of being able to communicate with each other from far away. "Imagine if I could talk to people in Australia!" they said.

In 1876 an Edinburgh-born American called Alexander Graham Bell invented the telephone, and the dream came true. After the Great War more and more people had telephones, and could speak to friends hundreds of miles away. When motor cars were invented, travelling became easier as well.

To start with, people couldn't understand how cars worked. "Did you see that?" they said. "A carriage going along without a horse!"

They were so scared, that cars were only allowed to drive slowly, with men walking in front of them waving red flags. When the red flag law was dropped, excited car owners held a race from London to Brighton to celebrate (people who own old cars still drive from London to Brighton every year to remember it). Children and animals scattered as they hurtled through villages. All over Britain travellers sold horses, pulled down stables and hurried to buy cars. Before the Great War only the very rich had them, but after it cars became cheap enough for ordinary people as well.

Aeroplanes were even more exciting. There are still arguments about who was the first person to fly a proper aeroplane, but the first to fly across the Channel was a Frenchman called Louis Blériot. Blériot took off from a cliff near Calais in a flimsy machine he had made himself out of wood and canvas. Its engine puffed black smoke and sometimes broke down in mid-air.

"Good luck!" everyone shouted as he dipped and swooped over the sea.

Halfway across the Channel, fog came down and Blériot got lost. But the fog lifted just in time for him to see the white cliffs of Dover, and he crash-landed on the grass while the crowds cheered and waved British and French flags.

Officers in the navy and army looked worried, though. "If armies can *fly* across the Channel," the sailors asked, "what use is the Royal Navy?"

"Aeroplanes will be able to bomb towns," the soldiers said. "And we won't be able to stop them!"

For the moment, though, aeroplanes seemed exciting, and pilots competed to break flying records. John Alcock, from Manchester, and Arthur Brown, from Glasgow, were the first to fly non-stop across the Atlantic. They set out from Newfoundland, but as they flew east it got colder and colder, and ice built up on the engines. They were worried the engines would stop, so Brown climbed out along the wings to hack the ice off. It was almost seventeen hours before they saw grass below them, and crash-landed in a bog in Ireland.

Amy Johnson became the first famous woman pilot. She flew solo to Australia, and was the first to fly non-stop to Moscow. She also flew from England to Japan in record time. The newspapers were full of stories about her courage and determination.

Finally, an Italian called Guglielmo Marconi came up with the idea of sending sounds through the air by radio waves. First ships used radio to speak to each other, then people used it to broadcast news and music. Just as everyone now has a television, every household then bought a radio, listened to new songs and – if they liked them – pushed back the furniture to dance.

And the radio played a new kind of music for them to dance to. It was louder than classical music, faster – and much more fun. It came from America and was called jazz.

"This is the jazz age!" couples screamed as they twirled around dance floors.

After the terrible slaughter of the Great War, it seemed as if the whole world had decided to throw a party. Women were fed up with wearing skirts too long to dance in, so they bought shorter ones.

"Disgusting!" complained old men when they saw girls' bare legs for the first time.

They cut their hair short as well.

"You look like a boy!" shrieked mothers as their daughters came back from the hairdresser's.

The girls didn't care. They were having fun!

Unfortunately, if one part of the world is rich and happy, you can be quite sure that things are going less well somewhere else. The jazz age got people dancing in London and New York, but in Ireland there was no dancing. There, everyone had more serious things to think about, for the old argument about Home Rule had started a civil war.

❖ War in Ireland ❖

ONE Easter, in the middle of the Great War, a group of Irish soldiers tried to start a rebellion. They seized the General Post Office in Dublin and declared Ireland free. When the British army arrived to drive them out, they closed the shutters and barricaded the door. But they didn't have many bullets, and some only had wooden rifles that they pointed out of the windows to make the British think them well armed, so the Easter Rising didn't last long. Today, if you go to Dublin, you can still see bullet holes in the post office walls where the British soldiers fired at the Irish until the last man surrendered.

But after the war the Irish were determined to win their freedom once and for all. Thousands had fought bravely for Britain in the Great War – wasn't it time they were rewarded?

"All the same, I bet the British cheat us again," muttered Irish soldiers as they returned home. "There's no point arguing for freedom in Parliament. The only thing they understand is fighting."

And so the fighting began. Irish republicans – people who wanted Ireland to be an independent country – set fire to English houses and attacked policemen. The British government retaliated by sending soldiers to Ireland. They were called Black and Tans because of the colour of their uniforms, and were ordered to bully the Irish into submission. Lorryloads of Black and Tans arrived in villages, beat up republicans and burned down Irish houses. The Irish Republican Army fought back, and the conflict became more and more bitter.

Even if fighting seems justified at the time, it always causes harm in the end. Violence brings more violence. It is like putting poison on a field – you might kill the weeds, but nothing can grow there for years afterwards.

And that was what happened in Ireland. The British government finally realized it couldn't keep Ireland by force, so it suggested a compromise. Ireland would become a free country, but would have to stay part of the British Empire, while the six provinces of Northern Ireland, where most people were Protestants, would go on being part of Great Britain. Protestants in Northern Ireland were proud of being British, and didn't want to live in a country where most people were Catholics.

Michael Collins, one of the leaders of the Irish Republican Army, went to Dublin Castle to become Ireland's first free prime minister. When the British governor complained that he was seven minutes late, Collins just laughed.

"We Irish have been waiting for freedom over seven hundred years," he said, *"you can have the extra seven minutes."*

But many Irish hated the British proposal, and didn't think the Irish Parliament, the Dáil, should have agreed to it.

"Freedom ought to mean freedom for the whole island of Ireland!" they said. "We'll never swear loyalty to the British Empire!"

And they killed Michael Collins and began a civil war. It went on for a year, but the Irish didn't really stop quarrelling until Ireland left the British Empire ten years later. Even then, the troubles of Northern Ireland were not over. Today the six provinces of Northern Ireland are still part of Britain, but Republicans and Loyalists still quarrel, and terrorists sometimes attack British soldiers. And Protestants and Catholics still look at each other with hatred and suspicion, never knowing if the violence of the past will explode into their lives again.

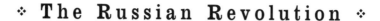

❖ The Russian Revolution ❖

IRELAND wasn't the only part of the world where fighting went on after the Great War was over. There was even more trouble in Russia, where communists began a revolution, killed the czar, and turned Russia into a communist state. Russia had never had a proper parliament or fair law courts. The czar decided everything. So when the Great War went badly for the Russians, it wasn't surprising they complained about the czar.

"Why should we die for a country we have no say in?" they asked each other.

To start with, the revolutionaries only wanted to set up a free parliament and make fair laws. "Just like in Britain and America," they said.

But at a time of revolution it is always the most violent and determined people who win out, just as they did in the French Revolution, a hundred years before. The communists' leader was called Vladimir Ulyanov. He had read Karl Marx's and Friedrich Engels's books about a world where the workers were in charge, there were no factory owners, everything was shared and everyone was equal. He had spent his whole life trying to start a revolution, and had even given himself a revolutionary new name – Lenin.

"Setting up a parliament won't give workers enough to eat," he shouted. "We need to change the whole system!"

Lenin was abroad when the revolution started, but he quickly caught a train back to Russia. The capital, Petrograd, was in turmoil, as soldiers rushed around the streets trying to keep order, politicians spent hours in meetings, and the czar issued orders that no one obeyed.

The disturbances went on for months, and for a time Lenin had to flee abroad, but that October he gathered his followers together. "We're going to take charge tonight," he told them.

That night, communist sailors from the navy directed their guns at the royal capital, communist soldiers attacked the czar's palace and factory workers marched into the city, waving the communists' red flag. Lenin and the communists drove all the aristocrats out of Russia, divided their palaces into flats for poor people, and gave factories to the workers and farms to the peasants.

"It's our land now," they said proudly.

They murdered the czar and his family, closed churches because they didn't believe in religion, and even changed Russia's name. It became the Union of Soviet Socialist Republics, or USSR.

For years countries like Britain and France had been frightened of the communists taking over; now there was a country where they actually *had*. Workers in Russia marched up and down the streets waving their huge red banners.

"Soon there will be revolutions everywhere!" they shouted.

Was that what the future held? Would workers take over Glasgow, Cardiff, London and Dublin, fly red flags over the Houses of Parliament, and turn Britain communist too? That was what British politicians feared. And when British workers went on strike, it looked to them as if the communist revolution was beginning.

❖ The General Strike ❖

MANY workers in Britain did want things to change. Although not many joined the communists, most belonged to unions and became members of the Labour Party, which became larger at every election, while the Liberal Party shrank.

The excitement of beating Germany didn't last long, for the Great War had been very expensive, and, after being the richest country in the world for centuries, Britain suddenly felt poor. People had been promised new homes and better schools after the war; instead they lost their jobs.

When coal miners in Wales were told their wages would be cut, they went on strike. The mine owners refused to listen to them, so the other unions called a general strike, and declared no one in Britain would work at all. There would be no electricity, no coal, no milk, no schools or newspapers, and all the factories would shut down. Everything in Britain would stop.

"This is the revolution!" the politicians said nervously to each other. "The communists are going to take over here as well!"

But most of the strikers weren't communists; they just wanted more money, better homes, decent heating and enough to eat. Britain was getting fairer, but not fast enough.

On the day the strike began, there were no buses in the streets and the stations were empty because there were no trains. Soon shops began to run out of food.

Many people began grumbling about the strikers. "If we don't give the workers what they want, they'll starve us to death," they said. "That's blackmail!"

"We're only asking for what's fair!" the strikers protested.

But most people didn't think Britain would be better if the workers ran the country. They could see what was happening in the USSR, where Lenin had died and a new leader, Stalin, had taken over.

"Who will make decisions now we're all equal?" the Russians asked Stalin.

"The communists will," Stalin answered.

"And who's in charge of the communists?"

"I am," Stalin said, and when the Russians looked around their towns,

they saw Stalin's face staring down from huge posters on every wall.

Stalin drove farmers off their farms and made shopkeepers give up their shops, while his secret police arrested anyone who disagreed with him.

"What's so fair about that?" asked people in Britain.

After the General Strike had gone on for a few days, the army started delivering food, while volunteers drove buses and trains. At last the strikers realized how few people supported them, and called the strike off.

Some things about Britain may have been unfair, but no one wanted a revolution.

❖ The Great Depression ❖

AFTER the General Strike, the factories opened again and the strikers went back to work. But if they hoped things would get better, they were disappointed. For soon afterwards the whole world was struck by an economic disaster that made the rich poor and left the poor with nothing.

In the old days people suffered when their crops failed. Today we suffer when the economy crashes. Everyone stops buying houses, so builders lose their jobs. Without work or money they stop buying things, so factory workers lose their jobs. Then *they* can't buy anything either, so more factories close and everyone gets poorer.

The crash, which became known as the Great Depression, started in America. Ever since the Great War, America had been the richest and most exciting country in the world. Ordinary American families lived like rich people anywhere else. Henry Ford designed a motor car cheap enough for everyone to buy, and his factory made thousands of Ford cars every week. Movies were invented and actors went to Hollywood to star in them. Musicians played jazz, and architects built huge towers they called skyscrapers. As companies grew richer, their shareholders grew wealthy as well, and some became millionaires. Then everyone wanted to buy shares, so the prices went up and up, and people got even richer.

But everyone had forgotten how risky it is to invest in shares. The boom couldn't last for ever – it was a bubble, just like the South Sea Bubble in England two hundred years before – and one day, the price of shares crashed. People withdrew their money from banks, so the banks ran out of money. Factories closed and workers lost their jobs. Some of the bankers, realizing their wealth was gone, killed themselves by jumping out of the windows of their skyscrapers.

The crash didn't only ruin America but Britain too, where millions of men and women lost their jobs. Children came home from school to find their fathers sitting on the sofa, head in hands. No work meant no more jazz records or rides in motor cars; it meant nothing to eat. Fathers spent hours standing in queues, only to be told there were no jobs to be had.

The north of England suffered worst. Once, the north had been called "the workshop of the world", and machines from Leeds and steel from Sheffield could be found everywhere from Africa to Afghanistan. Now the factory gates were shut, and nobody made anything.

"The politicians have got to listen to us," said some out-of-work men in Jarrow, on the Tyne, and they decided to march to London to ask the government to help.

Their leader was Ellen Wilkinson, one of the first women MPs, who was called "Red Ellen" not only because of the colour of her hair, but because red was the colour of the Labour Party. As they marched to London, people came out of their houses to watch the Jarrow Crusade go by with red flags flying. They handed packets of food to the hungry marchers, and at night friendly farmers let them sleep in their barns.

But when they reached London, the marchers found there was nothing the government could do to help. The whole world had fallen into the Great Depression, and the government had no money either. So the Jarrow marchers returned home as hungry as ever, and the Depression went on.

Terrible as the Depression was in Britain, it was even worse in Germany, the country that had lost the Great War. There, the Depression caused millions to lose their jobs and made the currency crash so badly that banknotes became worthless. It ruined cities and starved families. Worse than that, it brought a frightening new leader to power.

His name was Adolf Hitler.

❖ The Nazis ❖

AFTER the Great War, the German kaiser was driven from his throne and the communists began a revolution. Although they failed, German politicians never managed to put together a proper government, and no one was sure what to believe in any more. Wounded soldiers sat in the streets begging for bread. Old women sold their rings to buy food.

A group of people called fascists thought that Germany needed a strong leader to tell everyone what to do. Gangs of them, waving black flags, attacked gangs of communists, who waved red flags.

"Down with the communists!" shouted the fascists. "We need a leader to follow – a new hero for Germany!"

Adolf Hitler was their leader, although he didn't look much like a hero. He was small and weedy, and had no friends. He had fought in the Great War, but wasn't a very good soldier; he had studied to be an artist, but wasn't a very good painter. Unfortunately Adolf Hitler possessed the most dangerous weapon in the world. He was quite sure that what he said was right.

When people are feeling scared and unhappy, they often listen to those who are sure of themselves – even madmen they'd usually be sensible enough to ignore. "*He* seems to know what he's doing," they say. "It's good to have a leader who knows what he wants!"

The Germans were feeling scared and unhappy, so more and more of them listened to Hitler.

"We should have won the Great War," Hitler told the Germans. "It wasn't our fault we lost – it was the communists' fault!"

And his party, the Nazis, began attacking communists.

"Germany ought to be as great a nation as Britain or France!" Hitler insisted. "It isn't our fault we aren't." And he lowered his voice and hissed, "It's the Jews' fault!"

So the Nazis attacked Jews as well.

Jews had lived in Germany for centuries. They dressed and spoke just like other Germans, but on the Sabbath their synagogues were filled with candles and the chanting of prayers.

When people want to blame someone else for their own troubles, they often pick on outsiders, just as playground bullies pick on children who are smaller than everyone else, or who look different. Hitler told the Germans to blame communists and Jews for Germany's problems, and because they were scared and unsure of themselves, they listened to him and elected him chancellor of Germany.

Calling himself *Der Führer*, which is German for "the leader", Hitler passed laws to make Jews wear yellow stars on their clothes, so that everyone could see who they were. People spat at Jews in the street and refused them jobs. One night, the Nazis smashed up every Jewish shop in Berlin.

Some Germans remembered that their country had once been a peaceful place, famous for philosophy and music. "What is happening to us?" they whispered. But there were too few of them to stop the Nazis. Jews began to leave Germany. Some went to Palestine. Palestine (which was then run by Britain) had been the Jews' home centuries before, and they dreamed of starting a new Jewish country there. Others went to America, Holland or Britain. Sometimes a whole family couldn't afford to leave Germany, so the children were sent by themselves.

"Don't worry about us," their mothers and fathers said as they kissed them goodbye at the station. "We'll come and join you soon!" But when the train was out of sight, they said to each other, "At least our children will be safe. God knows what will happen to us!"

The children arrived in London carrying nothing but some clothes and a favourite book or teddy bear. London didn't look like home, or smell like it. The food was different, and passers-by stared at them as if they were animals from the circus. Even the street signs were strange, and the policemen wore odd uniforms. Strangers came up, asked questions they didn't understand, and plucked at the yellow stars on their coats.

"They mean to be kind," sisters explained to their brothers in German. "They're trying to help us."

In fact the British government did little – it had too many mouths to feed already. Instead, the refugees from Germany were looked after by British Jews, or by kindly people who saw them standing at the docks and befriended them. They were grateful for the help they were given, but couldn't stop thinking about home. And at night, unable to sleep, they fingered the dirty yellow stars they had unpicked from their coats, and wondered what was happening in Germany.

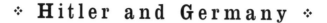

❖ Hitler and Germany ❖

IN Germany it wasn't long before the Nazis declared that there wouldn't be any more elections, and that they would rule for ever. Like bullies who force everyone else to play their game, they made everyone behave like a Nazi. All Germans had to use the Nazi salute, by sticking one arm straight out in front of them, and display the Nazi symbol, the swastika, which looked like a twisted cross.

And Germany wasn't the only fascist country in Europe. Italy had a fascist dictator, Benito Mussolini, who called himself *Il Duce*. In Spain there was a civil war between communists and fascists. Communists from Britain went to fight in the war, but Hitler sent his soldiers to help the Spanish fascists, and they won. Their dictator was called General Franco.

In Russia Stalin made everyone do what he wanted, even though he called himself a communist, not a fascist. Once, communism had sounded like a fair idea. In fact, "everyone being equal" turned out to mean "everyone being exactly the same"; and "no bosses" turned out to mean that the Communist Party was the boss. It had far too much power, and anyone who disagreed with Stalin was shot or sent to jail. Millions of Russians were condemned to prison camps, and forced to work until they died.

If you've read this far in this book, you'll know that the world is full of different people with different ideas, different customs and different religions. The only way for them to live in peace is if everyone agrees to respect those differences and leave each other alone. But the dictators who ruled Germany, Italy and Russia hated the idea of anyone being different. They wanted to control everything, and didn't mind how many they killed so long as they got what they wanted.

Quite often, today, you meet people who refuse to vote in general elections. "I'm not interested in politics," they say. "It doesn't make any difference who you vote for – politicians are all the same!"

They ought to go back to Germany in the 1930s to see what it's like living in a place where you aren't allowed to have your say. Then, perhaps, they'd realize how many people have died for the right to live in a free country, and how important it is to vote.

Hitler wasn't content with ruling Germany. He wanted to rule the whole world, so he took over Austria as well. He had been born in Austria, and many Austrians welcomed him. Instead of stopping him, the British and French hardly even complained.

"Whatever happens, we mustn't have another war," they said.

Then Hitler announced he wanted part of Czechoslovakia as well. People asked the League of Nations to help, but Hitler didn't care about the League of Nations.

"Anything but war," the British said. "The Great War was the last. There mustn't be another one!"

"If we let Hitler have Czechoslovakia, then he'll be content, and we can go on living in peace," said the British prime minister, Neville Chamberlain.

So he and the French prime minister, ignoring what the Czechs thought, made an agreement to let Hitler have part of Czechoslovakia. Most people cheered them for stopping another war, but some were ashamed of what Britain had done. One of them was a Conservative MP called Winston Churchill.

"The only way to deal with bullies," Churchill said, "is to stand up to them." Many people didn't trust Churchill because he was loud and a show-off, but he was quite certain Britain was doing the wrong thing. "We should stick up for our principles," he insisted. "Instead of trying to make friends with Hitler, we should build planes and ships, and fight to stop him!"

Sure enough, Hitler was not content with Czechoslovakia. Suddenly he announced that he and Stalin were going to divide up Poland between them, just as if it was a coat they both wanted, not a country full of free men and women. The German army had invented a new kind of warfare called *Blitzkrieg*, or "lightning war". Planes dropped bombs from the sky, while tanks advanced so quickly that no one had time to fight back. In just a few weeks, the Germans took over half of Poland while the Russians took over the other half.

There was no way the British could ignore that. They had promised the Poles that if ever they were in trouble, Britain would help. Neville Chamberlain made a broadcast on the radio to explain what had happened.

"I have to tell you now," he said sadly, *"that this country is at war with Germany."*

All over Britain families sat by their radios, listening in silence. They couldn't believe they had to fight Germany again. It was only twenty years since *"the war to end all wars"*. They remembered brothers who had been killed, and friends who had marched off to fight and never come back.

Now it felt as if they had all died for nothing.

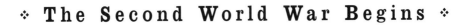

❖ The Second World War Begins ❖

AS soon as the war began, children who lived in cities started having nightmares. "I dreamed planes dropped bombs and blew up our home," they said.

Since the Great War, aeroplanes had become much stronger and faster. They could carry explosive bombs, and incendiaries which started fires. They could even carry bombs full of poisonous gas, so on the first day of the war gas masks were handed out to everybody.

"We'd better send the children away to safety," people said, "in case the Germans bomb us." So boys and girls from London and the other big cities packed suitcases and went off to live in the country.

Meanwhile, people left in the cities got ready for war. They dug air-raid shelters and prepared sirens to warn everyone if an attack was coming. On the coast scientists built radar stations to spot enemy aircraft approaching. Radar – which the Germans didn't yet know about – was a new invention that used radio waves to detect things much further away than you could see them.

But for months nothing happened and people started calling the new war against Germany a "phoney war". And then, just when they were starting to think it wouldn't be as bad as the last one, Hitler attacked Norway and Denmark. The British were taken by surprise and failed to stop him, and people were so angry with Neville Chamberlain that he had to resign. The Conservative and Labour parties agreed to form a joint government with Winston Churchill as prime minister.

Then Hitler invaded Holland, Belgium and France. His planes and tanks attacked so quickly that no one could do anything. Holland and Belgium were conquered, and the French army retreated, unable to stop the Germans. The British army, which was already in France, didn't even have time to dig trenches. All it could do was run before it was surrounded. Leaving their tanks and guns behind them, the British retreated until they reached the English Channel at a little town called Dunkirk, and couldn't go any further. There seemed nothing for them to do but surrender.

You can't fight a war without an army. It looked as if Britain and France had lost the war already.

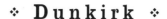

❖ Dunkirk ❖

THEN the government sent out a message on the radio. "Would everyone who owns a small boat please sail to Dover *immediately*!"

Hundreds of yachts and fishing boats set off from all round the coast. At Dover their owners were met by navy officers and told they were going to rescue the army in Dunkirk. Some of them had never crossed the Channel before, but they filled their engines with fuel and headed for France.

When they reached it, they saw hundreds of thousands of soldiers standing on the beach. The navy's ships were too big to get close to the shore and pick them up, but the little boats could go right up to the water's edge. Ignoring the German aeroplanes that flew overhead, they steered through breaking waves to where the soldiers waited patiently on the sand.

One boatload was taken off, and then another. Time and again the motor launches hurried back to the beach, and returned laden with exhausted and wounded soldiers. Time and again their skippers ducked as aeroplanes dived towards them. But they never gave up. To and fro they went until more than three hundred thousand men had been rescued and brought back to Britain. They had to leave all their guns and ammunition behind, but at least the British still had an army. And that meant they could go on fighting.

❖ The Battle of Britain ❖

HOWEVER, they had to go on fighting alone.

The French were angry that the British had escaped back to Britain. They couldn't hold out against the Germans by themselves, and a few weeks later France surrendered and the Germans marched into Paris. It seemed as if Adolf Hitler was unbeatable. He had captured Czechoslovakia and Poland, Belgium, Holland and France. Austria, Italy and Russia were on his side. Britain was the last free country left in Europe. How long could it be before German bombers and tanks came to conquer Britain as well?

But one person wasn't ready to give up: Winston Churchill.

People switched on the radio to hear his speeches. Thinking about Hitler made them scared, but Churchill's words made them brave again.

"What is our aim?" he said. *"Victory – victory at all costs, victory in spite of all terror; victory, however long and hard the road may be; for without victory, there is no survival!"*

Everyone expected the Germans to invade, so retired soldiers were organized into a second army, called the Home Guard. Most of them were middle-aged men who had fought in the Great War, and because they didn't have enough rifles, they practised drilling with pitchforks.

"Dad's Army!" people scoffed. All the same, they were glad Dad's Army was there to protect them.

Before Hitler could invade, though, he had to defeat the Royal Air Force. His own air force, the Luftwaffe, was much bigger, and its leader, Goering, told him he would soon smash the RAF. One day, people in France heard a droning noise above them and looked up to see thousands upon thousands of German planes flying towards Britain.

"The British haven't got a chance!" the French groaned, shaking their heads.

But thanks to radar, the Royal Air Force knew the Germans were coming.

"Scramble!" shouted RAF officers when the warning came, and pilots ran across the grass to their planes, parachutes bumping clumsily on their backs. They leaped into the cockpits and set off along the runway, travelling faster and faster until they were airborne.

Many of the pilots had only just left school. They weren't very experienced, and as they saw the German planes approaching, their mouths turned dry with fear. But when the fighting started, there was no time to be afraid. Their little planes twisted and wheeled in the air, trying to escape the bullets of the German fighters and shoot down the German bombers.

When the fight was over they landed again, guns out of ammunition and wings scarred by bullet holes. They hardly had time to refuel before another warning came. They fought and landed, but the sirens sounded yet again.

"Scramble!" shouted the officers, and the exhausted pilots ran out to their planes for the third time.

It seemed as if those days of fighting would never end. The Germans had so many planes they could attack time and time again, while the British pilots could never rest. They slept by their machines, so they'd be ready to take off at any moment. Their ground crews worked night and day to mend broken engines, patch bullet holes and reload guns.

People in Kent watched the Battle of Britain from the ground. Schoolchildren ran out of their classrooms when planes flew overhead, and sometimes saw one dive to the earth in flames, or spotted a parachute dangling in the sky. Sometimes planes crashed next to villages and people would go to see the twisted metal wreckage, marked with either the RAF roundel or the German swastika.

The British had one advantage: their planes were better. The Hurricane wasn't as quick as the German Messerschmitt but it was very sturdy, while the newest plane in the RAF, the Spitfire, was the best fighter in the world, quick to climb and swift to turn. Every evening the pilots gathered on their airfields to see which of their friends hadn't come back. As each day passed they grew more and more tired. But they never gave up or became downhearted. They knew that with each Messerschmitt they shot down they were one step closer to winning.

And one morning, the girls who worked the radar looked at their screens for the approaching Germans and saw nothing. Guards scanned the clouds with binoculars but found no German fighters. The pilots waiting by their

Spitfires stared up at the sky, but the Germans didn't come. It took a while for everyone to realize what had happened – the Germans had given up. They couldn't beat the RAF. The Battle of Britain had been won.

Afterwards Winston Churchill thanked the brave pilots who had saved Britain against such terrible odds.

"Never in the field of human conflict," he told the House of Commons, *"was so much owed by so many to so few."*

❖ The Blitz ❖

HITLER was furious. "How can the British hold out against me?" he snarled. "If we can't beat the RAF, we'll *scare* them into surrendering instead."

So he ordered the Luftwaffe to bomb British cities. All over London, sirens wailed. People going to work or on their way to the shops looked round in panic.

"Quickly!" wardens shouted. "Into the air-raid shelters! The bombers are coming!"

Some people had built shelters in their gardens. Others had put fortified cages under their dining tables. But most hurried to the nearest Tube station, where, deep underground, they hoped to be safe from German bombs. The trains stopped as crowds ran down the escalators and sat on the platforms. They felt the ground shake as the first bombs fell, saw the lights flicker if a bomb fell near by, and when there was a particularly loud explosion, they looked nervously at each other.

"Do you think that was the church being bombed?"

"Or the cinema?"

The Germans attacked day and night. People soon got used to sleeping in the Tube stations. Many of the children who had been evacuated to the countryside had come home by then, and when the sirens wailed their parents hurriedly woke them up.

"Don't forget your dressing gown!"

"Take a bottle of water!"

Families marked out their own areas of platform and brought blankets to sleep in. The children lay half awake, listening to the bombs exploding and wondering what it was like up on the surface.

But some people weren't allowed to take cover – firemen and air-raid wardens had to put out the fires and rescue the injured. Up on the surface, orange flames lit the sky, while bombs exploded and walls collapsed with a roar of falling rubble.

"Save St Paul's!" wardens shouted. "We mustn't let them burn the cathedral!"

So night after night they ran along the roof of St Paul's, desperately beating down fires. But hundreds of other buildings were destroyed. Each morning, when tired people came up from the air-raid shelters, they looked around to see a city they hardly recognized.

"Where's the town hall?"

"The butcher's gone!"

Sometimes the shop where they had bought a new toothbrush only the day before had become a crater in the ground. And sometimes, when they turned the corner of their streets, looking forward to breakfast and a cup of tea, families saw that their own homes had been bombed as well. They saw their beds hanging over broken floors, wallpaper flapping from the naked stairs, and smashed crockery on the floor of their ruined kitchen.

Thousands were killed in the Blitz. Shelters in gardens could keep off flying debris but not protect people from a fire. When the air-raid shelters were hit directly by bombs, everyone inside them was trapped.

Even Buckingham Palace was bombed. The king, George VI, was a shy man who had never expected to be king. His elder brother, Edward, had been crowned first, but Edward had fallen in love with a woman called Wallis Simpson, whom no one wanted to be queen, so he had to give up the throne. After their palace was hit, King George and his wife, Queen Elizabeth, visited bombed-out families in the East End to comfort them. The East End was hit hardest of all, because the Germans wanted to destroy the docks along the river Thames.

Three hundred years earlier, much of the city of London had been destroyed in the Great Fire. The Blitz destroyed even more.

Other cities were attacked as well. Plymouth was bombed because the navy used it as a base. Liverpool and Manchester were attacked. Sheffield was bombed because the Germans wanted to destroy its steelworks. Perhaps the worst hit of all was the great industrial city of Coventry. The Luftwaffe attacked it without warning, and in one terrible night the cathedral was burnt to the ground, along with most of the ancient city, while thousands of people were killed.

Hitler thought fear would make the British give up. But the Blitz had the opposite effect. When they saw their cities in ruins, people became more determined than ever to hold out against the Nazis.

❖ Life in the War ❖

A S the war went on, life became harder for everyone. Most of the men left home to join the army, so women went to work in the factories. Because farmers and miners were away fighting the war, girls were sent to the countryside to bring in the harvest and boys became coal miners. Everyone had to cover their windows at night so German pilots wouldn't see the lights of cities below. Drivers had to put black tape over their car headlights. In the countryside all the road signs were taken away, so that if the Germans invaded they wouldn't be able to find London.

The biggest problem was food. For years there had been too many people for the farmers to feed, and most of Britain's food came from other countries by ship. It was hard for ships to reach Britain any more because Hitler's submarines, or U-boats, were waiting to sink them, so no one had enough to eat.

The government turned parks into allotments for people to grow vegetables in, and rationed food so what there was would be shared equally. Each week everyone was allowed a small amount of meat, a tiny lump of cheese, a little butter. Each person had a ration book they had to show shopkeepers before they were allowed to buy anything. As the war went on, everyone grew hungry and thin.

It wasn't only food that ran short. Shops started to run out of needles for sewing; out of paper, cloth and paint. There wasn't enough fuel for heating so people shivered with cold. Some families drew lines on their baths to make sure they didn't use too much hot water. Women had to make their own clothes. During maths and history lessons, girls sat in class knitting socks for soldiers.

All the same, no one complained. They knew how evil Hitler was, and knew that if they let him win, the British would lose all the rights they had fought for over hundreds of years: to vote, to live how they wanted, and to be judged by fair courts under fair laws.

But it was all very well to say they wouldn't give in. The British were still alone, and Hitler ruled the whole of Europe. They might hold out, but how on earth could they beat him?

❖ The Allies ❖

FORTUNATELY Hitler made two terrible mistakes. A hundred and fifty years before, Napoleon had conquered all of Europe – except for Britain – and he too had seemed unbeatable. Then he had decided to attack Russia, a country so vast it could never be conquered, and a few years later his rule was over. Now Hitler decided to attack Russia as well.

"The Russians can never stand up to us Germans!" he announced. "Fascists are far better than communists."

A huge German army attacked the USSR. The Russians weren't ready, and retreated hundreds of miles. But Russia's length is measured not in hundreds of miles but in thousands, and for every thousand Russians the Germans killed or captured there were a million still ready to fight. The Germans ran out of food, their tanks ran out of petrol, their soldiers were exhausted, and there were always more Russians to attack them. Hitler had sent his men into a battle they couldn't win. The Russians had been enemies of Britain ever since the revolution, but after the German attack they became allies against Adolf Hitler and Britain was no longer alone.

Then an even stronger friend came to help.

Ever since the start of the war, the Americans had helped the British all they could by sending food and weapons across the Atlantic Ocean. The ships travelled in convoys, but many were sunk by German U-boats and their sailors drowned. Even so, enough food and weapons arrived to keep the British fighting.

The American president, Franklin Roosevelt, was a friend of Winston Churchill and hated Hitler. Most Americans didn't want to fight a war in Europe, though, so all Roosevelt could do was send supplies.

Then Hitler made his second mistake.

The Japanese, who were allies of Hitler, wanted to be the greatest power in the Pacific Ocean, so without even declaring war they attacked the American naval base at Pearl Harbor, destroying some of America's strongest ships. Only afterwards did the Japanese declare war; and a few days later Hitler declared war on America as well. At last Roosevelt had a reason to join the war and come to Britain's aid.

Meanwhile, although France itself had been defeated, many Frenchmen wanted to go on fighting. Their leader, General de Gaulle, was living in exile in London, and made a broadcast to them on the radio.

"Whatever happens," he said, *"the flame of French resistance must not and shall not die."*

All over France, despite the terrible danger, French resistance fighters attacked the Germans and helped British pilots who had been shot down. Britain was no longer alone. The Allies – Britain, America, Russia and France – were ready to fight back.

But the war was no longer just a war in Europe. It was a war all over the world.

❖ War All over the World ❖

IN every corner of the globe armies fought each other and aeroplanes dropped bombs from the sky. In the east the Japanese conquered Singapore and attacked Burma. Thousands of Australians and New Zealanders went to fight them, along with Gurkhas, Indians and troops from the Caribbean. The war in the east was particularly hard because the Japanese treated their prisoners badly, often starving and beating them.

Meanwhile, British soldiers fought the Italians and Germans in North Africa. And it was there they won their first victory. Hitler sent his best soldier, Rommel, to fight them, and Rommel drove the British all the way back to Egypt. But a skilful British general, Bernard Montgomery, attacked Rommel at the Battle of El Alamein and defeated him. That was the turning point, and soon Britain's 8th Army, the Desert Rats, were advancing across the sands of the Sahara.

"Before Alamein," said Churchill afterwards, *"we never had a victory – after Alamein we never had a defeat."*

A year later, the British and Americans invaded Italy, where Hitler's ally Mussolini was still in charge. Mussolini surrendered and Hitler had to send his own army into Italy to fight the British and Americans. Though the Allies were still far from winning, Hitler no longer had everything his own way. And the weary people of Britain, huddling around their radios to hear the news, had something to celebrate at last.

❖ The Holocaust ❖

BUT the news from Germany was more terrible than ever. It was difficult to know exactly what was happening, because German radio only broadcast what the Nazis allowed. Gradually, however, an awful rumour started to come out. To begin with, people could hardly believe it, even of Hitler. But at last they realized it was true. Hitler had always hated the Jews, and now he had decided to kill them – all of them.

According to the Nazis the Jews weren't people at all, so they treated them like animals, starving the women and children, and sending the men to factories to work until they died. The countries Germany had invaded in eastern Europe – Poland, Ukraine and Russia – were full of Jewish towns and villages. Hitler ordered the Jews who lived there to be rounded up and sent to concentration camps, where they were beaten and starved.

Some Jews tried to hide. Anne Frank, a Jewish girl who lived in Holland, hid for two years in the attic of her father's office. But the Nazi secret police, the Gestapo, found her and sent her to a concentration camp as well.

Hitler's camps filled up with Jews, along with the other races he hated, like the Roma; and the other people he feared, like homosexuals. The Gestapo built a special camp called Auschwitz and sent Jews there to be killed. When they arrived at Auschwitz, families were told to have a shower. They put down their suitcases, took off their boots and clothes, and soldiers herded them into the bathrooms. But when the showers were switched on, it wasn't water that came out of the taps but poison gas.

To kill someone else is the worst crime a person can commit. For a government to commit murder is even worse – governments are there to protect people. For a government to exterminate a whole race – which is called genocide – is the most evil crime imaginable.

Ever since, Jews around the world have called what happened under Hitler the Holocaust. It was the worst crime in history and will never be forgotten. And when the Allies heard the rumour about what Hitler was doing, they knew it was more important than ever to defeat him.

❖ The War in the West ❖

FOR the moment, there was only one way for the British to attack Germany: from the air. So they sent planes to bomb German cities, just as Hitler had bombed London and Coventry.

Every night, people were woken by the sound of aeroplanes flying overhead. The British bombers were much bigger than German ones; the Lancaster had four engines and needed seven men to fly it. Even so, flying into Germany was terribly dangerous. Guns fired at the bombers from the ground, and German fighter planes pounced on them out of the darkness. Often, through the cockpit windows, pilots saw their friends crashing to the ground in flames.

But they never saw what their bombs did to the cities below them. Most of Berlin was destroyed. Düsseldorf looked like an ancient ruin no one had lived in for centuries. One night, in Dresden, so many bombs were dropped that they started a fire too hot to put out. Burning winds sucked bystanders into the flames, and afterwards nothing was left of Dresden but smoking ruins and cellars full of bodies.

Some people wondered if it was right for the British to bomb cities. Should Britain fight in the same way Hitler did? "Wars should be fought against soldiers in uniform," they said, "not old men and children." Most people, though, just thought how brave the bomber crews were.

In any case, Hitler soon found a way to retaliate. His scientists invented exploding rockets. People walking down the street in London would hear a sound like a lawnmower in the sky overhead, then the sound would cut out and a rocket would dive out of the clouds and crash with a huge explosion. People called the rockets doodlebugs because of the noise they made. They were even more frightening than air raids because they came without warning, so no one had a chance to take cover. Later, Hitler's scientists came up with an even bigger rocket, which they called the V-2.

Even though the Russians had started to beat Hitler, people worried that he might still win the war by inventing weapons no one could fight against. It became more important than ever to defeat him quickly.

❖ D-Day ❖

A T last Roosevelt and Churchill came up with a plan to invade northern France and attack Germany from there. The British army wasn't strong enough to do it by itself, so thousands of American soldiers arrived in Britain to help. After four years of war, the British were pinched and thin. They looked tired and their clothes were shabby. The Americans were much better fed and richer. They drank Coca-Cola, listened to jazz records and liked to show off to English girls.

"Overpaid!" the British grumbled. *"Over sexed! And over here!"*

All the same, they were grateful for the Americans' help. And soldiers of both armies, along with Canadian and French fighters, started preparing for the great invasion.

The Allied commander-in-chief, General Eisenhower, called the day planned for the invasion D-Day. The Allies tricked the Germans into thinking they were going to land near Calais, where the Channel was narrowest. Instead Eisenhower decided to invade Normandy, from where William the Conqueror had attacked Britain a thousand years before. During the night, landing craft set out across the English Channel towards five beaches which the planners code-named Utah, Omaha, Gold, Juno and Sword. Some of the soldiers remembered being rescued from Dunkirk four years earlier. Now they were going the other way, to win France back again. The weather was bad, and the landing craft – square boats designed to take as many soldiers and tanks as possible – heaved up and down in the waves. Many of the soldiers were seasick.

But at dawn they saw the coast ahead of them.

"Get ready!" shouted the officers.

As soon as the landing craft reached shallow water, ramps were let down with a splash, and the soldiers charged through the breakers and up the beach. Now they would find out whether the Germans were ready for them. Luckily the trick had worked and most of the German army was still waiting at Calais. And the night before, parachute troops had dropped from the air to capture bridges across all the important roads. The British and Canadians landed quite easily, but on one of the American beaches, Omaha, the Germans fought back and thousands of American soldiers were killed.

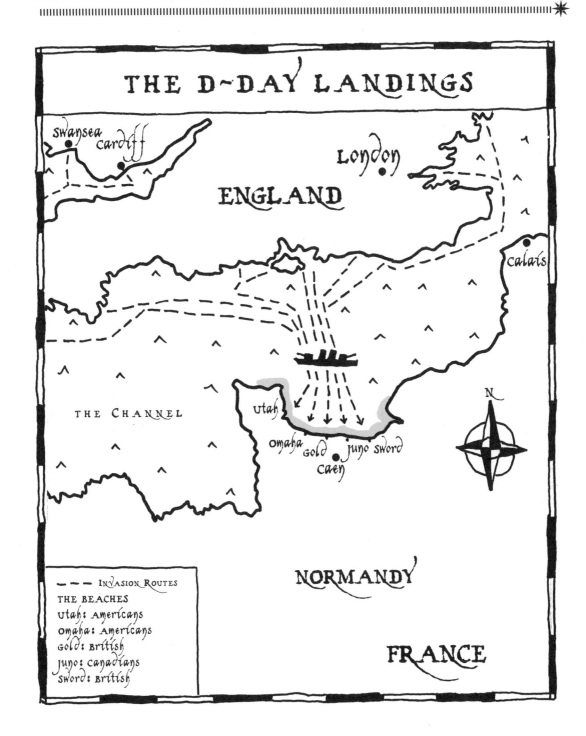

Next came the second part of the plan: to move inland and conquer France. The Allies needed a port to keep the army supplied, but the Germans still held all the ports, so the British built floating harbours, towed them across the Channel and anchored them by the beaches. Then ships could come alongside and unload all the food, bullets and spare petrol the army needed.

Inland, French families hung out British, French and American flags, and girls kissed the soldiers who came to free them from Nazi rule. Quite soon the Allies captured Paris, which became the capital of France again. Then they invaded Germany itself.

The Germans knew that with Russia, America and Britain against them, they had little chance of winning. They had even less food than the British, and their cities were in ruins. Even so, Hitler refused to give up. As the Russian army drew closer from the east, he hid in his concrete bunker under the streets of Berlin, shouted at his generals and made speeches blaming everyone but himself.

One day, the Allied soldiers reached Auschwitz. They found a fence of barbed wire and thousands of starving children in striped prison clothes. The children looked like walking skeletons, and hundreds of bodies lay in heaps around the gas chambers. When the soldiers pushed open the doors of the wooden huts where the prisoners lived, they found rows of Jewish men and women lying sick on their bunks, too weak even to call for help. Crows waited in the trees and everything stank of death.

Then the Allies knew that all the sacrifices of the past six years had been worthwhile. Hitler was so evil that he had to be defeated.

The Russians, advancing from the east, had the worst of the fighting, but at last they reached the first of the Americans, British and French advancing from the west. In the ruins of Berlin, where there wasn't a single building left standing, the Allied soldiers met, and the last German defenders came out of the rubble with their hands up.

But Hitler was not among them. He was already dead. He shot himself in the last hours of the war, and his soldiers burned his body.

❖ The Nuclear Bomb ❖

ALTHOUGH the war in Europe was over, the war against Japan still went on, because Japanese soldiers never surrendered but fought until they were killed. As the Americans advanced across the Pacific Ocean, the Japanese defended island after island – and each island meant another battle and more dead soldiers to send home to families in America. Meanwhile, British, Australian, Indian, Caribbean and African troops fought in the jungles of Burma, where it was so hot that weapons burned the soldiers' hands and flies buzzed incessantly around their heads.

The British general was called William Slim. He had once been an ordinary soldier, and knew what his men were suffering. Little by little he pushed the Japanese back, but still they refused to surrender. It seemed as if the war would drag on for years and thousands more soldiers be killed, so the Americans decided to end it once and for all by using a new and terrible weapon.

Their scientists had been working on an atom bomb. All of matter is made out of atoms, and splitting an atom releases huge amounts of energy. That energy can be used to run nuclear power stations, but Albert Einstein, the greatest scientist in the world, had realised that it could also be used to make a bomb.

One morning, Japanese in the city of Hiroshima looked up to see a single aeroplane flying overhead. Usually the American air force sent waves of bombers to attack them. A single plane couldn't mean an air raid, they thought, so most of them went on with what they were doing. Only a few kept watching. They saw a bomb drop from the plane and begin to fall. A moment later there was a bright flash of light. Before they could even hear the bang, most of the people of Hiroshima were dead.

From his cockpit, the American pilot saw a huge mushroom-shaped cloud rise into the air. It billowed up until it was as tall as a mountain. What have we done? he thought.

A few days later, the Americans dropped a second atom bomb on Nagasaki. Afterwards, when planes flew over to see what the two cities looked like, they found nothing left at all: no buildings, no trees, no people.

Japanese who went to visit Nagasaki said it was *"like a graveyard with not a tombstone standing"*. The atom bomb destroyed cities as if they had never been there.

And the terror it brought didn't even end with those huge explosions. In the weeks that followed, everyone who lived near Hiroshima or Nagasaki fell sick. Their skin began to peel off, then they started to vomit and died, for atom bombs released radiation, which caused radiation sickness and cancer.

Afterwards, Einstein would always regret that he had suggested making such a terrible weapon. But the Japanese knew they could not fight against atom bombs, so they surrendered. On 15 August 1945 the war in the east came to an end, and the Second World War was over.

The Great War – which people now call the First World War – had been terrible, but the Second World War was even worse. Around the world more than sixty million people had been killed – as many as there are living in the whole of Britain today. Cities had been destroyed, families uprooted, and races slaughtered.

The world had never seen such destruction before.

❖ The Welfare State ❖

IN Germany and Japan, the fascist leaders were captured and put on trial; and on victory night, fireworks were let off all over Britain. Soldiers came home to their families to see children they remembered as babies, and wives whose faces they had almost forgotten. But when the celebrations were over, they looked around and scratched their heads.

"Everything's changed," they said. "Where's the cinema? What's happened to the pub?"

The streets they knew were full of gaps where buildings had been bombed. Some of the soldiers found their homes gone, and their families living in temporary sheds. Everyone looked thin and tired.

"You wouldn't think we've just won a war," they said. "It feels more like we've been through a disaster!"

Factories had been bombed, shops were empty, and everything was shabby, for nothing had been mended for six years and there was no money to set things right. The war had cost a fortune, and Britain no longer had a fortune. Grey-faced and hungry, the British stood in queues to see the doctor, and in queues to buy bread. Everyone had thought food rationing would finish when the war was over; instead it got worse. Friends in Australia wrote about fresh fruit and meat. The British hadn't seen fresh fruit in years, and were only allowed to eat meat once or twice a week. At night cities stayed dark to save electricity. People looked sadly through magazines from before the war. Would they ever be able to afford new clothes again, new furniture, or new cars? They didn't feel like victors; they felt as if they were the ones who had been beaten.

"But at least we can make Britain fairer now," they told each other. "So much has been destroyed in the war, it's a chance for a fresh start."

And when the time came for a general election, they didn't choose Winston Churchill and the Conservatives. Instead, most people voted for the Labour Party and its leader, Clement Attlee.

"If there's one thing the war's taught us," they said, "it's to do things together."

The Labour government nationalized the coal mines and the railways, which meant that from now on they wouldn't be owned by bosses but by the whole country. Nye Bevan, a Welsh MP, started the National Health Service, so that everyone would be looked after when they were sick. Most people were proud of the NHS. But the Labour Party couldn't feed people, and it couldn't make them happy. The lights kept going out and, in wintertime, the old huddled under blankets because they couldn't afford coal for a fire. Everyone was grey, thin and ill.

The British had fought two great wars in thirty years, and they were exhausted.

❖ The End of the Empire ❖

AS soon as the war was over, Britain agreed it was time for India to become independent. The British Empire was the biggest there had ever been, and the British were proud of it. But in one way, there had been something wrong with it from the very start. People in Britain loved to talk about freedom, and believed everyone should have a say in choosing their government. So why shouldn't Indians have a say in choosing who governed *them*? And Africans? And Jamaicans?

The Indians had never lost their longing for freedom. "It's our right," they said. "Would the British want to be ruled by people from Delhi?"

They could see that the British ran India in a way that benefited themselves far more than the Indians. For example, cotton came from India, but Indians weren't allowed to build their own factories and make money selling cloth. They had to sell the raw cotton cheap to factories in Lancashire, and it was British factory owners who became rich.

But when Indians protested against the empire, the British government always stopped them. One day, at Amritsar, a British general ordered his soldiers to open fire on a crowd of unarmed men, women and children. The only place to take shelter was a well, and hundreds jumped into it and were drowned. The massacre at Amritsar was a bit like the Peterloo Massacre in Britain. It made people in India even more determined to change things.

Some of the British realized countries like India would have to be allowed to govern themselves one day, so they let Indians become judges and government officials. But just as in Ireland, change came very slowly, and it seemed to the Indians as if Britain would always find an excuse not to make them free. Some of them thought the only way to change things was by violence. However, the leader of the Indian reformers knew how damaging violence was. His name was Mohandas Gandhi and he refused to have anything to do with bombs or terror.

Gandhi had trained as a lawyer, but to show how close he was to ordinary Indian men and women, he dressed in a plain loincloth, ate simply, and gave no sign of being famous or important. Gandhi believed that the way to achieve justice was through peace and persuasion.

"Once fighting starts," he reminded his followers, "it's impossible to stop it. Violence only creates more violence!"

So instead of setting off bombs, his followers simply refused to obey British orders; and when Gandhi was sent to prison, he went on hunger strike and stopped eating until he almost died. Seeing how bravely he stood up to the British, more and more people joined Gandhi, and his Congress Party became strong and well organized.

During the Second World War, Indians stopped campaigning for freedom. Thousands of them joined the army and helped to fight the Japanese.

"Listen to Churchill's speeches!" they said. "The British are fighting for freedom, open elections and fair laws. That's exactly what we want in India as well!"

And when the war was over, the British agreed to grant India independence. But the difficulty was to decide how, for it was a huge country divided between many religions. Millions of Muslims lived alongside Hindus and Sikhs, but didn't want to be governed by them.

"All the leaders of the Congress Party are Hindus," the Muslims said nervously. "After independence they'll run India for themselves, and Muslims will be persecuted."

They were like the Protestants in Northern Ireland, who didn't want to live in a country where most people were Catholic.

"We want our own country," the Muslims said.

Everyone had forgotten the two lessons of toleration that John Locke had discovered centuries before – that religion should be kept apart from politics, and that people should respect each other's faiths.

And so India was divided, and a Muslim country called Pakistan was set up in the north (later, a third country called Bangladesh would be created as well). Muslims in the south sold their homes and set out for Pakistan, while Hindus in the north packed their bags and began the long walk south to India.

At midnight on 15 August 1947 India became free. It should have been a time of rejoicing. But instead, Muslims and Hindus began fighting. People walking north attacked people walking south.

"It's the Muslims' fault we have to leave our homes!" screamed the Hindus.

"The Hindus have taken our towns!" shouted the Muslims.

Gandhi was sad when he heard the news of fighting and death. He went on hunger strike to persuade Indians and Pakistanis to stop killing each other. But in the end Gandhi himself, who hated violence, was murdered by a Hindu terrorist who thought he had betrayed the Hindus.

Religion stops people thinking fairly because it makes them sure they're right and everyone else is wrong. India became free, but the moment of its freedom was spoiled by religion. Only Gandhi was wise enough to know that nobody understands everything, whatever religion they believe in. Once, somebody asked him if he was a Hindu. *"Yes, I am,"* he answered. *"But I am also a Christian, a Muslim, a Buddhist and a Jew."*

As we reach the last pages of this book, you will realize this is a story that doesn't have an end. The past turns into the present, and the present becomes the past. History goes on happening around us. And India and Pakistan are still quarrelling to this day.

When they saw that India was free to govern itself, the other countries of the empire demanded freedom as well. One by one, Kenya and Uganda, Jamaica, Trinidad and all the rest left to become new countries. Sometimes they fought wars to free themselves, and sometimes they became free peacefully. But sooner or later the Union Jacks were taken down from the government buildings, and new flags rose in their place. The British Empire was over.

Many in Britain were sorry to see it end. However, the truth was, Britain couldn't afford an empire any more. It cost a fortune to maintain armies in every continent in the world, to keep hundreds of ships sailing the seas, and to pay for officials, judges and teachers everywhere from St Kitts to Singapore – and the British didn't have a fortune any more. They were no longer the richest nation on earth.

Two new powers had appeared, and they were both much stronger. In the east was the communist empire of Stalin. And in the west was Britain's ally, the United States of America.

❖ The Cold War ❖

AMERICA and Russia couldn't have been more different. America was a democracy, Russia – the USSR or Soviet Union, as it was still called – a dictatorship. America was powerful because its businessmen and inventors had made it rich; the USSR was a communist country where no one was allowed to own anything. Americans lived as they pleased; people in the USSR did as the communists wanted. For as long as they were fighting Hitler together, America and the USSR were allies; but as soon as he was beaten, they became the deadliest of enemies. For the next forty years they lived on the brink of war.

At the end of the Second World War, the Americans advanced into Germany from the west, and the Russians from the east. When they met in the middle, Europe was divided in a line from north to south. Everything to the west became free and democratic like America, while the countries to the east – Czechoslovakia, Hungary, Romania, Bulgaria and Poland – were turned into communist states.

"An iron curtain has descended across the continent," said Winston Churchill sadly.

Germany was divided in two: West Germany was free, while East Germany became communist. Even the German capital, Berlin, was split in half, for the Russians built a wall through the middle to stop people moving to the west. There were machine guns on the wall, and anyone who tried to escape was shot.

In the west America's allies formed an alliance called NATO, the North Atlantic Treaty Organization, while the countries of the east joined an alliance with the USSR called the Warsaw Pact. People started preparing for a war between America and the USSR, but they quickly realized it would be even more terrible than the war against Hitler. The Americans already had atom bombs, and the Russians soon built A-bombs of their own. Then both sides invented H-bombs, which were even more powerful; missiles that could fly across continents in just a few minutes; and more missiles to shoot their enemies' missiles down.

It was like the time before the Great War when Britain and Germany had started a race to build battleships; but the American and Russian race was far more frightening, because their missiles could blow the whole world up a thousand times over. Five hundred years before, people had been amazed by cannon that shot a cannonball just a few hundred metres. Now the two superpowers had weapons that could destroy the whole planet. Were people getting too clever for their own good?

Children started having nightmares about atom bombs, dreaming they were living in a world ruined by a nuclear war. In their nightmares, cities were destroyed, millions died, the survivors were sick, and they lived in cellars in gangs, picking through ruined shops to find something to eat.

Fortunately the war never started. Both the Americans and Russians realized there could be no winners or losers in a nuclear war, for everything would be destroyed. So the years passed in a sort of war without fighting, and the superpowers' confrontation became known as the Cold War. During it, the Americans and Russians hardly spoke to each other. People in Poland couldn't watch American films or listen to British songs, while in America anyone who talked about sharing things or looking after the poor was accused of being a communist.

Because they didn't dare fight each other, the Americans and Russians got their friends and allies to wage wars for them, so communists and capitalists fought each other in Korea, Vietnam and Africa, using guns the Americans and Russians gave them. Just as the world had set up the League of Nations after the First World War, after the Second World War it started an organization called the United Nations to prevent wars from happening, but the United Nations was too weak to stop the superpowers quarrelling.

The Americans and Russians even carried on their rivalry in space. The Russians sent a man into space, using a rocket like the ones the Germans had designed to attack Britain. His name was Yuri Gagarin and he was the first astronaut. The Americans were furious that the Russians had beaten them at something, so they built an even bigger rocket, and in 1969 Neil Armstrong became the first man to land on the moon. Millions of people around the world watched on television as he set foot on its surface, and listened to the first words ever spoken on the moon.

"That's one small step for a man," Neil Armstrong said, *"one giant leap for mankind."*

The odd thing was that when astronauts looked back at the world from their spacecraft, they forgot about the quarrels of capitalists and communists, and the rivalry of America and the USSR. They just saw a small blue planet floating in an immense darkness, and wished the people who lived there could share it in peace.

❖ The Sixties ❖

BECAUSE of the rivalry between America and Russia, the people of Europe seemed much less important during the Cold War. That meant they had a chance to rebuild their countries after the terrible destruction of the two world wars. The Americans gave Europeans money to reconstruct factories, and it wasn't long before people started trading again, opening shops, repairing churches which had been bombed, and replacing homes which had been turned into rubble.

Europe started to get rich. Even Germany became wealthy, as the West Germans got rid of all traces of the Nazis, opened proper law courts, held elections, and made their country free and democratic, like Britain and France. The first half of the twentieth century was the most terrible Europe had ever known, but the second was the richest. And the people of Britain and Ireland became richer too.

In 1952 King George VI died and his daughter Elizabeth became Britain's first queen since Victoria. A Scot called John Logie Baird had invented television before the war, and thousands bought sets to watch Elizabeth's coronation.

But just as they had after the Napoleonic Wars and the Great War, many people felt restless after the Second World War. In particular, the young felt dissatisfied. They were fed up with hearing their parents talk about the empire, and tell stories about what it had been like in the war. They knew that Americans didn't talk about the past, but about the future. Americans challenged things rather than doing what they were told. American kids even had their own music, rock 'n' roll, which was loud and exciting. Grown-ups hated it, but the kids didn't care!

Copying the Americans, young people in Britain started wearing jeans and listening to rock 'n' roll. Four boys in Liverpool started their own band to play American-style music. They called themselves the Beatles and, during the 1960s, became the most famous band in the world. Other British bands like the Rolling Stones and the Who became world-famous too. Soon British music was just as important as American, and British kids were just as rebellious.

Boys let their hair grow long.

"You look like a girl!" their fathers shouted.

Girls no longer wanted just to get married and have babies. "Why shouldn't we go to university and get jobs?" they complained. "Why shouldn't we be treated equally?"

Young people in the sixties thought everything was going to change for the better. They would be free, and have a chance to do what they wanted. A miner's son could make a fortune; a shopkeeper's daughter could become a famous actor or entertainer.

And for a time, it seemed as if everything really could change for the better. But something was still wrong. They might have been rich and free, but the people of Britain were not content. They couldn't get used to the idea that their country wasn't so important any more.

❖ Britain in Trouble ❖

"WE used to have the biggest empire in the world," the British grumbled. "Now look at us!"

In just fifty years Britain had changed from being the most powerful country on earth to a small island on the edge of the Atlantic Ocean. The British didn't know where they belonged. The other countries in Europe started a club called the European Economic Community, but though Britain applied to join, the French wouldn't let them. Most British people weren't that keen either, and even after 1973, when Britain at last joined the EEC – which later became known as the European Union – they kept complaining about it.

"We're not really Europeans," they said. "We're different! Our empire used to cover the whole world!"

Their memories were like a burden the British couldn't put down. If you've run half the planet, it's difficult to get used to being a small island. France became richer than Britain; so did Germany, Japan and Italy. British factories were old-fashioned, and British designers couldn't come up with new ideas. Most of all, the unions seemed to have forgotten that unless their companies made money, Britain would keep on falling behind. They demanded pay rises even when their companies couldn't afford it, and called strikes for no reason at all.

"Britain's rich!" they said. "There's plenty to go round!"

Too much power always spoils people. And when they realized they could stop the whole country working, power spoiled the unions as well.

The coal miners went on strike. Soon there was no coal to run the power stations, so the electricity went off. Families sat huddled around candles in the cold and dark. Without electricity they couldn't even switch on the television or play records. There wasn't enough electricity for factories, so the government announced people would only work three days a week instead of five. Dustbin men went on strike, and rubbish piled up in the streets. Gravediggers went on strike, and bodies were left unburied.

That wasn't the only trouble Britain and Ireland faced. Fighting started again in Northern Ireland. Some Protestants began persecuting their Catholic neighbours, and though the British army was sent in to keep the peace, the Catholics thought it was there to help the Protestants. If they had listened to Parnell or Gandhi they might have fought for independence by peaceful means. Instead, they began a terrorist group they called the Provisional IRA to attack soldiers and set off bombs. They killed people in London and Manchester, in Belfast, Londonderry (which Catholics call Derry) and Enniskillen.

By the end of the 1970s it felt as if everything was going wrong again.

"It's all up with us now," people said gloomily. "Britain's finished!"

Maybe the two world wars had been too much for the British. Instead of looking for new things, they clung to old traditions, as if they knew their greatest days lay in the past and nothing exciting would ever happen again.

It felt as if the story of Britain was over.

❖ Immigration ❖

BUT Britain's story wasn't over. It was about to start all over again.

You might have thought that after the empire, people in places like India and the Caribbean would be angry, and want nothing more to do with the British. Instead, from all over the empire, Africans, West Indians and Asians set out for Britain to find a new life. And they brought new life to Britain as well.

The people of Britain had always been a mixture of different races: English, Welsh, Irish and Scots; Celts, Romans, Saxons, Vikings and Normans; Huguenots and Jews. That was what made them so special, for to be British didn't mean belonging to a particular race; it meant sharing a pride in the free life you could live here.

The first ship to arrive from Jamaica was called the *Empire Windrush*. The Jamaicans coming to Britain brought thick coats because they knew it would be cold. Some of them were doctors or teachers, and carefully packed their certificates, dreaming of the jobs they would find when they reached London. On the journey they talked about the country they were travelling to. They had all learned the story of Britain in school. They knew about Simon de Montfort and Queen Elizabeth I, about the civil wars and the Glorious Revolution. They knew about the Great Reform Act, the unions and the suffragettes.

"The British believe everyone is equal," they said. "It doesn't matter that we're black. We'll all have an equal chance."

"The British discovered how important it is to be tolerant," said others. "We'll be able to live the way we want."

"The British sailed all over the world to discover other nations. They'll be interested in our West Indian culture."

"I want to start a business," said one man. "That's easy in Britain. Think of the railways and factories! A new idea always has a chance in Britain."

But when they reached London, the immigrants had a terrible shock. London was not just cold but shabby. The great buildings were black with soot, and passers-by stared crossly at them.

"You can't stay here," snapped landladies. "I don't want black people in my house!"

"You should learn to talk proper," snarled pub landlords. "I can't understand a word you say!"

"Start a business?" laughed bosses when they asked for work. "Become a teacher? All you're good for is sweeping my floor!"

The West Indians moved to Brixton, in south London, where they could be closer together and felt safe.

"What's happened to the British?" they asked each other sadly. "When did they forget that everyone's equal?"

"When did they forget about toleration?"

"When did they stop being interested in new ideas?"

Asians moved to Britain from India, Pakistan and Bangladesh, and from Uganda, in Africa, where many Indians had lived during the British Empire. They found the same thing.

"What's happened to the British?" the Asians asked. "When did they become so small-minded?"

But gradually, as the years went by, things began to change. The new immigrants brought new ideas, new music, new talents and energy, just as the Huguenots and Jews had done before them. And the sound of new voices and the sight of new faces woke Britain up. How could it live in the past when the British looked so new?

It was time for the story of Britain to begin again.

❖ A New Start ❖

FIRST the British had to remember how to make money and become rich. In 1979 Margaret Thatcher was elected prime minister. She was the first woman prime minister Britain ever had (eleven years later, Mary Robinson became Ireland's first woman president). Her father had run a grocer's shop, and she believed in hard work and looking after yourself.

Many people were angry at the things Margaret Thatcher did. Because she wanted to stop the unions striking, she closed down the coal mines. Villages where miners had dug coal for generations were ruined, and thousands of families lost everything. She wanted everyone to be proud of Britain, so she fought a war to keep the Falkland Islands, one of the last, leftover bits of the empire.

"She shouldn't teach people to like war again," some said. "Haven't we learned that war is terrible?"

All the same, Margaret Thatcher did remind everyone how Britain had become rich in the first place, and she did stop the unions using their power unfairly.

"Britain won't stay rich just because we want it to," she argued. "We have to compete with other countries in the world. If we don't work hard and make money, we'll soon be poor."

And little by little Britain started getting richer again. New buildings were built, and the old ones cleaned. The last scars of the war were healed. At night in British cities you could hear the sound of laughter again, of people drinking, talking and becoming excited – just as they had in the old days before the empire. British businessmen came up with new ideas, and British scientists made new discoveries. In 1990 Tim Berners-Lee invented the World Wide Web, and the Internet was born.

At last politicians tried to sort out how the constitution worked. A new Labour prime minister, Tony Blair, stopped aristocrats from voting in the House of Lords, and Parliament moved a step nearer to proper democracy. Then he turned to Scotland and Wales. For years many Scots and Welsh had complained about the way Britain was governed.

"Why can't we run ourselves?" they asked.

Scotland and England had prospered as one in the empire. But since the empire was over, it was time to think again about how they worked together; and so, after three hundred years, a Scottish Parliament was elected and the Scots took over their own affairs again. Wales had never had its own parliament, and never been treated properly as the fourth nation of Britain, and at last that was put right. An assembly was built in Cardiff so the Welsh could elect representatives to discuss their own affairs.

In Northern Ireland, after many years of violence, known as the Troubles, the fighting finally came to an end. The terrorists announced that they would stop bombing, and the republicans sat down with the Irish and British governments to discuss how Northern Ireland should be run in future. Slowly peace came to the provinces of the north.

Meanwhile, the people of the Irish Republic had grown richer, now they were independent. The bitterness of the old days began to fade. They could live in peace and dignity with the British at last. And very gradually the new inhabitants of Britain – black, Asian or Chinese – were accepted as equal citizens, free to play their part in Britain's story.

It almost felt as if the British Empire had been a long dream. And the people of Britain had woken up to find themselves renewed and different, ready for the challenges that lay ahead.

❖ What Next? ❖

HISTORY never stops. This book doesn't have an end.

Once, all the stories you have just read weren't history; they were things that were happening to people like you.

Saxon boys heard the news that the Normans had won the Battle of Hastings and wondered what it meant for them. People in Yorkshire heard that King Charles I had been executed and wondered if the civil wars would go on, and whether Britain would be a republic for ever. When children in Coventry cowered in air-raid shelters with German bombs exploding above them, they didn't know if Coventry would even exist in future, if Britain itself would survive or if everyone would be killed by bombs.

They didn't know what the future held, and nor do we. By the time you have finished reading this book, there will be even more stories to tell. I don't know what they are, but I think I can guess what some of them will be about.

Perhaps, in the years to come, there will be more change in the way the people of Britain and Ireland govern themselves. Our relationship with Europe might shift; there might be change in Scotland, Wales or Northern Ireland. The important thing is that the people of Britain and Ireland share these islands in peace, remembering the stories, both good and bad, they have written together.

In 1989 the Cold War came to an end. People in Poland, Czechoslovakia and Russia were fed up living under the communists. They could see countries in the west getting richer and richer. Men and women in West Germany and France were allowed to say what they liked, read what books they chose, and travel where they pleased. Why couldn't everyone be as free as them?

In the communist countries of Europe citizens began demonstrating against the police. In Berlin, they climbed up onto the wall the communists had built between east and west, and pulled it down. One by one, the communist governments resigned. Although China remained communist, the great rivalry between democracy and communism was over.

That left America by far the strongest country in the world, and too much power always spoils people. Instead of using its power wisely, America began wars and angered its friends. Once, Americans had been loved all over the world; now, many started to hate them.

In particular some Muslims hated America for supporting Israel, the Jewish country that had been established in Palestine in the middle of their lands. Palestine was where the stories of the Jewish and Christian holy books took place. The British ruled it at the end of the Second World War, and because the Jews had suffered so terribly in the Holocaust, Britain and America agreed to give them a home there. But to do it they drove away the Muslim Arabs who had lived in Palestine for centuries, and after that many Muslims distrusted the west.

"We want nothing to do with America," they said. And they went back to studying the Koran, and praying for a return to the old ways.

Religion can be dangerous; it can persuade people to do things they'd never normally consider. A few fanatics became terrorists and destroyed the World Trade Center in New York. Some British Muslims even set off bombs in London, killing innocent passers-by. Those arguments haven't ended, and wars will go on being fought over them.

But the greatest challenge of all is what is happening to our planet, earth. In the industrial revolution people started digging up coal and burning it in steam engines. To make electricity, even more coal was dug up, along with oil and gas, to run power stations. Cars and aeroplanes were invented, and they burned oil as well.

"What marvellous inventions!" everyone said. "We've never had so much power before!"

"We've never been able to travel so easily!"

"To live so comfortably!"

No one realized that burning coal, oil and gas was doing terrible damage. Released into the air, the carbon locked up in them began to heat up the earth. Because of that the climate has started to change. Everywhere is getting hotter. The ice caps at the North and South Poles are melting, and the oceans rising. Perhaps people have been too clever for their own good. Perhaps our inventions, which have made life so much better, will end up destroying us.

Or perhaps we will find new answers to our problems. Perhaps we will make power from the wind and sun, and start to look after our country-side, which we have farmed for thousands of years. Perhaps we will learn to share our wealth more fairly. Perhaps we will remember how to respect each others' beliefs.

And then the people of Britain and Ireland can go on living peacefully in these islands, telling the stories that made us what we are, and writing the new story that will be our future.

TIMELINE

1909 ❖ Louis Blériot becomes the first man to fly across the Channel.

1914–1918 ❖ Britain and France fight the Great War against Germany. In 1916 thousands are killed and wounded at the Battle of the Somme.

1916 ❖ Irish soldiers try to start a rebellion in the Easter Rising.

1917 ❖ Lenin and the communists start a revolution in Russia, which they rename the USSR or Soviet Union.

1918 ❖ Women are finally allowed to vote, and the vote is given to all men as well, so Britain becomes a true democracy. A year later, Nancy Astor becomes the first woman MP.

1919 ❖ John Alcock, from Manchester, and Arthur Brown, from Glasgow, are the first to fly across the Atlantic Ocean.

1922 ❖ Treaty passed to make Ireland independent as the Irish Free State, but its first prime minister, Michael Collins, is killed the same year, and a civil war goes on until 1923.

1926 ❖ Unions call a general strike, but it lasts only ten days.

1929 ❖ The Wall Street Crash starts the Great Depression in America. It soon spreads across the world.

1933 ❖ Adolf Hitler becomes chancellor of Germany.

1936 ❖ Unemployed men from Jarrow march to London to demand work.

1938 ❖ Neville Chamberlain agrees to let Hitler take over part of Czechoslovakia.

1939–1945 ❖ The Second World War.

1940 ❖ The Germans attack Holland, Belgium and France. The British army is rescued from Dunkirk by "little ships" sailing across the Channel. Hitler fails to beat the RAF in the Battle of Britain, and starts to bomb British cities instead.

1941 ❖ Hitler attacks the USSR, which becomes an ally of Britain. Then the Japanese attack the USA at Pearl Harbor, so the Americans join the Allies as well.

1942 ❖ Montgomery and the Desert Rats defeat the Germans in Africa at the Battle of El Alamein.

1943 ❖ British aeroplanes bomb German cities.

1944 ❖ The British and Americans land in France on D-Day, and go on to capture Paris and free France, whose resistance fighters have been struggling against the Germans for four years.

1945 ❖ Berlin, the German capital, is captured, Hitler commits suicide and Germany surrenders. The Americans drop atom bombs on two Japanese cities, and the Japanese surrender as well.

1945–1951 ❖ The Labour government led by Clement Attlee nationalizes the railways and coal mines, and Nye Bevan starts the National Health Service.

1947 ❖ Gandhi wins

independence for India, which is divided into two countries, India and Pakistan. Later, a third country, Bangladesh, is formed as well. In the following years, the rest of the British Empire wins independence.

1945–1991 ❖ During the Cold War, America and the west of Europe are separated from the USSR, which runs a communist empire in the east of Europe, by the "iron curtain". Each side makes thousands of nuclear weapons, but fortunately they are never used.

1948 ❖ The *Empire Windrush* arrives in London from Jamaica, bringing West Indian immigrants to Britain. In the years that follow, immigrants will arrive from India, Bangladesh, Pakistan, Africa and China.

1952 ❖ Elizabeth II becomes queen.

1962 ❖ The Beatles are formed in Liverpool, and go on to become the world's biggest band.

1966 ❖ Fighting begins between Catholics and Protestants in Northern Ireland.

1969 ❖ The American astronaut Neil Armstrong becomes the first man to set foot on the moon.

1973 ❖ Britain joins the European Union, which is known at the time as the European Economic Community or Common Market.

1979 ❖ Margaret Thatcher, a Conservative, becomes the first woman prime minister of Britain. Five years later, she takes on the coal miners, who go on strike but are forced to return to work.

1989 ❖ The Berlin Wall falls and the communist countries of eastern Europe join the west. Two years later the communists lose power in the USSR, which changes its name back to Russia.

1990 ❖ Tim Berners-Lee invents the World Wide Web.

1998 ❖ The Good Friday agreement ends the troubles in Northern Ireland.

1999 ❖ The new Scottish Parliament and Welsh Assembly meet for the first time. In the same year, aristocrats lose their place in the House of Lords.

INDEX

A

aeroplanes 288–9, 303, 340
  Battle of Britain 305–7
Afghanistan 252
Agincourt, Battle of 74, 84
Albert, Prince 246, 247, 255, 272
Alcock, John 288, 340
Alfred the Great 14, 15, 18
America, discovery of 80, 84
American colonies 124, 139, 198
American Revolution 203–4, 224
Anderson, Elizabeth Garrett 267
Anglo-Saxons 11–15, 16, 18, 23, 25–9
Anne of Cleves 103–4, 130
Anne, Queen 168, 169, 184, 186, 187, 224
Arbroath, Declaration of 58, 84
aristocrats 191, 230, 335
Arkwright, Richard 237
Armstrong, Neil 327, 341
Astor, Nancy 287, 340
atomic bombs 319–20, 326
Attlee, Clement 321, 341
Augustine 13, 18
Australia 201–2, 224

B

Bacon, Sir Francis 156–7, 173
Baird, John Logie 329
Balliol, John 54, 83
Ban, Donald 33, 83
Bangladesh 324
Bank of England 189
Banks, Sir Joseph 201
Bannockburn, Battle of 57–8, 84

Beatles 275, 329, 341
Becket, Thomas 22, 36–8, 71, 83
Bede 13, 14, 18
Bell, Alexander Graham 287
Berners-Lee, Tim 335, 341
Bevan, Nye 274, 322, 341
Bill of Rights 170
Bismarck, Otto von 277
Black Death 66–7, 68, 84, 159
Black, Joseph 206
black people
  immigrants 333–4
  slavery 179–82, 221–2
The Black Prince 20, 64–5, 68, 84
Blair, Tony 335
Blenheim Palace 186
Blériot, Louis 288, 340
Bloody Assizes 167
Boleyn, Anne 99, 100, 101, 103, 104, 112, 130
Bonnie Prince Charlie 194–6, 224
books 81–2
Bosworth Field, Battle of 79, 84
Bothwell, Earl of 116
Boudicca 11
Boycott, Charles 261
Boyle, Robert 157
Boyne, Battle of the 170, 174, 211
British Empire 198–200, 201–2, 205, 252–8, 323, 325, 336
  and Ireland 290, 291
Brontë, Charlotte 247
Brown, Arthur 288, 340
Bruce, Robert 20, 56–8, 84, 114
Brunel, Isambard Kingdom 226, 239
Byron, Lord 177, 223

C

Cade, Jack 75
Caesar, Julius 10, 15, 18
Calcutta, Black Hole of 197
Calvin, John 98, 104, 114
Canada 198, 204
Catherine of Aragon 99, 100, 101, 104, 108, 130
cathedral architecture 36
Catholicism 108–9, 110
  and Charles II 164–5
  and Elizabeth I 112–13
  end of laws against 233–4
  in Ireland 211–12, 233–4, 331–2
  and James II 167–9
  and science 156
Cavaliers 143, 144
Caxton, William 81–2
Chadwick, Edwin 245
Chamberlain, Neville 301, 302, 303, 340
Charles I, King 140–2, 143–4, 146, 147, 148, 164, 173
Charles II, King 149–50, 151–2, 157, 163–5, 167, 173–4
  the Restoration 154–5
Charles V, Emperor 89
Chartists 263, 272
Chaucer, Geoffrey 21
  The Canterbury Tales 71, 82, 84
child labour 241
China 126
cholera 245
Christian Church
  Anglo-Saxons 13, 18
  Catholicism 109, 110, 112–13
  and Henry II 35, 36–8
  Puritans 136
  the Reformation 96, 97–8, 101, 130
  Romans 11
church architecture 36, 80, 321

Church of England 104-5, 112, 130, 136, 164, 165, 167. 168, 172
Churchill, John, Duke of Marlborough 186, 224
Churchill, Winston 274, 301, 303, 305, 307, 316
civil wars 143-5, 146-7, 156, 213
Clarkson, Thomas 222
climate change 338-9
Clive, Robert 199, 224
Cnut 15, 16, 18
Cold War 326-8, 329, 337, 341
Collins, Michael 291, 340
Columbus, Christopher 80, 84, 124, 151
communists 263-4, 292-5, 298, 300, 326, 327, 337, 340
compasses 48-9
Conservatives 265
Cook, Captain James 176, 201, 224
Covenanters 141, 143, 144, 146, 149-50, 165, 173
Coventry 309
Cranmer, Thomas 101, 105, 110, 130
Crécy, Battle of 63, 64, 84
crime and criminals 191, 192-3, 202
Crimean War 248-51, 272
Cromwell, Oliver 144, 146, 147, 149, 150-2, 164, 173, 213
Cromwell, Thomas 100, 101, 104, 130
Crusades 39, 40-1, 42, 83
Culloden, Battle of 195-6
Cumberland, Duke of 195, 196
Czechoslovakia 301, 305, 337

D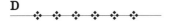

D-Day 316-17
Da Vinci, Leonardo 89-90
Dalrymple, John 183, 184
Danes 14, 15, 18
Darby, Abraham 237
Darnley, Lord 115-16
dates 15-16

Davison, Emily 268
De Montfort, Simon 46-7, 50-1, 83, 140
Defoe, Daniel 190
Despenser, Hugh 59, 60
Dickens, Charles 244
Diggers 149
Disraeli, Benjamin 227, 255, 265, 272
Domesday Book 27-8, 83
Drake, Sir Francis 87, 119-20, 124, 125, 126
Dudley, Robert 113
Dutch wars 163, 173-4

E

East India Company 126, 130, 199-200, 205
Edinburgh 205
Edward the Confessor 16, 17, 18
Edward I, King 47, 50-5, 56-7, 62, 72, 83, 140
Edward II, King 57-8, 59-61, 72, 84
Edward III, King 60, 62-4, 68, 72, 79, 84
Edward IV, King 75-6, 77, 84, 130
Edward VI, King 103, 105, 108
Edwardians 269-71
Einstein, Albert 319, 320
Eisenhower, General 316
El Alamein, Battle of 313, 341
Elizabeth I, Queen 86, 88, 103, 112-13, 119-25, 126, 129, 130, 135
and Mary Queen of Scots 114-17, 119
Elizabeth II, Queen 329, 341
Engagers 146-7
Engels, Friedrich 263-4, 272, 292
Erasmus, Desiderius 81
Essex, Robert Devereux, Earl of 122, 130
Ethelred the Unready 15

European Union 331, 341
Exclusion Crisis 164-5, 174

F

factories 237-8, 240, 241-5
Falkland Islands 335
Faraday, Michael 287
Fawcett, Millicent 267
Fawkes, Guy 138
Field of the Cloth of Gold 93
First World War 278-86, 290, 294, 340
Flamsteed, John 157
Flodden, Battle of 91-2
Ford, Henry 296
Fox, Charles 208
France 89-90, 303, 305, 316-18
Francis I, King of France 89-90, 91, 93, 130
Frank, Anne 314
French Revolution 208, 209-10, 211, 213, 224
French Revolutionary wars 213, 214-20, 224
Frobisher, Martin 124

G

Gagarin, Yuri 327
Galileo 156, 173
Gallipoli campaign 283-4
Gandhi, Mohandas 274, 323-4, 325, 332, 341
Gaskell, Elizabeth 244
Gaveston, Piers 59, 60
general strike 294-5
genocide 314
George I, King 184, 187, 194
George II, King 187, 194
George III, King 176, 187, 206, 207-8, 224
George IV, King (the Prince Regent) 187, 207-8, 224, 229, 235
George VI, King 309, 329

Germany 270, 329
  Berlin Wall 326, 337, 341
  Cold War 326–8
  First World War 277–86
  Nazi 297–302
  Second World War 301–20,
  321, 326
Gladstone, William 227, 265,
  272
Glencoe massacre 183–4, 224
Globe theatre 128–9, 130
Glorious Revolution 167–71,
  174, 183, 186, 188, 191
Godwinson, Harold 16–17, 18,
  23, 25–6, 33, 50
Gothic architecture 36, 80, 83
Great Depression 296–7
Great Exhibition 246–7, 252,
  272
Great War 272, 278–86, 290,
  294, 340
Grey, Edward 278
Grey, Lady Jane 86, 108–9, 130
Gruffudd ap Llywelyn 33
Gunpower Plot 136, 137–8, 173
guns 73, 90

H

Hadrian's Wall 11, 12, 18
Hardrada , Harald 16, 23
Hargreaves, James 237
Harvey, William 157, 173
Hastings, Battle of 25–6
Hawkins, John 124
Henry I, King 29, 30
Henry II, King 20, 31–2, 33, 50,
  83, 122
  and the Church 35, 36–8
  and Ireland 34–5
Henry III, King 46–7, 50, 83
Henry IV, King 72, 73, 74, 84
Henry V, King 72, 74, 84
Henry VI, King 72, 74, 75, 76,
  84
Henry VII, King (Henry
  Tudor) 79, 80, 84, 89–90,
  91, 130
Henry VIII, King 86, 91, 93–95,
  99–105, 108, 112, 114,

122, 130
Hereward the Wake 27
highwaymen 193
Hindus in India 324–5
Hitler, Adolf 297, 298–9, 300–2,
  305, 309, 310, 311, 314, 315,
  318, 340–1
Holbein, Hans 93, 103
Holocaust 314, 318
Hotspur (Henry Percy) 72, 84
Howard, Catherine 104
Huguenots 166
Hume, David 205
Hundred Years War 62–5, 72,
  74, 75, 84
Hunt, Henry "Orator" 230–1
Huskisson, William 239
Hutton, James 205
Hywel Dda 15

I

immigration 333–4, 341
India 126, 130, 197, 198,
  199–200, 224, 269
  Amritsar massacre 323
  independence 323–5, 341
Indian Mutiny 252–4, 272
Industrial Revolution 236,
  237–8, 338
internet 335, 341
Ireland 12
  Christianity 11, 13, 18
  civil war and
  independence 289, 290–1,
  340
  Cromwell's army in 149
  Elizabethan 122–3, 130
  English conquest of 34–5,
  83
  famine 259–60, 272
  and the Glorious
  Revolution 171
  Home Rule for 261–2
  Northern Ireland 290–1,
  331–2, 336, 341
  Phoenix Park murders 262,
  272
  the United Irishmen
  211–12, 224

Vikings 15, 34
Isabella the She-Wolf 60–1, 84
Israel 338

J

Jacobites 184, 187, 194–6, 224,
  229
Jamaica 151, 180, 333
James II, King 164–5, 166,
  167–71, 174, 184, 186, 211
James IV, King of Scotland
  91–2, 114, 130
James the Pretender 184, 187,
  194
James V, King of Scotland 114
James VI and I, King 117, 130,
  135–6, 140, 173
Japan 319–20, 321
Jarrow March 297
Jazz Age 289
Jefferson, Thomas 203–4
Jeffreys, George 167–8
Jews 51, 52–3, 83, 151, 299, 338
  the Holocaust 314, 318
Joan of Arc 75
Johnson, Amy 289

K

Kay, John 237
Keats, John 223
Keir Hardie, James 265–6, 272
Kingsley, Charles 244
knights 64
Knox, John 87, 114, 115, 116

L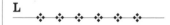

Labour governments 321–2,
  341
Labour Party 265–6, 272, 294
Lackland, King John 41, 43,
  44–5, 50, 83, 140

Laud, William, Archbishop of Canterbury 140, 141
League of Nations 286, 301
Lenin, Vladimir Ulyanov 292, 340
Levellers 146, 149, 151
Liberal Party 265, 266, 294
Light Brigade, Charge of the 248-9, 250, 272
Liverpool, Lord 232, 272
LLoyd George, David 266, 272
Llywelyn ap Gruffudd 50-1, 83
Locke, John 172
London
    the Blitz 276, 308-9
    Elizabethan 126-7
    factories 244
    Georgian 189
    Globe Theatre 128-9, 130
    the Great Fire 161-2
    Huguenots 166
    plague 159-60
    share trading 190
London, Tower of 77-8
Louis XIV, King of France 164, 166, 168, 186, 209
Louis XVI, King of France 209, 210, 224
Loveless, George 243
Luddites 242
Luther, Martin 97-8, 104, 130

M ❖ ❖ ❖ ❖ ❖ ❖

MacAlpin, Kenneth 14-15, 18
Macdonald, Flora 196
Magellan, Ferdinand 124
Magna Carta 44-5, 46, 50, 83
Malcolm IV, King of Scotland 33, 83
Marconi, Guglielmo 289
Marx, Karl 263-4, 272, 292
Mary of Guise 114
Mary I, Queen (Bloody Mary) 108, 109, 110-11, 112, 130
Mary II, Queen 168, 170, 174, 184
Mary Queen of Scots 86, 113, 114-17, 119, 130
Matilda 30, 31-2, 34, 83

Mayflower 139, 173
merchants 126-7, 188
Mompesson, William 160
monasteries 13, 14
    dissolution of 101-2
Monck, General 153, 154, 174
money 188-90
Monmouth Rebellion 167, 174
More, Thomas 86, 102, 130
Mortimer, Roger 60-1, 84
music 289, 329, 341
Muslims 40-1, 338
    in India 324-5

N ❖ ❖ ❖ ❖ ❖ ❖

Napoleon Bonaparte 213-15, 216-20, 224
National Health Service 322
navy 93, 229, 277
    Napoleonic wars 214-15
    Scottish 91
Nelson, Horatio 177, 178, 213, 214-15, 224
New Model Army 144, 146, 147, 148, 149, 152, 154
New Zealand 201
Newton, Isaac 157-8
Nightingale, Florence 250-1, 272
Nonconformists 172
Norman Conquest 16-17, 18, 23-6, 27, 33
Northern Ireland 291, 331-2, 336, 341
nuclear weapons 319-20, 326

O ❖ ❖ ❖ ❖ ❖ ❖

O'Connell, Daniel 226, 232, 233-4, 272
Offa's Dyke 12, 18
Ordainers 59, 84
Owain Glyn Dwr 21, 72-3, 84
Owain of Gwynedd 34, 50, 83
Owen, Wilfred 282

P ❖ ❖ ❖ ❖ ❖ ❖

Pakistan 324, 325
Pankhurst, Emmeline 227, 267-8, 272
Parliament 46-7, 50, 68
    and the American colonies 203
    aristocrats in 191, 230, 335
    and Charles I 140-2
    and Charles II 164, 165
    and the Civil War 143, 144
    and Cromwell 147, 151
    and George III 207-8
    and the Glorious Revolution 171
    the Good Parliament 68, 84
    Great Reform Act 235-6, 263
    and the Gunpowder Plot 137-8
    the Long Parliament 153
    Pride's Purge 147
    the Rump 150, 153, 154
    Scottish 183, 185, 335-6, 341
    Toleration Act 172, 174
Parnell, Charles Stewart 261-2, 332
Parr, Katherine 104, 105
Patrick, Saint 11, 18
Paxton, Joseph 246-7, 272
Peasants' Revolt 68-70, 71
Peel, Robert 245, 272
Pepys, Samuel 161-2
Peterloo Massacre 230-2, 272
Petition of Right 140, 141, 173
Picts 11, 12
Pilgrimage of Grace 102, 130
pirates 192
Pitt, William (the Elder) 176, 198, 212
Pitt, William (the Younger) 213-14, 221
plague 159-60
    the Black Death 66-7, 68, 84, 159
Poland 301-2, 337
poor people 191, 192, 244-5, 266
Popish Plot 165, 174
Princes in the Tower 21, 77-8

printing press 81-2
Protestants 98-9
    and Bloody Mary 110-11
    and the Glorious
        Revolution 167-8
    in Ireland 122-3, 212,
        331-2
    in Scotland 114
Puritans 136, 139, 140, 143,
    149-50, 164
Pym, John 141, 142

R

radar 303, 305
radio 289
railways 239-40, 272
Raleigh, Sir Walter 124, 126
Reformation 96, 97-8, 101,
    130
Remembrance Sunday 286
Renaissance 81
Restoration 154-5
Rhodes, Cecil 255, 272
Rhodri Mawr 15, 18
Richard II, King 68, 69-70,
    72, 84
Richard III, King 76, 77-8, 79,
    84
Richard the Lionheart 20,
    38-9, 41, 42, 43, 44, 52, 83
Richard of York 75, 84
Rizzio, David 115-16
Robespierre, Maximilien 210
Robin Hood 42-3, 83
Robinson, Mary 335
Romans 10-11, 18, 81
Romantic movement 223
Roosevelt, Franklin D. 316
Roundheads 143, 144
Royal Society 157
Rupert, Prince 143
Russell, Lord John 235-6
Russia 216-17, 248-9, 252,
    294-5, 300
    the USSR and the Cold
        War 326-8
Russian Revolution 292-3,
    340
Rye House Plot 165

S

Saladin 41, 83
Sancho, Ignatius 176, 221
scientists 156-8, 173, 205
Scotland 14-15, 18, 337
    and Britishness 229
    Church of 172
    Covenanters 141, 143, 144,
        146, 149-50, 165, 173
    and Edward I 54-5, 83
    Enlightenment 205-6
    Jacobite rebellions 187,
        194-6
    James IV 91-2
    James VI 135
    Mary Queen of Scots 86,
        113, 114-17
    Normans in 33, 83
    Parliament 183, 185, 335-6,
        341
    Robert Bruce 20, 56-8, 84,
        114
    union with England 183-5
Scots 12
Scott, Walter 229
sea voyages 48-9, 124-5, 201
Seacole, Mary 226, 251
Sealed Knot 151-2, 154
Second World War 301-20,
    321, 326, 340
    atomic bombs 319-20
    Battle of Britain 305-7
    the Blitz 276, 308-9
    Blitzkrieg 301
    bombing German cities 315
    D-Day 316-18
    daily life 310
    doodlebugs 315
    Dunkirk 303, 304
    El Alamein 313
    the Holocaust 314, 318
Seven Years War 197-8, 224
Seymour, Jane 103, 104
Shakespeare, William 87,
    128-9, 130
share trading 188-90, 296
Shelley, Percy 223
Simnel, Lambert 89, 130
slavery 179-82, 221-2
Slim, William 319
Smith, Adam 205

Snow, Dr John 245, 272
Solemn League and Covenant
    143
Somme, Battle of the 283, 340
South Africa 255
South Sea Bubble 188-90, 224
space race 327-8
Spain 89, 110, 151, 186
Spanish Armada 118-21, 124,
    130, 163
Spanish Civil War 300
Stalin, Josef 294-5, 300, 325
steam power 237-8
Stephen, King 31, 32, 34, 83
Stephenson, George and
    Robert 239, 272
strikes 294, 295, 331
Strongbow 34, 83
suffragettes 267-8, 272
sugar plantations 179-82

T

tanks 285
tea 126, 203
telephones 287
television 329
Tennyson, Alfred 249
Thatcher, Margaret 335, 341
Titanic 269-70, 272
Tolpuddle Martyrs 243, 272
Tone, Wolfe 177, 211, 224
Tories 165, 168, 170, 230, 235, 265
trade 48-9
Trafalgar, Battle of 214-15,
    216, 224
Tudors 79
Turpin, Dick 193, 224
Tyler, Wat 68-70
Tyndale, William 98
Tyrone, Hugh O'Neill, Earl of
    122

U

unemployment 296-7
Union Jack 185, 197, 201, 212

unions 243, 331, 335
United Irishmen 211-12, 224
United States 270, 296, 325,
    326-8, 337-8
    Second World War
    316-18

V

Victoria, Queen 227, 246, 247,
    255, 269, 272
Vikings 14, 15, 23, 34
Vortigern 12
voting 179, 191, 230, 300, 340
    Chartists 263
    reforms 235-6, 263, 265,
    272, 287
    suffragettes 267-8, 272

W

Wales 12, 15, 18, 337
    Assembly 336, 341
    English conquest of 50-1,
    83
    and the Industrial
    Revolution 238
    Normans in 33-4
    Owain Glyn Dwr's
    rebellion 72-3
Wallace, William 54-5, 84
Walpole, Sir Robert 207, 224
War of the Spanish
    Succession 186
Warbeck, Perkin 89, 130
Wars of the Roses 75-6, 79,
    80, 84
Warwick the Kingmaker 75-6,
    84
Washington, George 203-4
Waterloo, Battle of 218-20, 224
Watt, James 206
welfare state 321-2
Wellington, Duke of 177,
    218-20, 224, 229, 232,
    233-4, 235, 272
Whigs 165, 167, 168, 170,

172, 230, 265
    and the Great Reform
    Act 235-6
White Ship 29-30, 31, 83
Wilberforce, William 221-2,
    224
Wilkinson, Ellen 297
William I (the Conqueror)
    16-17, 18, 20, 23-6, 27-8,
    29, 31, 83, 316
William III, King (William
    of Orange) 168-9, 170,
    183, 184, 186, 211
William IV, King 235-6, 246
William Rufus 29, 83
Williams, Francis 221
Wolfe, James 198
Wollstonecraft, Mary 223
Wolsey, Cardinal Thomas
    94, 95-6, 99-100, 130
women
    Jazz Age 289
    voting rights 267-8, 272,
    287, 340
Woodville, Elizabeth 75,
    77
wool trade 48-9, 80
Wordsworth, William 223
Wyclif, John 95-6

Y

young people in the Sixties
    329-30

KINGS & QUEENS IN BRITAIN & IRELAND SINCE 1066

❖ ❖ ❖ ❖ ❖ ❖ ❖

In Wales and Ireland there were many kings but only a few managed to rule their whole nation. This list contains the most important.

WALES

❖ ❖ ❖

Gruffudd ap Llywelyn 1055–1063
Owain of Gwynedd "the Great" 1137–1170
Llywelyn ap Iorwerth......................... 1208–1240
Llywelyn ap Gruffudd 1258–1282

Wales became part of the English kingdom in 1284.

IRELAND

❖ ❖ ❖

Muirchertach O Brien...........................1096–1119
Turloch O Connor.................................1119–1156
Muirchertach O Mac Lochlainn........1156–1166
Rory O Connor 1166–1183

Henry II of England invaded Ireland in 1171.

SCOTLAND

❖ ❖ ❖

Malcolm III "Canmore" 1058–1093
Donald III (Donald Ban) 1094–1097
During the civil wars, Duncan II was also king in 1094.
Edgar.. 1097–1107
Alexander I 1107–1124
David I 1124–1153
Malcolm IV.. 1153–1165
William "the Lion"............................... 1165–1214
Alexander II... 1214–1249
Alexander III 1249–1286
Margaret "the Maid of Norway" 1286–1290
John Balliol..1292–1296
Robert I (Robert Bruce) 1306–1329
David II 1329–1371

THE STEWARTS

Robert II..1371–1390
Robert III..1390–1406
James I 1406–1437
James II... 1437–1460
James III 1460–1488
James IV 1488–1513
James V 1513–1542
Mary "Queen of Scots"........................1542–1567
James VI 1567–1625

James VI became King of England in 1603, uniting Scotland and England for the first time.

ENGLAND

❖ ❖ ❖

William I "the Conqueror" 1066–1087
William II "Rufus" 1087–1100
Henry I 1100–1135
Stephen 1135–1154

THE PLANTAGENETS

Henry II 1154–1189
Richard I "the Lionheart" 1189–1199
John 1199–1216
Henry III 1216–1272
Edward I 1272–1307
Edward II 1307–1327
Edward III 1327–1377
Richard II 1377–1399
Henry IV 1399–1413
Henry V 1413–1422
Henry VI 1422–1461
Edward IV 1461–1483

During the Wars of the Roses, Henry VI was
king again in 1470–1471.

Richard III 1483–1485

"Edward V" was one of the murdered
Princes in the Tower.

THE TUDORS

Henry VII 1485–1509
Henry VIII 1509–1547
Edward VI 1547–1553
Mary 1553–1558
Elizabeth I 1558–1603

Elizabeth was succeeded by King James VI
of Scotland, who became King James I of
England (and Wales and Ireland) in 1603.

BRITAIN & IRELAND

❖ ❖ ❖

THE STUARTS

James VI and I 1603–1625
Charles I 1625–1649

The Commonwealth 1649–1660

Charles II 1660–1685
James VII and II 1685–1688
William and Mary 1689–1694

After Mary's death in 1694, William ruled
alone as William III.

William III 1694–1702
Anne 1702–1714

THE HANOVERIANS

George I 1714–1727
George II 1727–1760
George III 1760–1820
George IV 1820–1830
William IV 1830–1837
Victoria 1837–1901
Edward VII 1901–1910

THE WINDSORS

George V 1910–1936

The south of Ireland became independent
in 1922.

BRITAIN & NORTHERN IRELAND

❖ ❖ ❖

Edward VIII 1936
George VI 1936–1952
Elizabeth II 1952–

ACKNOWLEDGEMENTS

Lots of people helped write this book, but most of all
I'd like to thank Martha, Joe and Nicola for reading the stories,
Andrew Lownie, P. J. for his brilliant pictures, Martha again
for the maps, John Goodall for his helpful comments, and everyone
at Walker who made the book such fun – Beth, Genevieve,
Georgie, and most of all Caz Royds who's done more
than anyone to help tell the story of Britain.

FOR
MARTHA & JOSEPH

P. D.

FOR
THE BREEN FAMILY

P. J. L.